International Library of Psychology
Philosophy and Scientific Method

Charles Peirce's Empiricism

CHARLES PEIRCE'S EMPIRICISM

By
JUSTUS BUCHLER

With a Foreword by
ERNEST NAGEL

1966
OCTAGON BOOKS, INC.
New York

Originally published 1939 by Kegan Paul, Trench, Trubner & Co. Ltd.

Reprinted 1966
by special arrangement with Routledge & Kegan Paul Ltd.

OCTAGON BOOKS, INC.
175 FIFTH AVENUE
NEW YORK, N. Y. 10010

LIBRARY OF CONGRESS CATALOG CARD NUMBER: 66-17508

Printed in U.S.A. by
NOBLE OFFSET PRINTERS, INC.
NEW YORK 3, N. Y.

To

MY PARENTS

CONTENTS

PREFACE

If there be a reader who cannot understand my writings, let
me tell him that no straining of his mind will help him : his
whole difficulty is that he has no personal experience of the world
of problems of which I am talking. . . . (3.419).

BERTRAND RUSSELL once complained, of certain present-day
thinkers, that they attain clarity at the expense of pro-
fundity. Quite the contrary was the case with Peirce, who
characterized himself as "a mere table of contents, so
abstract, a very snarl of twine". The purpose of the
following pages is to clarify Peirce in some measure, partly
by restatement, partly by filling the lacunae in his thought
with what I take to be its implications. But it cannot be
stressed sufficiently that this exposition is limited to the
methodological side of his thought, his empiricism, which
should emerge fairly well defined from the discussion of
what may be regarded as its major constituents, critical
common-sensism, pragmatism, and the theory of the formal
sciences. For it might otherwise (and might in any case)
be held against me that I make little or no mention of
metaphysics and of phenomenology, in general, of all that
allegedly distinguishes Peirce's originality, imaginativeness
and historical penetration.

The most superficial reader has no difficulty detecting
the existence of two strains in Peirce, one empirical, the
other metaphysical and to a considerable degree extra-
empirical. Whether these two strains are ultimately compatible is a question with which I am not concerned except
briefly (§ 39). I happen myself to believe that Peirce is
primarily an empiricist: there is a good deal in his metaphysics that is incongruous with empiricism, but it seems
to me of secondary importance; much, moreover, that
appears to be incongruous is in fact not, and can be explained
as due to the reverence for traditional philosophy early
implanted in him. Professor Dewey has emphasized that
"Peirce . . . was an empiricist, with the habits of mind, as

he put it, of the laboratory".[1] But the justification of this exposition does not depend upon acceptance of the view that empiricism is the dominant strain in Peirce. It is necessary only to maintain that the empiricism which is to be found in him can stand on its own feet as a self-sufficient philosophy, and it would seem that this is beyond doubt. For those, then, who hold that Peirce is essentially a metaphysician, what follows will be an abstraction from his writings (and I am content to show that what is abstracted is self-sufficient); for those who hold that Peirce is radically inconsistent, it will simply be an exposition ignoring one side of the inconsistency; and for those, finally, who regard Peirce as essentially an empiricist, it will perhaps be a stimulus to further study of him. Such further study would, I believe, reveal that many of his views which are other than methodological fit the empirical framework; above all, those which constitute his phenomenology or theory of the categories.

Each section in this essay assumes acquaintance with all of the sections that precede it. Some apology may be necessary for the first eight or ten, which I suspect are a little tedious. Unlike the rest, they are concerned primarily with the restatement of actual articles, namely, two of the three papers of 1868. So fundamental to Peirce's empiricism do I consider these papers, that I have felt obliged to give especial attention to the theory of knowledge which they contain. It is worth noting that virtually every principal theme of Peirce's thought is unmistakably present in the earliest of his writings, which, relatively few in number, appear between 1867 and 1871.[2] The fact that after four

---

[1] "The Development of American Pragmatism", in *Studies in the History of Ideas*, Vol. II, p. 354.

[2] These comprise the 1867-8 contributions to the *Proceedings of the American Academy of Arts and Sciences*, the 1868 papers in the *Journal of Speculative Philosophy*, the 1867 review of Venn's Logic of Chance in the *North American Review*, the 1870 paper "Description of a Notation for the Logic of Relatives, etc." in *Memoirs of the American Academy*, and the 1871 review of Fraser's edition of Berkeley's Works in the *North American Review*.

decades of attempted elaboration and self-correction his work should have remained a table of contents is indicative not, as one might at first think, of the refractory character of his ideas, but of their wealth and force.

My thanks are due to Professor Herbert W. Schneider and Professor John H. Randall, Jr., for their kindness in reading the manuscript and offering acute suggestions. Of equal value were the comments of my friend Dr. Milton K. Munitz. I am most indebted to Professor Nagel, not merely for our interesting conversations on Peirce, but for all that I have gained from him over a long period of time. For me he has always been a standard of sanity in matters philosophical, and I would like to think that I have been able to reflect some degree of this influence.

J. B.

BROOKLYN COLLEGE,
    NEW YORK.

FOREWORD

IT was the ambition of Peirce to construct a system of philosophy so comprehensive that for a long time to come achievements in all departments of research, in mathematics, in the natural sciences, in history, in sociology, would appear simply as details filling out its outlines. However, whether because of outward circumstance or inner instability, he was no systematic writer; and it is his contributions to logical theory, the least fragmentary of his writings but dealing with issues uppermost in his mind, which assure him a permanent place in intellectual history. He himself relates that he was incessantly occupied with the study of methods of inquiry almost since he had learned to read; and it is this concern with the procedures for acquiring stable beliefs, even more than his technical contributions to mathematics and formal logic, which makes him a vital contemporary influence. He began to publish at a time when Kant, Hegel, the Scottish realists and sensationalistic empiricists dominated Anglo-American philosophy. If the tendencies which these names represent no longer occupy the centre of the contemporary stage, if the conceptions of mind and nature for which they stand no longer seem credible, the change in the climate of opinion is in no small measure due to the direct or indirect influence of Peirce's contributions to the theory of inquiry. James, Royce, Dewey in America, Russell and Ramsey in England, to cite only a few names, and through them an indefinite number of others, are the beneficiaries of Peirce's intellectual labours.

Recent literature in philosophy illustrates the exploitation of two fundamental insights, both of which are integral to Peirce's thought and to the development of both of which he made important contributions: the recognition of the central rôle played by symbols or language in human behaviour and knowledge; and the recognition that human knowledge is an achievement of biological organisms functioning in social contexts. The first has been accompanied by a renaissance of researches in formal logic oriented toward mathematics, and by a renewed consciousness of the need for examining the conditions for significant discourse; the second has supplied a powerful impetus for freeing theories of knowledge and science from the preconceptions of individualistic, atomic psychology. Nevertheless, thinkers who contribute to the development of both tendencies are rare; for the most part, workers in these fields either ignore the researches of others who cultivate an alternative approach, or exhibit what are frequently well-founded suspicions of the uses to which these researches have been put by partisans of philosophic schools. The advantages of pursuing specialized interests are manifest in the marked progress made within each field of interest since the turn of the century. None the less, the development of these specialized studies has itself persuaded many of those who profess them, that these distinct approaches to the theory of inquiry are intimately related and require to be supplemented by one another. Indeed, the construction of a comprehensive logic conceived as a theory of inquiry, which would assimilate the findings of a biologico-social approach as well as the brilliant results of modern formal researches, has come to be recognized as one of the pressing needs of the day. In spite of some notable essays in this direction within recent years, such a logic is still incomplete.

The writings of Peirce have much to offer toward the completion of such a theory of inquiry. His dual concern with formal logic and mathematics and with the analysis of methods leading to stable knowledge, grew out of his conception of semiosis as a unitary process, involving signs, their referends, and their users, in distinguishable but inseparable relations to one another. He regarded himself, as indeed he was, as a pioneer or backwoodsman in the work of opening up semiotic, and much of the territory

still remains virgin land. And it is essential for an understanding of his conception of logic to bear in mind that he
thought of it as the general theory of signs, which must be
comprehensive enough to include within a unified framework
of ideas types of analysis and approach such as have been
indicated, but commonly kept in air-tight isolation from
one another.

"The genius of a man's logical method", Peirce once
declared, "should be loved and reverenced as his bride,
whom he has chosen from all the world." Dr. Buchler's
study provides us with the first full-length portrait of the
Beatrice who inspired Peirce profoundly and in whose
behalf he fought with all his intellectual might; and for
a systematic account of the details of Peirce's contributions
to the theory of inquiry, the reader must turn to Dr.
Buchler's sympathetic but critical exposition. But a few
broad features of that theory are perhaps worth stressing
in this place. Peirce conceived inquiry as a process
beginning with specific problems and terminating in their
resolution, and he identified knowledge as the end-product
of inquiry. Accordingly, knowledge cannot be divorced
from the character of the methods employed in reaching it,
so that, as Peirce repeatedly emphasized, science is more
assured of the general, long-run validity of its methods
than of any one of the specific conclusions obtained with
them. The notion that science is a body of final knowledge,
rather than the *pursuit* of those who are devoured by a
desire to find things out, is therefore incongruous with the
facts in the case; the history of science itself exhibits its
conclusions as essentially corrigible, though supported by
the character of the inquiry they terminate. No conclusions
are above criticism, because there is no ultimate "last
analysis" and no intrinsically indubitable basis for our
knowledge, though not all conclusions are in fact dubious.
This is the substance of Peirce's fallibilism, perhaps the
most far-reaching of his methodological principles. Consequently, he rejected a psychological as well as an ontological

atomism. For he saw clearly that inquiry neither begins
nor terminates with simples, although it may isolate certain
relatively less complex features of a subject-matter explored
in order to explore and control it more successfully. And
by holding fast to his fundamental characterization of the
relation between inquiry and knowledge, he avoided the
traditional puzzles of philosophy and logical theory; for
these derive almost entirely from isolating knowledge from
the procedures which lead up to it, so that it becomes
logically impossible to attain it. It is not the least merit
of Peirce's conception of scientific method that he identified
knowledge as the terminus of inquiry, capable of being
studied as to the conditions of its occurrence, as to its
functions and consequences, by the same methods which
serve to unravel the mutual relations of other facts of
nature.

Peirce's analysis of the conditions for significant discourse
is intimately related to his general theory of signs, as
Dr. Buchler clearly demonstrates. The pragmatic criterion
he proposed for the clarification of ideas, in terms of their
applicability to matters of observation and experiment,
has become an almost universally adopted intellectual
disinfectant in almost every branch of inquiry. He was
the first, or among the first, to work out an empiricism
which could combine recognition of the indispensable
function in inquiry of strict logic and other regulative
principles, with a recognition of the equally indispensable
rôle of sensory observation. Perhaps far too little attention
has been given to his interpretation of the meaning of terms
and propositions as habits of (organic) action, possessing
generality or universality in proportion to the range of
their applicability to particular situations. This suggestion,
never adequately worked out by Peirce himself, provides
a clue for understanding how principles are generated out
of the non-cognitive matrix of inquiry, how they acquire
operative efficacy, and how they can serve as norms or
standards of procedure. On the other hand, Peirce's views

on the status and rôle of mathematics, topics which have always been the Achilles-heel of traditional empiricism, have come to play a dominant rôle in contemporary researches upon the foundations of the subject—although it should be added that they have been arrived at independently of him and elaborated with a fulness and subtlety of which he knew little. It was in consonance with his general theory of signs that he advanced what in his day were remarkably bold views on the nature of mathematics: the validity of mathematical demonstrations rests entirely upon the syntactical properties of systems of signs, and the function of mathematics in inquiry lies in the transformations of discourse it performs. Peirce's views on the subject are a touch-stone of the empiricism he espoused; they enabled him to offer an account of mathematics free from obscurantism, from irrelevant ontological interpretations, and from the sensationalism which bedevilled traditional empiricists.

Peirce once explained that his writings are for people "who want to find out", and that "people who want philosophy ladled out to them can go elsewhere. There are philosophical soup shops at every corner, thank God!" Peirce makes no easy reading, and Dr. Buchler's book, in supplying the details and the background of Peirce's empiricism, does not minimize its difficulties. He does not present Peirce's logical theory as a tightly-knit system of ideas, for such a system is not to be found in Peirce; he does organize and clarify the remarkably rich and suggestive ideas of Peirce, and indicates their interrelations, their excellencies, and their shortcomings. The present book is therefore an invaluable critical guide to a rich mine of ideas awaiting further exploration. Dr. Buchler does not ladle out Peirce, and his essay also is for people who want to find out.

ERNEST NAGEL.

COLUMBIA UNIVERSITY.

CHARLES PEIRCE'S EMPIRICISM

PART I

CRITICAL COMMON-SENSISM

I wish to state, as accurately as possible without sacrificing typical details, Peirce's doctrine of critical common-sensism.[1] Peirce is habitually obscure and very often confused, but it is not so much the content as the order of his ideas that requires reconstruction. The designation 'critical common-sensism' first appears in 1905,[2] after almost forty years of thinking and writing. It must be said at once that I use the term to cover much more in Peirce's thought than he himself does. In his own sense the doctrine is a "variety" of the Scottish philosophy of common sense marked by certain "distinctive characters"; it is first adumbrated, he says, nine years before his formulation of pragmatism, which means in 1868. He acknowledges his "adhesion, under inevitable modification, to the opinion of that subtle but well-balanced intellect, Thomas Reid, in the matter of Common Sense. . . ." (5.444; cf. 5.504). But the similarities between Peirce and the Scottish school cannot be found by a superficial comparison. In fact, the series

[1] The Collected Papers of Charles Sanders Peirce are in six volumes (Harvard University Press, 1931-1935) of an originally projected series of ten. The editors are Charles Hartshorne and Paul Weiss, who have entitled these volumes as follows : I " Principles of Philosophy "; II " Elements of Logic "; III " Exact Logic "; IV " The Simplest Mathematics "; V " Pragmatism and Pragmaticism "; VI " Scientific Metaphysics ".

Following the practice of the editors, all citations of the text will here be by volume and paragraph number. Thus ' 4.320 ' will mean ' volume 4, paragraph 320 '. If a paper by Peirce is cited simply as appearing in an independent source of publication, this means that it has not been reprinted in the Collected Papers.

Italics in quotations from Peirce are his if not otherwise specified. In the one or two cases where I have added my own italics to his in the same quotation this is indicated explicitly.

[2] In " Issues of Pragmaticism ", the *Monist*. (Coll. Papers, 5.438-463.)

of 1868 papers [1] referred to by him not only lacks mention of that school but is based on an opposition to it. If the 1905 paper together with manuscripts of the same period states the similarities, then the 1868 papers state the dissimilarities—historically more important. In the second of these papers Peirce says that he writes in a "spirit of opposition to Cartesianism". We shall see later how, by breaking with certain dogmas best expressed in Reid and Stewart, Peirce did in fact break with the Cartesian tradition; [2] and we shall also see how he made use of opinions of Reid and Stewart to formulate critical common-sensism in the narrow, i.e. in his own, sense (§ 14 ff.). 'Critical common-sensism' as we use it designates collectively all the subjects considered in the sections that follow.

Thus, in this broader sense, the doctrine is both an attack on certain presuppositions employed by Scottish philosophy (the aspect which concerns us in the first half of this Part), and an adoption of the Scottish emphasis on 'common sense' beliefs in the light of this critique (which we show later).

I do not intend to deal with Peirce chronologically, but for various reasons it is desirable to begin with the papers of 1868. In §§ 1-8 I shall dwell on them [3] to a large extent, and state their burden with the help of some conceptions

---

[1] " Questions Concerning Certain Faculties Claimed for Man ", " Some Consequences of Four Incapacities ", " Grounds of Validity of the Laws of Logic ", in *Journal of Speculative Philosophy*. (Coll. Papers, 5.213-357.)

[2] Aside from internal evidence, there is no explicit statement by Peirce that those whom he had in mind when attacking the ' Cartesian ' psychological tradition in 1868 were the Scottish representatives of this tradition. But it is significant that in a note at the beginning of the first 1868 paper he calls attention to the meanings of ' intuition ' given by Hamilton in the Notes on Reid appended to his edition. The term ' cognition ', which is perhaps the most prominent in the 1868 papers, is a term systematically introduced into British philosophy by Hamilton. That Peirce was thoroughly familiar with Reid and Stewart is quite certain. His close knowledge of Hamilton's Reid, which would help to confirm the supposition that he had these men in mind in 1868, is attested by other statements and references to the Notes. Cf. e.g. 6.590, 5.608, and 2.533.

[3] Strictly, on the first two of the three papers.

of later date. Of these papers James said, "They are exceedingly bold, subtle and incomprehensible and I can't say that his [Peirce's] vocal elucidations helped me a great deal to their understanding";[1] and further, that these "very acute and original psychologico-metaphysical articles . . . are so crabbedly expressed that one can hardly get their exact sense."[2]

1. **Terminology.** The most important and most frequently occurring terms in the papers of 1868 are 'cognition', 'intuition', and 'thought'. 'Cognition' and 'thought' are synonymous. As in most other writers, cognition is spoken of sometimes participially, to mean the act of cognizing, and sometimes substantivally, to mean an instance of knowledge (as when we speak of '*a* cognition'). Cognition in both senses corresponds to Locke's 'thinking': it is the most general term for mental operation or kind of knowledge. Reasoning, abstraction, belief, sensation, conception, etc. are each a kind of cognition. What applies to cognition in general, applies of course to each kind of cognition: belief, for instance, is used both in the sense of a mental process and of an assertion entertained in this process. It is hardly necessary to mention the point except in order to note that the confusion between the two senses does not occur in Peirce; and it will not be necessary to point it out again when we use such words as 'belief' and 'judgment'.

'Cognizing' (and 'cognition'), 'knowing' (and 'knowledge'), 'thinking' (and 'thought') are, to repeat, synonymous; a cognition, a thought, and an instance of knowledge are identical. Whatever peculiarity may at first appear in this usage will be dispelled later. I prefer, in what follows, to use the term 'cognition' most often, first because Peirce himself does, second because it is less awkward than 'instance of knowledge', and third because it is more suggestive of

---

[1] Letter to Henry Bowditch, 1869 (in Perry, *Thought and Character of William James*, I, p. 292).
[2] Letter to Bowditch, 1869 (*Ibid.*, I, p. 296).

knowledge than is 'thought' (though to use the latter term will sometimes be convenient).

Cognitions are of two fundamental classes: first, cognitions which are 'determined' by previous cognitions; second, cognitions which are not determined by previous cognitions. A cognition of the second class Peirce calls an 'intuition'. 'Determined by' means, roughly, 'inferred from'. An intuition, then, is a "premiss not itself a conclusion" (5.213). But Peirce holds that an intuition would have to be 'determined' directly and immediately by its 'object'. We shall therefore shortly distinguish different senses of 'determine'.

2. Cognition; Material Quality of Cognition; Theory of Signs. A basic distinction in Peirce is that between a cognition and the 'material quality' of a cognition. For instance, we are said to have a 'sensation of redness'. In this 'sensation' two elements can be distinguished. There is, first of all, the brute feeling of redness. This brute feeling is private, cannot be duplicated in another person by mere linguistic description, and is a fact, like any other fact in the physical world. But, secondly, we may speak of a knowledge of redness, of redness as a cognition. Knowledge is public, and communicable in language. For Peirce the reason why redness-as-a-cognition is more than a mere qualitative feeling-occurrence is that it is a *representation* or *sign*. In order to understand his distinction, we must sketch very briefly what is involved in his notion of a sign.

A sign is something that *stands for* something else. The mark 'house' on paper is a sign, because it is said to stand for a house; and we are able to talk about the house because we can manipulate the sign which stands for it, together with other signs, according to rules agreed upon. The house is the *object* of the mark 'house'. This mark consists of five individual marks in black type. So that it not only stands for an object but has a definite *material quality* of its own. Every sign has an object, and every sign has some material quality. Signs may be very complex. The sign 'This house is red' has a different material quality from 'house', and its object is, roughly, the fact that the house is red. But something further is required to fulfil the function of a sign. No sign can function as such unless there are (a) other signs in terms of which the given sign is describable and understandable, and (b) some mind which interprets the given sign in terms of these other signs. A man who uses a sign is always able to, and does, translate it into another sign (or other signs) in terms of which he understands it. A material sign thus has the function of representing or standing for something (to some one) by means of a sign or signs which interpret it. In addition, then, to the material quality of a sign, and the object of this material sign, we must distinguish the interpretation or translation (i.e. another sign), which is the third essential feature. Peirce calls the sign that functions as interpretation or translation the *interpretant* of the given sign. For example, the interpretant of 'house' might be 'square structure with entrance and windows'. The interpretant of a sign is what would ordinarily be called the meaning of a sign.[1] In general, the conception of sign or representation involves a triadic relation between a physical object or quality (the material thing taken as a sign), something which this denotes or refers to (its object), and another sign which it is said to 'mean' or 'connote' (its interpretant).[2]

Let us return to cognition. According to Peirce, every cognition is a sign (e.g. 1.538, 5.250). We should now understand why a cognition is more than a mere brute feeling. The feeling is merely the *material quality* of the cognition, and there is no cognition without some material quality. Every cognition or thought is in one sense a feeling, it is a particular event. But on the other hand the thought stands for something, it is a thought *of* something; and moreover, it is interpreted or translated by a subsequent thought, its interpretant. Every thought *A* has an interpretant thought

---

[1] We reserve exactitude on this point for Part II (cf. § 30).

[2] Strictly, as we have indicated, there is a fourth element, the mind or interpreter (cf. § 30).

B. *B* is itself a sign of the same object of which *A* is a sign, and is interpreted by another subsequent thought *C*. *C* is a sign of the object of which *B* and *A* are signs, and is interpreted by another thought *D*. And so on.[1]

3. **Every Cognition is Judicative.** It follows from the nature of cognitions as signs that every cognition is at least a tacit predication or judgment. If a mere image involving absolutely no judgment were called a cognition, it could not be distinguished from the material quality of a cognition. In order that brute feeling, such as an image of redness, should occur, it is necessary only that the sense organs should operate. But in order that there should be said to be a cognition, some possibility [2] of interpretation is essential. We cannot call a mere qualitative feeling of redness a sign, because there is no sense in speaking of an interpretant of such a feeling. Redness is not 'translated' or 'interpreted'; it simply occurs as an instantaneous feeling, and is followed perhaps by a feeling of a different quality. In order, therefore, that a sensation of redness should involve cognition, it must consist not merely in a brute feeling but in *tacitly predicating red of some object*. Only then can it be called a representation, and be said to have an interpretant.[3]

4. **Different Senses of 'Determine'.** Peirce distinguishes three senses of 'determine', not in 1868 but in 1905 (5.441). (1) A cognition may be determined by another cognition or by several cognitions, in the sense that it is consciously inferred from them. By 'consciously inferred' is meant

---

[1] " Thought . . . is in itself essentially of the nature of a sign. But a sign is not a sign unless it translates itself into another sign. . . ." (5.594 ; cf. 5.138).

[2] " It is not necessary that the Interpretant should actually exist " ; an interpretant " *in futuro* will suffice " (2.92).

[3] Both ' feeling ' and ' sensation ' are often used by Peirce in a cognitive sense. We shall, however, use ' feeling ' in the non-cognitive sense, i.e. as synonymous with ' material quality of cognition ', except where otherwise indicated. We shall, on the other hand, use ' sensation ' in the cognitive sense, except where otherwise indicated.

inferred according to a rule of inference or, as Peirce calls it, a 'leading principle' of inference.[1] It is not necessary that such a leading principle should be explicitly in the mind of one who makes the inference, in the sense that he should be able to express it precisely (cf. 4.476), but only that he should be conscious of such a principle as governing the inference. Thus a cognition as conclusion may be determined by other cognitions as premisses, in the sense of being inferred in this way. Such determinations or inferences Peirce calls *reasonings*. "Reasoning . . . at the very least conceives its inference to be one of a general class of possible inferences on the same model, and all equally valid" (6.497). Thus the inferences drawn by mathematicians are properly called 'reasonings' because they employ conscious rules for validity, such as the rule of replacement, which govern a whole class of inferences of a given form. (2) A cognition may be determined by another in the sense that it is inferred from that other in a conscious inference but without one's being aware that the inference is governed by a leading principle. Of such a rudimentary inference Peirce gives as example the familiar 'cogito, ergo sum'. These instances of determination he calls *acritical inferences*. (3) In still other instances, a cognition may be determined by another "without our being at all aware of it" (5.441). Such determinations he calls *associational suggestions*, and we shall give examples of them in § 14.

There is a fourth sense of 'determine', not mentioned by Peirce perhaps because of its obviousness, but all the more worthy of mention; namely, (4) causal or physiological determination. In this sense there is no doubt that a cognition may be determined by its object, as well as by other cognitions. Thus when we look at a book and involuntarily think 'This book is large', we may in a proper sense regard the thought as determined by the book and its bulk. For Peirce determination is a *logical* relation, hence his usage comprises only the first three senses mentioned. Tacitly, of

---

[1] Sometimes, 'guiding principle'.

course, he must admit the fourth sense. But what he does not admit—a denial which in fact constitutes the thesis we are at present concerned with—is that a *cognition* may be determined (even in the fourth sense) *immediately* by its object. This denial we shall elaborate gradually in the following sections.

If we consider, then, a series of thoughts succeeding one another, we may say that any thought is determined (in the fourth sense) by the object to which it refers, as well as by other thoughts. But every thought determines (in one of the first three senses) another succeeding thought, its interpretant. So that thoughts are related to one another inferentially. However, only a thought occurring in that kind of cognition known as external perception can be said to be somehow causally determined by its 'object'; the thoughts determined *by* this thought may also be said to be determined by their object, but not in the same way. They are determined *via* this thought. They refer to their object by referring to the thoughts from which they are inferred (cf. p. 110, i). Every thought is, as we have said, a sign of its object. The interpretant of every thought is a sign of the same object,—but only because it is a sign of the thought whose interpretant it is. In the series of thoughts each thought is thus (as interpretant) a sign of the preceding thought, and hence, indirectly, a sign of the same object.

5. **Peirce's Thesis; Further on the Usage of ' Intuition '.** The dominant idea in the papers of 1868, recurring constantly in Peirce's work, is that *there are no intuitive cognitions.* That is to say, no thought in the series of thoughts is determined directly and immediately, in the fourth sense or, a fortiori, in any of the other three, by its object. In still other words, no thought that can be genuinely called a thought arises solely and immediately on sensory contact with its object: *every* thought is inferred, in one of the first three senses, from some other thought. Any thought *has*

an interpretant thought and *is* the interpretant of some other thought.[1] A thought directly determined by its object would be an intuition. It is important to remember that for Peirce 'intuition' means 'intuitive cognition'. It does not mean sense appearance; that is, it is not to be confused with the material quality of cognition. Peirce does not deny that *this* is determined directly and immediately by an external object. This "mere feeling . . . is determined only by an inexplicable, occult power" (5.291). For Peirce an intuition is understood to be a cognition, but a cognition not inferred from any other. As a cognition, an intuition would be a predication, it would be judicative; and so the thesis that there are no intuitions should be understood as meaning that there are no intuitive judgments. Those who hold that empirical intuitions [2] do exist are primarily interested in showing that some of our cognitions yield immediate and certain knowledge. They often hold that this certain knowledge is nothing other than 'direct experience'. But 'direct experience' is simply, so far as Peirce is concerned, a term synonymous with 'material quality of cognition'. Consequently, "Direct experience is neither certain nor uncertain, because it affirms nothing—it just *is*. There are delusions, hallucinations, dreams. But there is no mistake that such things really do appear, and direct experience means simply the appearance. It involves no error, because it testifies to nothing but its own appearance. For the same reason it affords no certainty. It is not *exact*, because it leaves much vague; though it is not *inexact* either; that is, it has no false exactitude" (1.145). Thus only cognitions can be said to be certain or uncertain.

Perhaps it is advisable to add another elucidation of the distinction between cognition and its material quality (cf. 5.261, 5.467). Suppose two persons A and B, and two

---

[1] Cf. 1.339, and p. 110 below.

[2] 'Intuition' in Peirce's use means only empirical intuition. It is non-discursive cognition in the sense that it is uninferred, not in the sense that it is asymbolic or mystical.

physical objects, one called 'red', the other 'blue'. Both
A and B agree on the use of the names 'red' and 'blue' for
the respective objects. But the feeling which A has when
he sees the 'blue' object is the feeling which B has when he
sees the 'red' object; and the feeling which A has when he
sees the 'red' object is the feeling of B when he sees the
'blue'. Nevertheless, despite this difference in the qualitative feelings which A and B have, they always agree that
the red object is 'red' and the blue object 'blue'. All their
actions and manipulations with respect to these objects likewise agree, and each is therefore able publicly to confirm
statements of the other in which the names 'red' and 'blue'
occur. Thus while the *material quality* 'red' differs for A
and B, the *cognition* (or tacit predication of) 'red' is identical
for both.[1]

6. **Associational not the Same as Causal Determination.**
Peirce's thesis is that every cognition or thought-sign is
logically determined by some previous cognition. Where,
then, does the third type of determination mentioned above,
namely, associational suggestion, fit in? If one thought
should call up another associationally, or by random suggestion, what logical connection is there between the thoughts?
May not a thought be intuitive despite the fact that it
happens to be associationally suggested by another? We
shall show later that determination by association is logical
determination fully as much as the other two kinds. Here
it is sufficient to point out that associational determination
is not to be confused with determination in a physiological
or causal sense, though 'association' might perhaps be
described in physiological terms. The fact that one cognition temporally precedes another may mean that if the
first had not occurred the second would not have occurred.
But two such cognitions may not at all be logically related.
The relation would not then be what Peirce understands by

[1] Cf. *North American Review*, Vol. 113 (1871), p. 455 (Review of Fraser's
edition of Berkeley's works).

associational suggestion, which, though it may be involuntary, is regarded by him as a species of inference.

The thesis of Peirce that we are discussing can be treated best in detail if we divide it into three parts. First, in §§ 7-8 we give Peirce's argument that it is not necessary to *assume* intuitive cognitions (the approach of 1868); next, in § 12, we show that there cannot *be* cognition that is intuitive; finally, in § 14, we explain the thesis in *positive* terms, viz. that all thought is inferential, and the sense in which it is.

7. Why Intuitive Cognitions Need not be Assumed.

(1) *How would we Know whether Cognitions were Intuitive?* Peirce shrewdly raises the question, What is the character of our evidence that there are intuitive cognitions? If we can show that this evidence is not itself intuitive, then it is at least always open to doubt that there are intuitions. Suppose that at a given time we are said to have a cognition. Can we judge intuitively that this cognition is or is not intuitive? (*a*) We cannot argue that we have this power on the ground that we 'feel' it: this begs the question. For in the first place, is this 'feeling' a cognition or not? and secondly, if a cognition, is it an intuitive or a mediate (determined, inferred) cognition? On the argument at hand, we should have to answer this second question by citing another 'feeling' that the first feeling was an intuitive cognition. But this too would be subject to the same question; and so on ad infinitum. (*b*) If we had this power of intuitive discrimination, there would be a relatively small variation of opinion regarding it. But (i) philosophers have strongly disputed as to which cognitions are intuitive, and (ii) it is well known that witnesses in courts of law find it difficult to distinguish between what they have actually seen and what they have inferred. (*c*) While dreaming we mistake the dream for an intuition in the sense of a wholly novel cognition; but in actual fact everyone believes that dreams are determined by previous cognitions, e.g. according to the

laws of association. (*d*) Before the publication of Berkeley's *Essay Towards a New Theory of Vision* it was generally believed that the third dimension of space was immediately intuited; after its publication it was generally believed that this was known by inference. (See 5.214-224, 6.416.)

(2) ' *Self-Consciousness* ' *not Intuitive but a Result of Inference.* Any assertion, then, that such-and-such a cognition is intuitive, is only probable and not itself intuitive. But is the evidence such as to make it at least highly probable that there are intuitions? For instance, it is maintained that we must suppose an intuition of a 'private self'. But (*a*) investigation of growing children reveals either a total absence or a very imperfect sense of self-consciousness. The child becomes conscious of himself through the *testimony* of those around him. He becomes aware, in time, of error; but error will have no significance for him unless he arrives at the notion of a self as that which is capable of error. (*b*) Consider the following argument for intuitive self-consciousness: We cannot have inferred our own existence from any other fact; for we are more certain of our own existence than of any other fact, and a premiss cannot determine a conclusion to be more certain than it is itself. Peirce in reply grants that we are more certain of our own existence than of any other fact, but he denies the main contention on the ground that while "a conclusion cannot be more certain than that *some* one of the facts which support it is true, . . . it may easily be more certain than *any* one [i.e. any given one] of those facts" (5.237; my ital.). Thus, if a dozen witnesses testify to an occurrence, then a belief in that occurrence depends upon, and is not more certain than, the belief that each of the witnesses is generally to be believed. Yet the belief in the occurrence is made more certain than that any given witness is generally to be believed. Similarly, the evidence for a man's belief in his own existence consists in every other fact, so that it cannot be more certain than the belief in some fact; but it may be more certain than the belief in any one fact. In general, Peirce's discussion refutes the claim for

intuitive self-consciousness by showing, first, that genetically the self is inferred; second, that there is no positive evidence that the adult mind is intuitively aware of the self. (Cf. 5.225-237.)

(3) *How Different Kinds of Cognition are Discriminated.* In every cognition there is "something represented, or that of which we are conscious, and some action or passion of the self whereby it becomes represented. The former shall be termed the objective, the latter the subjective, element of the cognition" (5.238).[1] Now, must it not be supposed that we discriminate between two 'kinds' of cognition, say perception and imagination, by intuitively distinguishing their 'subjective elements'? Do we not know immediately (and certainly) whether we are 'perceiving' something or 'imagining' it? Peirce holds (*a*) that the great difference in the *objects* of perception and imagination sufficiently accounts for our distinguishing between them; and (*b*) that if we take two kinds of cognition, say belief and conception, which appear not to differ in their objects, we can distinguish them by means of a "peculiar feeling of conviction" which accompanies the former, and which we (presumably) *learn* to recognize as its concomitant. Thus we learn to consciously discriminate perception from imagination by examining the objects that occur in each, and we learn to distinguish what we believe from what we merely conceive by associating a feeling of conviction with the former. (Cf. 5.238, 5.241-243.)

(4) *We have no Power of 'Introspection'.* Thus neither the 'self' nor its cognitions considered as mental activities or processes is known intuitively. Now the self and its cognitions thus considered comprise what are ordinarily regarded as 'internal' phenomena. As opposed to these, there is a set of facts ordinarily called 'external'. By 'introspection'

---

[1] This 'subjective' element of the cognition, ordinarily called mental 'act' as distinguished from mental 'content' or 'object' (the 'objective' element), is not to be confused with the material quality of the cognition. The latter is the qualitative character of the content represented, the former the process occurring during a given kind of cognition.

Peirce means "any knowledge of the internal world not derived from external observation" (5.244). Having maintained thus far that there is no intuitive cognition of the internal world, he now goes a step further and holds that there is no cognition at all (intuitive or mediate) of the internal world which is not derived from external observation. (a) An objection at once presents itself in the view that, since the feeling e.g. of redness "is as it is, owing to the constitution of the mind" (5.245), a cognition of this feeling would be knowledge of the internal world not inferred from external observation. That is to say, our introspection might presumably consist in the judgment 'I now have the feeling of redness'. But according to Peirce this is not a purely internal cognition. We can only reflect upon the redness after being aware that it is a predicate of something external. Thus we would judge 'I have the feeling of redness' only after judging (tacitly) 'Such-and-such is red'. (b) But it may be argued that what we call the emotions are purely mental qualities with no representative element, and that a cognition of an emotion, say anger, is a purely internal cognition. But Peirce disagrees that the emotion itself has no cognitive element. He believes that when a man is angry, "it can hardly be questioned that there is some relative character in the outward thing which makes him angry, and a little reflection will show that his anger consists in his saying to himself, 'this thing is vile, abominable, etc.' and that it is rather a mark of returning reason to say, 'I am angry'" (5.247; cf. 1.250). So that emotions are really predications about objects. (c) Volition as a mental category has been traditionally distinguished (as in Kant, or in Locke) from cognition, and it may be argued that it is necessary to suppose a power of introspection to cognize it. But Peirce distinguishes two senses of 'volition': If it means 'desire', then it can be known only by inference from some object desired. As distinguished from desire, volition "is nothing but the power of . . . abstracting. Hence, the knowledge of the power of abstracting may be inferred from abstract objects, just as the knowledge of the power of seeing is inferred from colored objects" (5.248).[1]

Peirce concludes from his denial of the power of introspection that "the only way of investigating a psychological question is by inference from external facts" (5.249). I do not propose to dwell on what is implied by this brief statement. But some misunderstanding may be avoided if a word is added on the sense which 'introspection' has for Peirce. In experimental psychology we speak commonly of introspection. And ordinarily it is wholly permissible to speak of concentrating the attention (i) on the quality of a feeling, in order to describe it; (ii) on the character of cognition as a complex mental process; for instance, we ask whether thought is independent of conventional language; (iii) on the character of a cognition considered logically, i.e. as a type of assertion; (iv) on the relation between the discursive and non-discursive elements in cognition (i.e. between cognition and mere feeling); and so on. If this concentration were not possible Peirce could not himself have made the distinctions we have considered. He often uses the term 'introspection' in connection with alleged examination of the quality of feelings. He does not deny that we can carry on such examination, but holds that in so doing we represent the feeling as the quality of an object, not as something purely psychical. That the feeling is something mental is always an inference. And *this* process of examining feelings Peirce would call not introspection but attention; an act of introspection being definable as an act of attention that is *purely internal*. He would hold that when attention to feelings takes the form of deliberate laboratory examination, though it may be taken for granted by the investigator that

---

[1] "It is the external world that we directly observe. What passes within we only know as it is mirrored in external objects. In a certain sense, there is such a thing as introspection; but it consists in an interpretation of phenomena presenting themselves as external percepts. We first see blue and red things. It is quite a discovery when we find the eye has anything to do with them. . . ." (Review of Karl Pearson's *Grammar of Science*, in *Popular Science Monthly*, Vol. 58, 1900-1901, p. 301).

he is examining a mental quality, nevertheless in the actual process of examination the feeling will not be attended to as such (cf. 1.250, 1.254, 5.462). Peirce also emphasizes the point—closely connected with the foregoing, and by now a commonplace—that deliberate attention to a feeling for the purpose of describing it tends to be unsuccessful, since in the process of attending, the feeling either no longer remains the same or has in consequence disappeared completely (cf. 1.310, 1.115).

8. **No Necessity of Assuming a 'First' Cognition.** It may be argued that if our cognitions are determined by previous cognitions, and these by others previous to them, there must have been a first cognition (i.e. an intuition) in this series. Peirce's answer, employing an analogy, is as follows: Suppose that we trace the series of cognitions backward, from any cognition to some preceding cognition which determined it, to the cognition which determined the latter, etc. Cognitions which arise earlier in time may be regarded as having a less 'lively consciousness', so that a given cognition will be livelier than the one by which it is determined. Let us now imagine an inverted triangle (i.e. apex downward) about to be dipped into water. The surface of the water will make horizontal lines across the triangle as it is gradually immersed, and the deeper the triangle is immersed the longer will be the horizontal line across it. Let each horizontal line be a cognition; let the shorter line represent the earlier and less lively, the longer the subsequent and more lively, cognition; so that by gradual immersion the shorter lines or cognitions will give way to (i.e. determine) longer. (A cognition B may be determined by a cognition A even though temporally other cognitions may intervene. These other cognitions do not determine B except perhaps physiologically, because they are irrelevant and not cognitions 'of the same object', as A and B are.) "The apex of the triangle represents the object external to the mind which determines both these cognitions. The state of the triangle before it reaches the water, repre-

sents a state of cognition which contains nothing which determines these subsequent cognitions" (5.263). To say that there must be a first cognition in this series is to say "that when that triangle is dipped into the water there must be a sectional line made by the surface of the water lower than which no surface line had been made in that way. But draw the horizontal line where you will, as many horizontal lines as you please can be assigned at finite distances below it and below one another. For any such section is at some distance above the apex, otherwise it is not a line" (*ib.*). Peirce holds that if this is a paradox, it is identical with the Achilles paradox. If as a result of that paradox motion is to be denied, then so must the process of cognitions determining one another. His implication is that we do not rule out motion because of an a priori argument, and that similarly the fact that there need be no first cognition does not mean that there can be no cognition.

On this interesting matter it is hardly fair to confine ourselves to this brief conclusion of 1868. Peirce's view might be rendered somewhat as follows: The objection against the view of cognition here presented, like that against motion, should be discussed both on logical and on empirical grounds. From an empirical point of view, the Achilles paradox is an a priori sophism, because we falsely speak of Achilles as *in actual fact* making distinct steps that are sharply demarcated from one another. We likewise have no right to speak in this way of 'cognitions', which in actual fact merge gradually into one another and are not each perfectly isolable. ". . . Cognition arises by a *process* of beginning, as any other change comes to pass" (5.263). The mind "performs its act in one continuous process" (5.181). No less than motion, Peirce argues, cognition is continuous and has no actual first step. Objections against this conception of motion and cognition may be met on logical grounds, i.e. on grounds analyzing what is implied in the notion of a continuum. Now we may legitimately speak of Achilles' pursuit and of the process of cognition as *analyzable* into steps and cognitions, and of these as preceding and succeeding one another. But we may not speak of absolute predecessors and successors. The arguments of Zeno make contradictions inevitable only because they rest on a self-contradictory supposition, namely, that "a continuum has ultimate parts"; the truth being that "a continuum is precisely that, every part of which has parts, in the same sense" (5.335). The series of cognitions is always *further* analyzable, and what we call 'cognitions' could be regarded as composed of constituent 'cognitions'. We may deal with the objection that if there is no first cognition in the series of cognitions, then that series could not have had a beginning in time. This does not follow in the case of a continuous series (5.327, 5.311), for an origin in time does not imply that an *analysis* of the members of a continuous series must terminate in an ultimate earliest member. Peirce denies, not that cognition begins (for this would be senseless), but that there is a first *cognition*, an absolutely individual judgment coming first in a series of inferred judgments. Cognition (in time), like a line (in space), has a beginning but no atomic first term. We may also dispose of the objection that if the series of cognitions is infinitely analyzable into individual cognitions, a given series would contain an infinite number of individual cognitions and cannot therefore be thought in a finite time. This no more follows than it follows that we cannot pass over a given distance in a finite time because that distance is infinitely divisible (cf. 6.179, 2.666).

We shall later (§ 14) delineate the process of cognition in more positive terms, showing that it consists of a definite kind of inferences constituting a series in which no 'first premiss' need be assumed.

9. **Peirce's Use of ' Self '.** I want to digress briefly for a remark on § 7. In Peirce's discussion of self-consciousness he says that by 'self-consciousness' he means "a knowledge of ourselves. Not a mere feeling of subjective conditions of

consciousness, but of our personal selves" (5.225). We saw
that he denies this knowledge of the self to be intuitive; and
it is not merely inferred but inferred from external observation. But what does he mean by 'self' or 'mind', and does
the conception of a substantival self intrude? To be conscious of self, he says, is to be conscious not of mental
activity but of something else. It is possible to employ the
word 'self' empirically and unambiguously. For instance,
it may mean the class of activities generated by the operation
of the sense organs; or more specifically, the class of such
'mental' activities, as distinguished from the activities of
the biological organism in general, 'mental' being in turn
empirically definable. I do not know what Peirce means by
'self', but it is not unlikely that in 1868 he would, if pressed,
have given an empirical account. This is made probable by
his denial of the faculty of 'introspection'. For this denial
is at least equivalent to the opinion that the self is not an
object cognized in the same sense in which an external object
is cognized; it is inferred from knowledge of the external
world. Just what it is that is inferred remains vague. Here
and there we have one or two positive suggestions that seem
to lead in an empirical direction, but they are bare. Peirce
speaks of "the mind as seen from within, which by an ego-
tistical anacoluthon we call *our* mind" (2.444). In an unpublished manuscript, quoted copiously by Professor Perry,[1]
he says:

> "Everybody will admit a personal self exists in the
> same sense in which a snark exists; that is, there is a
> phenomenon to which that name is given. It is an illusory
> phenomenon; but still it is a phenomenon. It is not quite
> purely illusory, but only mainly so. It is true, for instance,
> that men are *selfish*, that is, that they are really deluded
> into supposing themselves to have some isolated existence;
> and in so far, they *have* it. . . ."

---

[1] " Questions on William James's *Principles of Psychology* ", in Perry,
op. cit., II, p. 107.

10. ' **Percepts** ' and ' **Perceptual Judgments** '. The fundamental distinction between cognition and the material
quality of cognition is never abandoned by Peirce. But the
term 'material quality' as applied to the quality of *mental*
signs is hardly used after 1868. There the term applies
equally to the quality of redness and the quality of anger,
that is, to both image-qualities and 'feeling'-qualities. For
the feeling- or emotion-qualities Peirce later has no fixed
term, sometimes using 'feeling', sometimes 'quality', most
often and better, 'quality of feeling' (e.g. 5.44, 5.85). He
has, however, a term which he often uses for the qualitative
image, namely, 'percept'. If the kind of cognition with
which we are dealing is 'perception', then (in the 1868
manner of speaking) the 'percept' is the material quality of
the 'perceptual judgment'. (This will seem less peculiar if we
remember not to confuse the perceptual judgment or cognition
with the written or spoken perceptual statement. The latter is
explicitly linguistic, the former quasi-linguistic. Both involve
logical assertion in the same sense, but clearly they have
material quality in different senses.)　In this substitution of
usage there are two points to which attention should be called.

(1) Peirce is very emphatic in distinguishing the perceptual judgment from the percept (e.g. 2.141, 5.54). The
percept is the 'direct experience' which cannot be said to
be certain or uncertain, exact or inexact (cf. 2.142). The
percept 'redness' does not "proclaim itself" as a sensation:
it simply appears (1.254).[1]　Nevertheless, in certain places
Peirce makes statements like: "The science of psychology

[1] Peirce often speaks of ' percepts ' as ' signs ' (e.g. 4.543, 1.313). Are
we wrong, then, in saying that a ' percept ' is only the material quality
of a perceptual cognition and not itself cognitive ? It is easy to explain
why we are not.

Peirce makes three fundamental divisions of signs, based on the point
of view from which they are analyzed (cf. 2.243). One division is from
the point of view of the way in which the sign may denote its object :
thus it may be either an ' icon ' (sign that diagrams or pictures), an
' index ' (sign that indicates or points, e.g. a weathervane), or a ' symbol '
(conventional sign). Another division is from the point of view of the
way in which the sign may connote : thus it may be either a term, a

assures me that the very percepts [are] mental constructions, not the first impressions of sense" (2.141). Or, ". . . Our very percepts are the results of cognitive elaboration" (5.416). In the case of the second of these statements the context shows, I think, that Peirce is using 'percept' loosely for 'perceptual judgment'.[1] In the case of the first statement he is unmistakably speaking of percepts, but what he means is that percepts are *complex* (cf. 5.494). No image is an absolutely pure, specific and (retrospectively [2]) unanalyzable quality; if it were, it would be a 'first impression of sense'. Certain passages in the 1868 papers too make it sometimes appear that Peirce is arguing for the view that every *percept* is 'determined' by previous percepts (e.g. 5.222), in which case 'determined' would have a physiological sense similar to but of considerably less significance than that mentioned in § 4 which was intended for perceptual judgments and cognitions generally.[3] How easy it was for

sentence or an inference. A third division is from the point of view of the *material quality* of the sign : thus it may be either a 'qualisign' (e.g. a feeling of redness), a 'sinsign' (a given sentence considered as a spatio-temporal set of marks), or a 'legisign' (a given sentence considered as an assertion, independent of particular physical occurrences). Now a percept is a sign in the sense that it is a qualisign. But a qualisign, while a necessary condition of perceptual cognition, and while capable of occurrence independently, cannot *merely* as a qualisign function as a 'sign' properly speaking. It must be in addition, say, a term, which is a tacit predication.

[1] In 6.497 Peirce speaks of 'percepts' as 'premisses'.

[2] "A feeling is necessarily perfectly simple, *in itself* . . ." (6.18) ; "a feeling may certainly be compound, but only in virtue of a perception which is not that feeling nor any feeling at all" (6.18 n.).

[3] Misleading usage occurs also in 5.291 : that which would not be "determined" Peirce refers to as an "intuition, or first impression of sense". What he has in mind in this confused use of 'intuition' and 'determine' is : Intuition, if assumed, as it is, to be immediate, must turn out not to be *cognitive* (for the genuinely cognitive cannot be purely immediate) but only the material quality of the cognitive, which alone is immediate. Peirce's confusion is thus between the *intended* sense of 'intuition' (distinguished from the material quality of cognition) and the sense to which it reduces after analysis (not distinguishable from the material quality of cognition). Moreover, even in the latter sense of 'intuition', it would be a percept-complex, not a 'first impression of sense'.

Peirce to become confused on the matter under consideration can be seen from the following passage: "I see an inkstand on the table: that is a percept. Moving my head, I get a different percept of the inkstand. It coalesces with the other. What I call the inkstand is a generalized percept, a quasi-inference from percepts, perhaps I might say a composite-photograph of percepts."[1] Now a 'generalized percept', a 'quasi-inference from percepts' and a 'composite-photograph of percepts' are not at all the same. The property 'generalized' belongs to concepts (strictly speaking, to linguistic terms), not to brute percepts (cf. 1.253). And an inference, of whatever kind, is from judgments, not percepts. On the other hand, 'composite-photograph' is legitimate and clear: it means that percepts are in some degree complex and not perfectly simple or specific (though this complexity is revealed by subsequent analysis of, or reflection on, the percept). But if we dwell on the intent rather than the letter of Peirce we understand that by 'generalized percept' he really means 'tacit perceptual judgment', and that by 'quasi-inference from percepts' he means to express the fact that perceptual judgments arise as a result of the stimulus of percepts which link them by association to previous cognitions or other judgments. (On this point we expand in § 14.) I call attention to the present matter only to illustrate how much is compressed in Peirce's language, and how necessary it is to make some such examination of his usage and fundamental ideas as we have attempted thus far.

(2) According to Peirce, the perceptual judgment 'interprets' the percept, it ascertains and asserts what the character of a percept is (5.54, 5.115). This appears to conform to ordinary usage: we 'judge' what we 'see', we tell what it is that appears to us. According to this way of speaking, it would not make very good sense to call the percept the 'material quality' of the perceptual judgment; we could not very well say that the judgment ascertained what its 'material quality' was. But the usage of 1868 is not invalidated.

---

[1] Review of Pearson, *loc. cit.*, p. 301.

It is permissible but not quite accurate for Peirce to say that the judgment 'ascertains the character of the percept'. What he means is that the judgment ascertains the character of the *object*. The percept may legitimately be called the material quality of the perceptual judgment in this sense, that when we judge 'This is a brown chair' the judgment depends upon the appearance of a given set of related qualities. Had the qualities appearing to us been different, the judgment would have differed. The perceptual judgment 'Such-and-such is brown' does not occur without the appearance of brown. We must once more remember that the perceptual judgment is not necessarily an explicit linguistic symbol but rather a cognition. Cognition, though something more than sense feeling (the percept), is inseparable from it.

11. **Generality and Vagueness.** An argument against the possibility of intuition emerges in Peirce if we give some form to his views on the subject of vagueness and generality. Despite the scattered and fragmentary character of these views, Peirce was a pioneer in the conscious analysis of the subject. He says, in fact, "I have worked out the logic of vagueness with something like completeness" (5.506), though if this refers to written work it is not substantiated even by his mss. In what follows, not all that is said is strictly relevant to the next section, but it is perhaps justifiable on its own account.

(*a*) It is necessary, first of all, to be clear on the relation of various terms that occur in Peirce: 'vague', 'general', 'definite', 'determinate', 'singular', 'individual', 'precise'. The contrary of 'vague' is 'definite', which is synonymous with 'precise'. The contrary of 'general' is 'individual', which is usually synonymous with 'singular'. A term is indeterminate if it is either vague or general: vagueness and generality are species of indeterminateness. Hence to say that a term is perfectly determinate may mean either that it is absolutely definite (precise, non-vague), or that it is absolutely singular (individual, non-general). It should be added that 'vague' and 'indefinite' do not always in Peirce mean 'unprecise'. Sometimes he applies these terms to the subject of the traditional existential proposition, e.g., 'Some men . . .'; but most often for this sense he confines himself, in accordance with tradition, to 'indefinite'. (We shall consider the relation of vagueness and generality shortly.)

(b) In the Century Dictionary Peirce's definition of 'vague' is: "Uncertain as to characters and specific designation, yet limited in scope and application; restricted in logical breadth, without any corresponding fullness of logical depth. . . ." In Baldwin's Dictionary of Philosophy and Psychology he calls a proposition 'vague' (though the same applies to terms) "when there are possible states of things concerning which it is intrinsically uncertain whether, had they been contemplated by the speaker, he would have regarded them as excluded or allowed by the proposition [or term]. By intrinsically uncertain we mean not uncertain in consequence of any ignorance of the interpreter, but because the speaker's habits of language were indeterminate; so that one day he would regard the proposition [or term] as excluding, another as admitting, those states of things ".[1] The Century definition thus tacitly emphasizes vagueness of connotation or depth; the Baldwin definition, vagueness of application or breadth.

(c) According to Peirce, "no Sign is absolutely precise . . ." and "indefiniteness is of two kinds, indefiniteness as to what is the Object of the sign, and indefiniteness as to its Interpretant, or indefiniteness in Breadth and in Depth" (4.543). The notion of vagueness in depth thus amounts to vagueness of definition or signification; the notion of vagueness in breadth implies inability to ascertain the exact limits of a term's extension or application, i.e. inability to identify any given instance as included in or excluded from a term's extension. The question arises, What for Peirce is the relation of vagueness in depth to vagueness in breadth? May a term be vague in depth and yet relatively precise in breadth, or vice versa? Does increase in precision of breadth

[1] Vol. II, p. 748.

affect increase in precision of depth, or vice versa? Peirce discusses at length the relations of breadth and depth, and their traditionally supposed inverse proportionality, making some very fine distinctions (2.391-434), but he does not discuss the relation of *vagueness* (or precision) of breadth to that of depth. The notion of increase of precision in depth is not the same as the notion of increase in depth (and similarly with breadth). But I wish to postpone for a moment a suggestion of what Peirce's view on this matter probably was. (See (*e*).)

(*d*) What is the difference between generality and vagueness? According to Peirce "anything is *general* in so far as the principle of excluded middle does not apply to it and is *vague* in so far as the principle of contradiction does not apply to it" (5.448). Thus "a triangle in general is not isosceles nor equilateral; nor is a triangle in general scalene" (5.505). As for vagueness, Peirce means that if, for example, we say 'This is a melancholy day', the statement may be both true and false, since 'melancholy' is used vaguely. If it were made more precise we should not have to say, as we often do, that 'in a sense' the statement is true and in a sense false; we should decide that it must be one or the other. Now since Peirce holds that "*no* sign is absolutely precise", this means that whatever is general is also to some degree vague (unprecise). He is not very clear or consistent on the question whether every sign has some degree of generality, though it would seem that an unprecise sign must in some degree be general. But for the moment he can be taken to hold at least that all linguistic [1] signs (including cognitions or mental signs, which are quasi-linguistic) are in some degree general.[2] This does not affect the truth that

[1] As opposed to ' natural ' signs, such as the pointing of a finger.

[2] In addition to saying that every sign is in some degree vague or unprecise, Peirce says that every sign is in some degree indeterminate (3.93, 5.506). These two statements do not strictly imply that every sign is in some degree general. If, however, no sign were purely demonstrative, every sign would be general. We attempt to show later that no sign is purely demonstrative (pp. 101, 106).

generality and vagueness are for Peirce genuinely distinct. A term may be general and yet *relatively* precise (e.g. 'man'); or vague and yet *relatively* specific (e.g. 'around here').[1]

(*e*) The notion of increasing or decreasing generality is a fairly clear one. We decrease the generality of 'triangle' by specifying an additional differentiating attribute, e.g. 'isosceles'. We are said to generalize a concept, on the other hand, when we define it in such a way that its extension will include a greater variety of instances. But the notion of increase or decrease in *vagueness* is much less clear, involving as it does the subsidiary notions of *vagueness in breadth and in depth* and the relation between the latter two. (The addition of a differentiating property is not sufficient for decrease of vagueness; e.g. 'glorious' and 'intensely glorious' are equally vague.) It seems likely, from the Baldwin definition, that Peirce would hold it possible for precision in breadth to be high while precision in depth was low. An example, presumably, would be the case where the members of a given language-community could identify with ease the objects signified by a term without being able to give a clear definition of that term. On the other hand, it seems unlikely that Peirce would hold it possible for precision in depth to be high while precision in breadth was low. That is to say, if the defining characters of a term are clearly known and expressed, the application of that term must be correspondingly facilitated. The reason why this is probably his view lies in the character of pragmatism, which states what is involved in the meaning of terms and sentences; and we shall better understand the justification of the opinion just ascribed to him when we discuss that doctrine.

(*f*) A prevalent contemporary view, also that of Peirce, is that the predicates 'vague' and 'precise' are applicable chiefly to signs, not, for instance, to objects. The object

---

[1] Most words are 'symbols' (conventionally established signs), but some are 'indices' (signs that have some kind of physical relation to their objects). An index may be either a natural or a linguistic sign, the former exemplified in the gesture of pointing, the latter in a demonstrative pronoun.

simply is as it is, but the sign which refers to the object may
be more or less precise. Sometimes the form in which the
view is expressed is that vagueness and precision are properties of our knowledge; [1] but so far as Peirce is concerned,
this would amount to the same thing, knowledge for him
consisting of thought-signs in relation to an object and to
one another. But an interesting question arises, with respect
to mere *percepts*. Can we say that these are in any sense
vague? We have already (§ 5) quoted Peirce as holding
that percepts cannot be called certain or uncertain, exact or
inexact, for they simply 'are' (1.145). But we find him to
hold that there are no "absolutely determinate images" in
perception or in any other mental operation (5.299-306);
and he speaks of "vagueness in immediate sensation" (3.93),
and says that "not even a percept" is "absolutely precise"
(4.543). To say that an image is absolutely determinate
means for Peirce that "every possible character, or the
negative thereof, must be true of such an image" (5.299).
Thus if we had an absolutely determinate image of a man we
should be able to say whether he was of the white race or
not, precisely how tall he was, what the colour of his eyes
were, etc. Obviously we cannot predicate all these specific
properties in the case of any percept, and we may safely say
with Peirce that no percept is 'absolutely determinate'.
Now if we are to use the terms 'determinate' and 'indeterminate' with respect to percepts as well as signs, then it
would seem that we can use the terms 'vague' (or 'precise')
and 'general' (or 'specific') likewise. It seems to me that
a sense can be given in which percepts are said to have the
properties of generality and vagueness. What Peirce intends
here by ascribing 'indeterminateness' to percepts we may
call 'generality' (he did not use the terms 'general' and
'vague' at the time of this ascription, i.e. 1868). Every
image has a certain amount of generality, that is, is not
specific as to all the properties that might significantly be

[1] E.g. B. Russell, "Vagueness", *Australasian Jour. of Psych. and Phil.*,
Vol. I (1923).

predicated of it. Peirce's view is a sound criticism of that of Berkeley. But he sometimes seems to be using 'indeterminate' in another sense, for instance, as expressing the variation in sense quality of an image from some standard appearance of that image. In any event he gives no clear account of the matter, and in 3.93 even seems to confuse 'vagueness in immediate sensation' with generality as we have just understood it. But having suggested a sense in which percepts are 'general', I now want to state a sense in which percepts may be said to be 'vague'; the relevance of this being that the Baldwin definition of vagueness in *signs* may be shown to require some modification.

(g) A percept may be said to be vague, not *qua* appearance but in relation to a term, in particular the term that is said to describe it. Thus we can speak of a vague image of a house in the sense that the term 'house' is usually applied to an image of different quality, whether sharper in outline, more prominent in colour, etc. In this case it is obviously not because the *word* 'house' is to a certain extent vague that we have difficulty in identifying the percept; it is rather because of special perceptual conditions. The Baldwin definition of vagueness calls a term 'vague' if it is uncertain or doubtful whether an object comes within the extension of that term. But in the example just given it is uncertain whether the object seen (the 'percept') comes within the application of 'house'; yet we should not say that it is on account of the word's vagueness but on account of certain perceptual conditions, resulting in vagueness of the percept, that we are doubtful of the application. Peirce would appear to have anticipated this objection by saying (cf. Baldwin statement above) that the uncertainty of the extension of the term to the object must be 'intrinsic' uncertainty, which he defines as uncertainty resulting from indeterminacy of usage. But it may easily be, and perhaps is, the case that as a result of vagueness in percepts we are *as often* in doubt about the application of a term as we are sure of it; yet we do not on this account regard the term as vague. The point is that the emphasis on vagueness in breadth is misleading; the definition in terms of indeterminacy of language habits or usage is inadequate. It is not merely because we decide to alter our habit in the use of a word and legislate that hereafter it shall be restricted or extended to such-and-such objects that the term is made more precise; but because we do this when conscious of new defining characters. In saying this we must guard against the opposite extreme, which would emphasize exclusively the interpretant rather than the object, contrary to the spirit of Peirce's pragmatism.

This returns us to (e), where we said it appeared to be the view of Peirce that greater precision in depth entailed greater precision in breadth (in harmony with pragmatism), but that greater precision in breadth did not entail greater precision in depth. It is the latter view that we have just been protesting, holding that increase in determinacy of application without increase in precision of depth does not occur.

We said that presumably the members of a language-community might know with great precision to just which objects a term applies without being able to define the term at all precisely. To a certain extent this is an empirical question and can only be decided as such. I am inclined to believe that the assumption is dubious, and that while the application of a term may be relatively accurate for practical purposes and as a result of conditioning, borderline cases cannot easily be identified without awareness to a rather precise degree of abstract distinguishing characters. But even if conditioning should make possible precise discrimination in applying a term, without awareness of abstract characters, it is still questionable whether vagueness or precision in breadth depends upon the mere fact of usage by a majority of members in a language-group. Every term used in a language can, after all, be placed in the domain of a special discipline, and it would seem proper for the vagueness or precision of that term to be relative to the usage of trained investigators. This does not mean that such investigators arbitrarily decree what usage shall occur. It means that the precise application of a term will involve its precise signification, formulated probably by experts. But we must, it is true, remember that precise signification in turn involves precise application, likewise determined by experts.

(*h*) For the purpose of Peirce's essential argument against intuition which we shall try to state, it was not strictly necessary to distinguish between generality and vagueness (though we make use of the distinction in stating the argument), especially since Peirce's view is that all linguistic signs are to a certain degree both vague and general. What it is important to emphasize is simply that all terms are to a certain degree indeterminate (3.93). But it is rather important also to further supplement Peirce by distinguishing purely abstract and empirical terms, between which there is a difference with respect to vagueness and generality. An abstract term cannot be free from generality, but it may be free from vagueness; an empirical term can be free neither from vagueness nor from generality. (i) In an abstract system a term may be precisely defined in terms of arbitrarily selected primitives. We are not bothered by the question of empirical reference or interpretation. The question of refining the primitives in point of precision never occurs, and is in fact meaningless.[1] (ii) But logical atomism, or perfect freedom from generality in abstract systems, is impossible, because the primitive terms being selected conventionally, we may always introduce new primitives by means of which we can define the old less generally. (iii) Turning to empirical terms (though it applies to all terms), let us note that absolute generality and absolute vagueness amount to the same thing, and so do perfect freedom from generality and perfect precision (cf. 5.506). That is, an absolutely general empirical term would be absolutely vague, and vice versa; and an absolutely specific term would be absolutely precise, and

[1] If (i) is the view of Peirce, then the assertion that " no sign is absolutely precise " must be modified to apply only to terms with objective reference. (See an incompatibility in statements of 4.237 and 6.496, the former affirming the existence of perfect precision in mathematics, the latter denying it.)

vice versa. It seems obvious also that absolute precision (or vagueness) in *depth* implies absolute precision (or vagueness) in *breadth*, and vice versa. Now to say that a term is absolutely non-general is to say that it requires no definition at all in terms of general characters, i.e. that it is purely demonstrative or non-connotative. To say that a term is perfectly precise in depth means that it is definable by perfectly precise terms. These latter terms could not be further definable; so that a term perfectly precise in depth would be 'definable' only in purely demonstrative terms, i.e. again, it would itself be a purely demonstrative term. Finally, a term perfectly precise in breadth, being also perfectly precise in depth, would be purely demonstrative. Thus if Peirce does not admit that there are purely demonstrative terms he cannot admit that an empirical term can be perfectly precise and non-general. He does hold explicitly, as we saw, that no cognition and in general no sign is absolutely precise. But why? It is not necessary to hunt stray considerations. For a purely demonstrative sign would be a sign with an object but with no interpretant, and this violates the general theory of signs. 'Blue' does express a feeling, but it expresses something more—for a feeling is no interpretation or translation. 'Blue' is the name of a property which stands in relation to other properties, and the definition or interpretant of which takes cognizance of such relation. The precise definition of 'blue' makes use of general characters, and its precise application makes use of instruments of measurement. Absolute exactness of measurement cannot be attained; moreover, the process of measurement makes use of many assumptions, both in the form of physical principles and of special conditions prevailing at a given time, and these will not be free from vagueness; so that the definition and application of 'blue' will never be *perfectly* precise.

12. **Why Intuitive Cognition is not Possible.** In §§ 7-8 we represented Peirce as showing that there was no necessity of

assuming intuition. We now want to show how on his view there can *be* none. Before we do so it may be worth noting that to deny intuitive cognitions and to deny intuitive sentences amount to the same thing. For what we mean when we speak of an intuitive sentence is one known intuitively; and on the other hand, every cognition is in some degree judicative and, if a genuine cognition at all, can be expressed in a sentence. We should also call attention to the fact that the following expressions are all synonymous: (i) intuitive judgments (cognitions, sentences, propositions); (ii) immediate judgments; (iii) judgments known certainly to be true; (iv) purely demonstrative judgments; (v) ostensive judgments; (vi) uninferred (undetermined) judgments; (vii) conclusively verifiable judgments; (viii) unalterable or incorrigible judgments; (ix) atomic judgments.

We may divide the argument into four parts: first, an argument from the generality of terms and sentences; second, one from the vagueness of terms and sentences; third, one from the vagueness of percepts; fourth, one from the nature of knowledge in general.

(1) If every empirical word has some degree of generality, it follows that every synthetic judgment has, including the perceptual judgments (5.151-157). We are most interested in these perceptual judgments, for they are supposedly the intuitive judgments. If we recall what it means for a term to be general we soon see why there can be no intuitive judgments. Such a term is always definable by means of others themselves further definable. We can never exhaust the enumeration of the empirical properties implied in the meaning of any empirical term. From the statement containing such a term, therefore, an infinite number of other statements is deducible (cf. 5.157). These state the properties implied in the original predication of a property. Clearly all of these properties cannot be given in perception. But to say that a perceptual judgment is intuitive means that we immediately verify all of its consequences, which is absurd. Consider, for instance, the perceptual judgment 'This is

blue'. In order to determine whether it is true, we must ascertain by tests whether the designated object has the exact property of blueness. To ascribe blueness to an object is to ascribe a number of properties generally taken as definitory of blueness. We specify a set of properties or conditions which, if possessed or fulfilled by an object, justifies the predication of the name 'blue'. The ascertainment of whether the given object actually possesses these defining properties or fulfils these defining conditions is no instantaneous affair. It employs instruments of measurement which require numerous assumptions. So that a *rigid* ascertainment of the truth of even a simple perceptual judgment is a relatively complex matter, involving the truth of other statements, which in turn involve the truth of still others, and so on ad infinitum. Every synthetic statement, then, remains theoretically corrigible. There is no reason, after all, why we should be mistaken in judging 'This is vermilion' and yet not be capable of false judgment in 'This is blue'.

(2) If every empirical word has some degree of vagueness, so has every synthetic statement. But to say that every such statement is vague is to say that we are not absolutely certain of its meaning. And clearly if we are not absolutely certain of its meaning we cannot be absolutely certain of its truth.[1]

---

[1] Opposed to this is the present-day view of G. E. Moore, who holds that there are propositions which we " know, with certainty, to be true ", yet of whose meaning we cannot be said to be absolutely certain. Moore distinguishes between *understanding* the meaning of a proposition and *giving a correct analysis* of the meaning of that proposition. We understand the meaning of the propositions which we know certainly to be true, but we cannot (as yet) give a ' correct ' analysis of that meaning. It is not clear just what Moore intends by ' correct ' analysis of a proposition's meaning. I would suggest that the justice which Moore craves for common sense in his ' certainly true ' propositions is achieved by Peirce's theory of ' indubitables ' (see below), and that Moore's common-sensism, lacking a theory of ' fallibilism ' (see below), is not so *critical* a common-sensism as Peirce's. (See Moore, " A Defence of Common Sense ", in *Contemporary British Philosophy*, 2nd series, ed. Muirhead, pp. 193-223.)

(3) We saw that a distinction can be expressed between the vagueness of a term and perceptual vagueness, and that Peirce (5.299-306) sensed the importance of the latter notion even if he did not satisfactorily describe it. Its importance in the matter of intuitive cognition lies in the fact that we can never, while judging, be certain that our judgment was made under standard perceptual conditions. What do we mean by 'standard conditions'? We mean conditions which prevail when standard tests confirm the judgment. That we cannot be certain while judging that the judgment is made under standard conditions means that we cannot be certain whether special perceptual factors cause us to judge differently from what others would judge, or from what standard tests would decide, or from what we would at other times have judged. These special perceptual conditions always exist to a certain extent and are responsible in part for perceptual vagueness. That they always exist to some extent, does not prevent us from being able to define a set of standard conditions. But the essential point is that the determination of whether the standard conditions obtain or not is no momentary matter, and consequently no perceptual judgment is known immediately to be true. All of this is, I think, implied in a point stated by Peirce (5.544) as follows: There is a distinction between the mere operation of the senses (and the consequent percept), which is momentary, and the forming of a judgment, which is not momentary. Every perceptual judgment is thus, strictly speaking, a reference to a memory of a percept. Actually we do not judge that something looks red but that (a moment ago) it looked red,—and we may repeat this from moment to moment. Memory is notoriously unreliable. We always have in mind the possibility that a percept in the past might have been different in quality from one in the present, and consequently that our past judgment, be it never so recent, might always have been made under different perceptual conditions from those which prevail when we make the same judgment again. (Cf. 2.141, 5.142.)

(4) The preceding arguments are really special ways of stating the more inclusive argument against intuition, based on the nature of knowledge.   Knowledge or cognition is constituted by thought-signs in relation to one another and to some object.   Any thought has another thought interpreting or translating it and it has an object.   A thought not capable of translation, i.e. of yielding consequences, would not be a thought (5.594).   Suppose our thought to be a perceptual judgment.   If this judgment were intuitive or purely demonstrative it would have no interpretant judgment but would be purely referential, which is contrary to Peirce's theory of the nature of knowledge.   Every thought is susceptible of interpretation, and there is none whose full meaning and complete truth (or falsity) are immediately and simultaneously given in perception (cf. 5.253).

The foregoing arguments aim to show more than that there are in fact no intuitions.   If we accept Peirce's analysis of knowledge, we must conclude that the concept of intuitive *cognition* is self-contradictory, and that the term 'intuitive cognition' becomes a violation of proper usage.

There are two remarks which must be appended to the conclusions represented in this and the preceding section. We have ruled out purely demonstrative linguistic signs. But there are some inconsistencies in Peirce's theory of signs, affecting the argument against purely demonstrative signs, and hence affecting the argument against intuition.   We shall have occasion to examine and explain these inconsistencies in Part II (esp. § 31).   The argument against intuition depends upon the argument against purely demonstrative linguistic (and mental or quasi-linguistic) signs.   The argument against such signs depends on the nature of knowledge, which depends on the nature of the sign in general.   The argument against purely demonstrative signs is also directly connected with the pragmatic theory of meaning, which we shall explore in Part II.   The inconsistencies in the theory of signs just mentioned do not affect the pragmatic theory as such, but they do affect its scope; and it is conceivable

that certain signs are not to be interpreted pragmatically
and are purely demonstrative, so that our argument against
intuition threatens to waver. With this matter too we shall
deal at greater length.

Whereas in §§ 7-8 we showed that there was no necessity
of assuming intuition, and in § 12 that there could *be* no
intuition, we now want to round off the picture by a positive
account of just what thought does amount to when intuition
is eliminated. Such an account, if satisfactory, is itself of
course an argument against intuition, or at least a fortifica-
tion of such an argument. We said that every cognition is
inferred from some previous cognition.[1] It should be fairly
evident that the bulk of thought consists not of deliberate
inferences but of what we have found Peirce to call 'associational suggestion.' We have also seen that this associational connection of thoughts is a continuous process. We
now want to analyze this process and describe its logical
form. And in order to do this we must again for a
moment refer to Peirce's theory of signs, this time not to
the general concept of representation but to a particular
kind of sign.

13. **Abduction and Induction.** Peirce makes various classifications of signs, depending upon the purpose he has in
mind.[2] One is into terms, sentences and inferences (or
'arguments', in Peirce's terminology). Thus the sign 'lover'
is a term, the sign 'All men are lovers' is a proposition, and
the sign known as the syllogism in Barbara is an inference.
Now Peirce makes a fundamental division of inferences into
explicative (analytic, deductive) and ampliative (synthetic).
Ampliative inferences are of two kinds, induction and abduction (sometimes called 'hypothesis', 'hypothetic inference'
or 'retroduction'). Ampliative inferences are probable: the
premises, assumed to be true, constitute evidence but not
(except in the case of complete induction) demonstrative

---

[1] ". . . Inference is the essential function of the cognitive mind "
(2.444 n.).   [2] Cf. p. 20, note.

evidence for the truth of the conclusion.[1] An induction is an argument which, from the knowledge that certain members of a class, chosen at random, have a certain property, concludes approximately that all the members of the class have that property. Inductions are arguments by which we seek to establish scientific hypotheses (e.g. 6.526). These hypotheses have consequences predicting "the results of possible experiments" (2.96). Experimentation confirms a number of these predictions, and by induction we conclude that the hypothesis is established with a certain degree of finality. But then how is the hypothesis itself arrived at? The usual view regards hypotheses in science as fruitful guesses or 'flashes of insight'. Peirce holds the apparently paradoxical view that hypotheses are indeed flashes of insight, or even 'conjectures' (5.189, 5.480), and yet at the same time inferences—abductions. An abduction is an inference which consists in passing from a fact (or facts) observed to a hypothesis, or explanation of this fact, the statement of the fact being a necessary consequence of the hypothesis. The form of the inference is somewhat as follows:

"The surprising fact, C, is observed;
But if A were true, C would be a matter of course,
Hence, there is reason to suspect that A is true" (5.189).

The element of insight or guess here consists in the perception that from A, C would follow as a factual result; and our conclusion that A is probably the case results, inferentially, from the affirmation of the consequent of the second statement. Thus abduction is the adoption of a hypothesis. This process of adopting a hypothesis is an inferential process. The hypothesis adopted is 'probational' (1.68, 2.96), being subject to test by induction from those of its consequences which are experimentally confirmed. Abduction,

---

[1] Ampliative inference is not the only, and in fact not the most important, kind of probable reasoning for Peirce ; for he recognizes ' probable deduction '. Both probable deduction, which is ' explicative ', and ampliative inference, are forms of probable reasoning (cf. p. 189, note, and § 50).

on Peirce's view, differs from both deduction and induction in that it is the source of new ideas, and the sole source (5.145, 5.171). He distinguishes abduction and induction in the following way: ". . . the essence of an induction is that it infers from one set of facts another set of similar facts, whereas hypothesis infers from facts of one kind to facts of another" (2.642). (Cf. § 37.)

14. **The Abductive and Inductive Character of Thought.** On Peirce's view the associational connection of thought is either an abductive or an inductive relation of cognitions (thought-signs). Now, according to him, all cognition can in a sense be reduced to two fundamental kinds, sensation and attention (or abstraction) (5.295). (1) We have seen that sensation (as opposed, of course, to non-cognitive 'feeling') is a process of forming perceptual judgments. This process, the most rudimentary in cognition and in fact the source of all cognition, is analyzed by Peirce to be a process of abduction. On such an analysis, although every perceptual judgment is 'determined by', i.e. inferred from, some previous cognition, it is yet possible to account for the fact that through perception new elements (strictly, new predications) enter into thought. For this 'determination' is abductive inference, the formation of a hypothesis, which is the source of new thought. Our perceptual judgments are the simplest and best evidenced of all our hypotheses. (2) Whereas perception is abductive, attention or the abstracting process of thought is held by Peirce to be inductive, attention bearing the same relation to sensation as induction, inferentially considered, to abduction.

(1) *Perception as Abduction.* To say that a perceptual judgment is a hypothesis, that is, a judgment inferred abductively, is another way of saying that it is interpretative. One of the best pieces of evidence for the interpretativeness of perceptual judgments is to be found in the well-known psychological phenomena resulting from mental 'adjustment'. ". . . We perceive what we are adjusted for inter-

preting. . . ." (5.185). For instance, when we wish to awaken in the morning at a certain hour, our actual awakening, resulting from mental preparation and adjustment, comes closer to the actual hour than if we were to judge it while awake. Or, while sitting in a room busily engaged, say in study or contemplation, we commonly fail to perceive the striking of the clock, though the tone would ordinarily be regarded as quite audible. This interpretativeness of the perceptual judgment was familiar to psychologists before Peirce. But Peirce's analysis of the judgment as a hypothesis makes clear, as we shall see, the logical and methodological significance of the interpretativeness. (It is worth mentioning that the theory of perception as abduction fits in with another point made by Peirce. We saw that a cognition inferred from another may be regarded as the interpretant of that other. Peirce holds, in line with this, that the conclusion of an inference is the interpretant of the premises [e.g. 2.95, 253; 4.540; 5.175, 179]. If we were to return to the terminology used above, we should state the present thesis as being that every perceptual judgment is the interpretant of some other, specifically, the abductive interpretant.[1])

We now want to go into detail and state more specifically and accurately just what Peirce's thesis means. It seems that we can distinguish two descriptions of the form of perceptual hypothetic inference, one in 1868, the other in 1891, the latter being clearer and somewhat fuller.

First the earlier description, obscure but helped somewhat when taken in conjunction with a passage from a paper of 1867, the first year in which Peirce published.[2] Consider an example, 'This is red'. This perceptual judgment is a hypothesis in the sense that (a) the term 'red' is ordinarily applied to objects that have certain properties; (b) we judge the given object to have some or all of these properties; (c) we conclude (hypothetically) that the object is red. Consider

---

[1] It is not the case, conversely, that every interpretant is a conclusion.
[2] He printed privately in 1866 (cf. Collected Papers, Vol. II, Appendix).

another example. It is clear that in judging 'This is silk' we tacitly assume the name 'silk' to apply to whatever has certain properties (e.g. smoothness and gloss) discovered in touch and sight; upon discovering these properties we judge the cloth to be silk (cf. 5.221). The perceptual judgment is a hypothesis in that it substitutes a simple predicate for a complex set of predicates. This hypothesis is the conclusion or result of an inference "from definition to definitum" (5.291). What does Peirce mean by reasoning 'from definition to definitum', and in what sense is it hypothetic inference? This seems to be answered by 2.426: "The definitum implies the character of being designated by a word, while the definition, previously to the formation of the word, does not. . . . The definition is the predicate and the definitum the subject, of the defining proposition, and this last cannot be simply converted. In fact, the defining proposition affirms that whatever a certain name is applied to is supposed to have such and such characters; but it does not strictly follow from this, that whatever has such and such characters is actually called by that name, although it certainly *might* be so called." Thus to pass from the discovery of certain properties to the assertion that a given object is 'red' or 'silk' is hypothetical. We might state the form of the inference as follows:

We discover an object with the properties a, b, c;
But if the object were 'red', these are the properties it
    would have;
Therefore, it is red. (Cf. scheme p. 37, above.)

The second premiss is a 'defining proposition'. The first states defining properties. The conclusion is a hypothesis obtained by affirmation of the consequent.

The later account of perceptual abduction is to be found in a review [1] of James's *Principles of Psychology*. Peirce devotes his entire discussion of the second volume of the book to the brief section entitled "Is Perception Unconscious Inference?" That James was not jesting in the remarks

[1] *Nation*, Vol. 53 (1891), pp. 32-33.

quoted above (§ 1) concerning his inability to understand
Peirce's 1868 papers, is here proved, for in this section he
makes no mention of Peirce, going rather to the traditional
German view of perception as 'unconscious inference'.
Peirce considers both James and the Germans to be confused. He attempts to show that James's refutation of their
view is not a refutation at all but actually a confirmation—
provided the view is properly stated. The attempted refutation depends upon a confusion of 'reasoning' with 'associational suggestion' ('associative suggestion' in the review), of
inference in a narrow sense with inference in a generalized
sense. James agrees that perception involves association,
and moreover, that this association is in a broad sense
inferential. His complaint is: "Only one sees no room in
it for any unconscious part. Both associates, the present
sign and the contiguous things which it suggests, are above
board, and no intermediary ideas are required." [1] Peirce
points out that James is not clear as to what 'unconscious
inference' means, or should properly mean. Reasoning
(conscious inference) always involves the "side-thought",
"so it would be in every analogous case (or in most cases)";
i.e. it involves the awareness of a leading principle of inference. As for associational inference (or 'suggestion'), the
following is its form:

   (i) "A well-recognized kind of object, M, has for its
        ordinary predicates P_1, P_2, P_3, etc., indistinctly
        recognized.
  (ii) The suggesting object, S, has these same predicates,
        P_1, P_2, P_3, etc.
 (iii) Hence, S is of the kind M." [2]

"This is hypothetic inference in form. The first premiss is
not actually thought, though it is in the mind habitually.
This, of itself, would not make the inference unconscious.
But it is so because it is not recognized as an inference; the
conclusion is accepted without our knowing how" (ib.).

[1] *Principles of Psychology*, Vol. II, pp. 111-112.
[2] *Loc. cit.*, p. 32.

Thus, the first premiss above represents the habit; the second represents the stimulus (suggestion); the third is the perceptual cognition which, by virtue of the habit and the suggestion, is evoked as an associational response. (Cf. 4.541.)

We must add a few words on reasoning and associational inference, as well as on 'acritical inference', already mentioned (§ 4). Now reasoning involves awareness of some leading principle, even if not formulated, as governing the inference. Acritical inference is conscious inference without awareness of a leading principle; and finally, associational suggestion is inference that is unconscious, hence, a fortiori, unaware of a leading principle. But it is a view of Peirce that leading principles do in fact play a certain part in acritical inference: they are not explicit rules but *habits* of inference; they constitute part of our 'home-made' logic, or *logica utens* (see 2.186, 3.164). In fact, most often Peirce speaks of leading principles as being the habits that govern the various kinds or classes of inference we make. Leading principles are not merely explicit linguistic rules, but, more generally, habits of inference verbally expressed (cf. 3.160); and we find Peirce using the expression "leading principle of a habit of inference" (2.589). Thus sometimes 'leading principle' means the actual habit of inference, sometimes the habit in so far as it is formulated, and sometimes, though least frequently, a rule that may not necessarily express a habit but be arbitrary. But do leading principles also play a part in associational inference? It seems to follow from Peirce's views on leading principles that we may regard the habit, (i) above, as the leading principle of the inference (cf. 3.160); that is to say, the habit of conjoining the name of an object with certain properties enables us to pass from one sign, (ii), to another sign, (iii), the latter the interpretant, hypothesis, or response. For although Peirce carefully distinguishes the leading principle of an inference from the premisses of that inference, he nevertheless holds that a leading principle may sometimes function as a premiss (or premiss function as leading principle). The assertion that from (ii), (iii) follows, would by itself be an inference; but (i) would be tacitly assumed as regulating the transition. (i) is not a 'logical' leading principle, i.e. it is not a rule for an analytic inference; it is what Peirce calls a 'material' or 'factual' leading principle (cf. 2.589), such principles governing other than apodictic inferences (cf. § 45).

What about (ii) in the above inference, or our judgment a while ago that the cloth has certain properties? James objects that these are likewise perceptual judgments, and on the view in question are themselves the results of associational inference, thus leading to infinite inferential regress. Peirce's reply to this objection we have already to some extent seen (§ 8). Perceptual cognition is a continuous process. It has a beginning in time (5.327), but has no atomic term that can be called the 'first' cognition. When we represent this situation abstractly, as we have just done, we characterize it as consisting of a series of inferences that can be traced back indefinitely. We can always point to some perceptual judgment as preceding a given one, and to some habit by means of which we infer a later judgment from an earlier one. There is no first premiss to this series of inferences in terms of which we state our analysis. But to call this analysis a description of the actual movement of thought, which seems to be what James has in mind when he objects, is to make the same mistake as the Achilles sophism, which assumes that Achilles must make distinct or atomic efforts to overtake the tortoise and thus purports to describe what actual motion in space amounts to. Thought "does not have to make separate acts of inference, but performs its act in one continuous process" (5.181). Nevertheless thought can be *analyzed* into inferential steps, and it is only because of such analysis that we are able to understand why it is that knowledge is of a hypothetical character. The case is the same with any other abstract analysis which does not describe but which explains.

In physiological terms, the reason why our conclusion (the

response) is hypothetical, is that the same stimulus *may*, depending upon the conditions which prevail, give rise to any one of a number of responses. And in logical terms, the perceptual judgment is a hypothetic conclusion because an object with the suggesting properties P_1, P_2, P_3, etc. *may* be of another kind than M. Or, to use the earlier version, it may be that *another* object than one called 'red' should have the discovered properties a, b, c.

(2) *Attention (Abstraction) as Induction.* Attention or abstraction, Peirce believes, "is roused when the same phenomenon presents itself repeatedly on different occasions, or the same predicate in different subjects. We see that A has a certain character, that B has the same, C has the same; and this excites our attention, so that we say, '*These* have this character'. Thus attention is an act of induction; but it is an induction which does not increase our knowledge, because our 'these' covers nothing but the instances experienced. It is, in short, an argument from enumeration" (5.296). (An 'increase' in knowledge is in any case, strictly speaking, due only to an abduction, though Peirce sometimes speaks of increase in knowledge as being due to ampliative inference in general.) The inductive character of attention is seen if we consider, analogously to the case of perception, the effects of attention on the nervous system. The formation of a habit is for Peirce an induction. Suppose that a, b, and c are particular instances of an event l. "A habit arises, when, having had the sensation of performing a certain act, m, on several occasions a, b, c, we come to do it upon every occurrence of the general event, l. . . ." (5.297). In other words, from the judgment 'Every case a, b, c, is a case of m' we infer the judgment 'Every case of l is a case of m'.[1]

15. **Peirce and the Scottish School.** I suggested at the beginning of this discussion of critical common-sensism that

[1] For the physiological interpretation of inference in general, see 6.144-146, 2.643, 2.711-713. E.g., "Induction . . . is the logical formula which expresses the physiological process of formation of a habit " (2.643).

Peirce's emphasis against intuitive cognition and what is implied by it could best be understood if regarded as in opposition to the view of the Scottish philosophers. This does not mean that Peirce's own description of the 1868 papers as written "in a spirit of opposition to Cartesianism" is incorrect. On the contrary; for, in so far as the general character and presuppositions of their psychology is concerned, the Scottish philosophers follow Locke, who in turn follows Descartes. I believe we are now ready to illustrate, by means of quotation first from Reid and then from Dugald Stewart, the respect in which Peirce's 1868 papers are a reaction against certain of their opinions. This will enable us the better to understand how he profits by the *positive* influence which they exercise upon him.

It will be recalled that for Locke there are a number of 'operations of the mind', such as perception, abstraction, belief and imagination, which, by means of 'reflection' or 'internal sense', we can observe and discriminate, just as by external sense we observe and discriminate physical objects. The writings of Reid and Stewart are an extension and elaboration of Locke's general scheme of the mind.

(1)   ". . . Consciousness is only of things in the mind, and not of external things. It is improper to say, I am conscious of the table which is before me. I perceive it, I see it ; but do not say I am conscious of it. . . . That consciousness by which we have a knowledge of the operations of our own minds, is a different power from that by which we perceive external objects." (Hamilton's Reid, pp. 222-223.)

". . . By consciousness we know certainly the existence of our present thoughts and passions." (*Ibid.* p. 231.)

"When a man is conscious of pain, he is certain of its existence ; when he is conscious that he doubts or believes, he is certain of the existence of those operations. But the irresistible conviction he has of the reality of those operations is not the effect of reasoning; it is immediate and intuitive." (*Ibid.* p. 442.)

Reid distinguishes between 'consciousness' and 'reflection', which he thinks are often confused by Locke.

(2)   "All men are conscious of the operations of their own minds, at all times, while they are awake; but there are few who reflect upon them, or make them objects of thought. From infancy, till we come to the years of understanding, we are employed solely about external objects. And, although the mind is conscious of its operations, it does not attend to them; its attention is turned solely to the external objects, about which those operations are employed. Thus, when a man is angry, he is conscious of his passion; but his attention is turned to the person who offended him, and the circumstances of the offence, while the passion of anger is not in the least the object of his attention. . . . We may have [consciousness] without any degree of [reflection]. The difference between consciousness and reflection, is like to the difference between a superficial view of an object which presents itself to the eye while we are engaged about something else, and that attentive examination which we give to an object when we are wholly employed in surveying it." (*Ibid.* p. 239.)

"[Consciousness] . . . is insufficient of itself to give us clear and distinct notions of the operations of which we are conscious, and of their mutual relations and minute distinctions." (*Ibid.* p. 443.)

Reflection requires attention and is a habit which must be inculcated. But

(3)   "This reflection is a kind of intuition, it gives a like conviction with regard to internal objects, or things in the mind, as the faculty of seeing gives with regard to objects of sight. A man must, therefore, be convinced beyond possibility of doubt, of everything with regard to the operations of his own mind, which he clearly and distinctly discerns by attentive reflection." (*Ibid.* p. 232.)

The distinction between intuitive and non-intuitive judgments is described as follows:

(4)   "One of the most important distinctions of our judgments is, that some of them are intuitive, others grounded on argument. . . . In propositions that are submitted to our judgment, there is this great difference—some are of such

a nature that a man of ripe understanding may apprehend them distinctly, and perfectly understand their meaning, without finding himself under any necessity of believing them to be true or false, probable or improbable. The judgment remains in suspense, until it is inclined to one side or another by reasons or arguments. But there are other propositions which are no sooner understood than they are believed. . . . There is no searching for evidence, no weighing of arguments; the proposition is not deduced or inferred from another; it has the light of truth in itself. . . ." (*Ibid.* p. 434.)

These intuitive judgments are called by Reid 'dictates of' or 'principles of common sense'.

The points made in the foregoing passages are: (i) The objects of 'consciousness' are the operations of the mind; (ii) This consciousness is immediate and intuitive, and the existence of its objects is therefore beyond doubt; (iii) Whereas consciousness reveals with certainty the existence of the operations, 'reflection' reveals with certainty their nature and mutual relations; (iv) All judgments either require other judgments as evidence for their truth or falsity, i.e. are inferred; or are immediate, i.e. known to be true or false simply by understanding their meaning.

For purposes of comparison, it may be worth calling attention to certain confusions in Reid. In the first place, he is not clear as to the kind of statement that is to be called intuitive. Most often this seems to be a demonstrative statement about internal or external sense. But he also says, for instance, that "I hold, as a first principle, the existence of everything of which I am conscious." [1] This and other examples seem to imply that a statement like 'Whatever I am conscious of, exists', which is of course general and not demonstrative, is intuitive. Secondly, Reid fails to make clear, in distinguishing between consciousness and reflection, whether and to what extent consciousness or reflection, or neither, or both, are judicative. Thirdly, there

[1] Hamilton's Reid, p. 442.

seems to be considerable confusion in calling reflection the result of habit and close attention and yet intuitive. 'Reflection' is what Peirce calls 'introspection', Peirce holding, as we saw, not only that it is not intuitive but that it is not a purely internal process at all.

Stewart calls Reid's intuitive principles of common sense 'fundamental laws of human belief'. Belief in these is "necessary for the preservation of our animal existence; and it is accordingly coeval with the first operations of the intellect." [1] I want to quote Stewart on two points, in which he somewhat modifies the opinions of Reid and reveals a degree of affinity with Peirce. Concerning an intuitive consciousness of the *self*, as distinct from consciousness of its operations, he says:

(1)   "We are conscious of sensation, thought, desire, volition; but we are not conscious of the existence of mind itself; nor would it be possible for us to arrive at the knowledge of it . . . if no impression were ever to be made on our external senses. The moment that, in consequence of such an impression, a sensation is excited, we learn two facts at once; the existence of the sensation, and our own existence as sentient beings. . . . It appears to me, therefore, more correct to call the belief of our own existence a concomitant or accessory of the exercise of consciousness, than to say, that our existence is a fact falling under the immediate cognizance of consciousness. . . ." (*Elements of the Philosophy of the Human Mind*, Pt. II, ch. 1.)

"If this distinction be just, the celebrated enthymeme of Descartes, *cogito, ergo sum*, does not deserve *all* the ridicule bestowed on it by those writers who have represented the author as attempting to demonstrate his own existence by a process of reasoning. To me it seems more probable, that he meant . . . to direct the attention of his readers to . . . the impossibility of our ever having learned the fact of our own existence, without some sensation being excited in the mind. . . ." (*Philosophical Essays*, Ess. I, ch.1.)

---

[1] *Outlines of Moral Philosophy*, sec. 70.

Concerning the relation between intuition and reasoning, he says:

(2)   "Although . . . I have followed the example of preceding writers, so far as to speak of intuition and reasoning as two different faculties of the understanding, I am by no means satisfied that there exists between them that radical distinction which is commonly apprehended. . . . I look upon the distinction between our intuitive and deductive judgments as, in many cases, merely an object of theoretical curiosity." (*Elements*, Pt. II, ch. 2.)

Stewart is unable to say clearly just what the status is of knowledge of the 'self'. This knowledge he holds to be certain, yet to be neither an 'immediate cognizance' nor the result of a 'process of reasoning'. If we bear in mind that Stewart wrote a mere forty years before Peirce, it becomes evident how remarkable are the 1868 papers, which not only break with a powerful psychological tradition but contain in germ almost every major theme in Peirce's thought.

16. **Three Categories of the Mind; 'Immediate Perception'.** We have distinguished cognition or thought proper from the material quality of cognition. It must not be supposed that this material quality is a mere abstraction from a single actual process called cognition. For it may be the case that mere feeling occurs without our being justifiably said to think or know. Hence, from a certain point of view, we may distinguish as mental categories the element of pure feeling, instantaneous and qualitative, from the element of knowing, which is discursive. We may, however, say that if feeling can occur without knowing, the converse is not the case, for every instance of knowing involves some kind of feeling. There is yet another mental category recognized by Peirce which we have not mentioned since it was not essential for our purpose, but which is also said by him to be involved in cognition. This category is what Peirce substitutes for volition in the traditional Kantian division of the mental categories into feeling of pleasure and pain, voli-

tion, and cognition (though the other two categories do not quite mean in Peirce what they mean in Kant or subsequently). In 1868 he calls it the 'pure demonstrative [or 'denotative'] application' of the thought-sign, a vague appellation for a kind of physical relationship which he was trying to describe as obtaining between a cognition and its object, or between one cognition and another. But in later years his writings abound with this mental category, called by him the 'polar sense' or 'sense of duality'. It is a sense of opposition between the knowing mind and the external world, or even between the non-cognizing mind and the world; a sense of a 'within' and a 'without'; a sense of 'hitting and getting hit', of 'actual action and reaction', of struggle (1.380; cf. 1.377).[1]

There is one familiar point on which I have not quoted Reid, namely, immediate perception. Peirce declares that he holds Reid's doctrine of immediate perception (5.56, 5.539). Reid, it will be remembered, distinguished between the mind, the act or operation of the mind, and the external object, and attacked Locke for having introduced what he took to be a fourth entity, the 'idea'.[2] But Peirce's interpretation of 'immediate perception' is not quite the same as that of Reid or Kant, and his belief in it is consistent with his belief in non-intuitive cognition as the sole kind of cognition. For according to Peirce, the doctrine of 'immediate perception' is simply the recognition that there is a 'sense of duality' in perception. It is this sense, which is present in *all* cognition, that justifies us in calling perception

[1] The three mental categories are manifestations of Peirce's three general categories, which he calls by the names Firstness, Secondness and Thirdness. These categories are "modes of being" (1.23), or better, are the most general characters that can be discriminated in all experience. Roughly, Firstness is quality, Secondness is actual fact, Thirdness is law or generality. Thus feeling would be an instance of Firstness; the sense of duality, which is a sense of the brute factual element in thought, would be an instance of Secondness; and cognition, or thought proper, would be an instance of Thirdness. (The three kinds of 'interpretant' distinguished in § 30 are also instances of the categories.)

[2] Hamilton's Reid, p. 278.

'immediate' or 'direct'. The "perception represents two objects reacting upon one another", and "it is downright nonsense to dispute the fact that in perception two objects really do so react upon one another" (5.55). It is necessary to quote Peirce in greater detail on this sense of duality.

> "Besides Feelings, we have Sensations of reaction; as when a person blindfold suddenly runs against a post, when we make a muscular effort, or when any feeling gives way to a new feeling. Suppose I had nothing in my mind but a feeling of blue, which were suddenly to give place to a feeling of red; then, at the instant of transition, there would be a shock, a sense of reaction, my blue life being transmuted into a red life. If I were further endowed with a memory, that sense would continue for some time, and there would also be a peculiar feeling or sentiment connected with it. This last feeling might endure (conceivably I mean) after the memory of the occurrence and the feelings of blue and red had passed away. But the *sensation* of reaction cannot exist except in the actual presence of the two feelings blue and red to which it relates. Wherever we have two feelings and pay attention to a relation between them of whatever kind, there is the sensation of which I am speaking. But the sense of action and reaction has two types: it may either be a perception of relation between two ideas, or it may be a sense of action and reaction between feeling and something out of feeling. And this sense of external reaction again has two forms; for it is either a sense of something happening to us, by no act of ours, we being passive in the matter, or it is a sense of resistance, that is, of our expending feeling upon something without. The sense of reaction is thus a sense of connection or comparison between feelings, either, *A*, between one feeling and another, or *B* between feeling and its absence or lower degree; and under *B* we have, first, the sense of the access of feeling, and second, the sense of remission of feeling" (6.19).

It is not necessary for us to remember these different forms of the sense of duality (or action and reaction), but simply that this sense is in itself non-cognitive. Peirce is emphatic on this point (5.539, 5.607), despite his use in the foregoing passage of the words 'attention to a relation', 'perception of relation', etc., and despite his declaration that "every philosopher who denies the doctrine of Immediate Perception . . . by that denial cuts off all possibility of ever cognizing a *relation*" (5.56). The sense of duality is a *sense* of a relation of duality, not a *cognition* of such a relation. A cognition involves generality, and to mistake the sense of duality as cognitive is to miss "the *here*ness and *now*ness which is its essence." [1] Thus our three categories or elements of mind are: Feeling, devoid of all relation; the Sense of Relation between feelings, or between a feeling and the external object responsible for it, between "ego and non-ego",[1] etc.; and Cognition, or the representation of relations, which alone is communicable. Mere feeling may occur without the sense of relation or cognition; the sense of relation may not occur without feeling, but it may occur without cognition; while cognition necessarily involves the other two.

According to Peirce, it is the distinction between the sense of duality and cognition that distinguishes the immediate perceptionist from the representative perceptionist. In every instance of perception there is of course some feeling or percept. The representationist regards this percept as an appearance or picture from which by a mental act we 'infer' an object which is its 'hidden cause'. Peirce, on the other hand, holds "that perception is a two-sided consciousness in which the percept appears as forcibly acting upon us, so that in perception the consciousness of an active object and of a subject acted on are as indivisible as, in making a muscular effort, the sense of exertion is one with and inseparable from the sense of resistance" (5.607).[2]

Certain objections arise against Peirce's conception of a sense of duality, not by way of criticism, but from the stand-

---

[1] Letter to James (in Perry, *op. cit.*, II, p. 429).

[2] "It is the external world that we directly observe" (*Pop. Sci. Mo.* 1900-1901, p. 301); also, ". . . We have *direct experience of things in themselves*. Nothing can be more completely false than that we can experience only our own ideas" (6.95).

point of its congruity with his other principal conceptions. First, if this sense of relation is non-cognitive, it would not seem to be so different from feeling as to be constituted a special mental category. It appears to be not something different from feeling but rather a kind of feeling. Second, if we allow a non-cognitive sense of relation at all, we open the door once again to intuitive knowledge. For how shall we draw the line between the relations which can be immediately sensed and those which can only be cognized? Third, there is one respect in which *any* feeling may be called a feeling of a relation, viz. that the feeling may subsequently be analyzed; and Peirce likewise fails to take this into account. It would seem to be most proper and in greater consonance with Peirce's other opinions to admit the *sensing* of relations only in this last sense. For to sense dual or dyadic relations is another way of saying that we can sense facts (cf. 3.416), which in turn is another way of admitting intuitive knowledge. There is no reason why the 'sense of duality' may not be cognitive and yet compatible with the doctrine of direct perception, i.e. perception of external objects without a medium of hypostatized percepts. Peirce does not realize it because he seems to think that in the very *act of perception itself* we must have the guarantee that we perceive directly. (See the statement of 5.607 in the preceding paragraph.)

I now want to turn to that part of Peirce's critical common-sensism which comes closer to the special sense in which he used the term and which he regarded as influenced positively by the Scottish school. I have not quoted Reid and Stewart with the similarities in mind, partly because their views on the fundamental beliefs are somewhat familiar, but chiefly because their influence, while real, is hardly so great as Peirce would make it. It is a peculiar trait of Peirce that he sometimes minimizes or fails to mention a rather important influence that is obvious, while he exaggerates an influence that may even be remote. (See § 28, on his view of the classical predecessors of pragmatism.)

17. **The ' Indubitable ' Propositions.** According to Peirce there are certain propositions which are "indubitable" (e.g. 5.440). These propositions are not "inferential" (5.516). They are "ultimate premisses" (5.515), and are our "original beliefs" (5.516). What are these indubitable beliefs? Peirce gives very few examples, and one is not certain whether at a given place of discussion he has in mind perceptual judgments or statements of a more general character. Both kinds, in fact, are to be classed as 'indubitables'. An example of the general kind of statement which he gives is "[the belief] that there is an element of order in the universe" (6.496), or "the belief in the criminality of incest" (5.445). In the "Lectures on Pragmatism" of 1903 (5.14-212), he says that "perceptual judgments are the first premisses of all our reasonings and . . . they cannot be called in question" (5.116). They are "uncriticizable" (5.55, 5.157). It would seem at first glance that an argument for such indubitable or uncriticizable judgments contradicts the anti-intuition arguments. But it may be said at once that there is no inconsistency, and we shall see how the two arguments coalesce. With the same breath that Peirce declares the perceptual judgments to be uncriticizable, he proclaims that we cannot "pretend to absolute certainty about any matter of fact". The perceptual judgments are not intuitive. As for the other class of indubitables, the 'original beliefs', there is a possibility that must be ruled out at once, namely, that they are a priori though synthetic. Peirce emphatically holds that experience alone can settle matters of fact: all "a priori arguments . . . about positive fact are rubbish" (2.137). All the indubitables are empirical.

18. **The Theory of Doubt and Belief.** In order to understand what Peirce means by 'indubitable', it is necessary to understand his opinions on the nature of doubt and belief, a subject of considerable intrinsic interest. For Peirce the act of doubting is not a matter of simple choosing: we cannot doubt at will (e.g. 5.443)—and this point cannot be too

heavily emphasized. There is a great difference between saying that we doubt and genuinely doubting. Genuine doubt "has an external origin, usually from surprise" (*ib.*), so that it is just as impossible to doubt at will as it is to surprise oneself at will. The opposite of doubt is belief. There is a difference in feeling between doubt and belief (5.370), but we must not regard this as the essential difference (5.510; cf. 5.242). Doubt is marked by a state of uneasiness, belief by a state which is on the whole calmer and more pleasurable. We generally struggle to end doubt and to attain belief, as we struggle to free ourselves from any kind of irritation (5.374). It is easier to believe than to doubt. A belief is something intimately connected with a habit. Sometimes Peirce says that a belief *is* a habit, sometimes that it is associated with a habit; but this detail is not important. ". . . A genuine belief, or opinion, is something on which a man is prepared to act, and is therefore, in a general sense, a habit" (2.148). What is important is that a man who genuinely believes is prepared to act in a certain way, and does act in a certain way: ". . . different beliefs are distinguished by the different modes of action to which they give rise" (5.398). When a belief is said to be established a habit of action or of preparation to act is thereby established. This is the only test by which genuine belief can be distinguished from mere pretense, or by which one belief can be distinguished from another. That is to say, a person who really believes is prepared to act in a definite way, and a person who does not, is not prepared to do so; and to say that a person has two different beliefs is to say that he has established two different habits of action or of preparation to act.[1] (Peirce sometimes speaks of 'habits of belief' or 'belief-habits', e.g. 3.160, 5.397.) A genuine doubt may

---

[1] Sometimes Peirce emphasizes that a belief "is a habit of which we are conscious" or "something that we are aware of" (4.53, 5.397, resp.); sometimes he emphasizes that a belief "need not be conscious" and is "mostly unconscious" (2.148, 5.417, resp.). It is a rather peculiar inconsistency, because he obviously wishes to stress the preparation to act rather than the action itself. In that case "a deliberate, or self-

be defined as a doubt which influences, or interferes with, a habit of action, i.e. a belief. The difference between doubt and belief is thus not merely sensational but practical. We do not act the same way when we believe as when we doubt. But we can neither believe nor doubt at will. The (tacit) supposition that we can doubt at will is what Peirce regards as the 'Cartesian error' (5.524; cf. 5.265). According to him, Descartes's initial scepticism was not genuine doubt, because neither he nor anyone else can escape at will from the prejudices and beliefs which he actually has and which govern his actions. It may of course often happen that we come to doubt what we originally believed, but only because we have a 'positive reason' to doubt. "The breaking of a belief can only be due to some novel experience, whether external or internal" (5.524). Experience cannot be "summoned up at pleasure" (*ib.*), for then it would not be experience.[1]

19. **The Meaning of 'Indubitable'.** Now there are certain beliefs that we do not doubt, e.g. that Scott wrote *Waverley*. But this is not an indubitable belief. What we call an indubitable belief is, of course, one that is free from actual doubt. But this is not sufficient. We must distinguish between an indubitable belief and a belief that is not actually doubted. An indubitable belief is one that *cannot* be doubted, not in the sense that the negation of it is self-contradictory, but in the sense that the social or biological situation of those who have the belief excludes conditions that *might make* for doubt. Of a belief which is merely not in fact doubted, it may also be said in a sense that it 'cannot' be doubted, namely, in the sense that we cannot doubt it at will. But certain factors, a new experience, for instance, might at any moment arise and tend to create doubt; and this is not the case with the beliefs Peirce calls indubitable.

controlled, habit is precisely a belief " (5.480) ; a belief can only be " a habit of deliberate behaviour " (5.538). (But see § 21.)

[1] ". . . Belief is partly determined by old beliefs and partly by new experience " (3.161).

For these beliefs are so vital a part of the social and biological environment that they may virtually be said to be
characteristic of that environment: to genuinely call them
into question is to alter the environment, or rather to be
liberated from it in some important respect.

According to Peirce, the following characteristics distinguish his own theory of common sense (i.e. literally, of
common beliefs) from that of the Scottish school. For him,
first of all, the indubitables are especially vague; second,
these beliefs (for instance, the belief in a uniformity of
nature) are indubitable only in so far as they apply to a
'primitive mode of life'; and finally, his theory, in its
capacity as a critical common-sensism or theory of the
validity and comparative value as knowledge, of common
sense, encourages genuine doubt and its cultivation (cf.
5.498). It is clear that in these points Peirce is thinking
primarily of our 'original instinctive beliefs' rather than of
the perceptual indubitables. In fact, it is most often of them
that he is thinking when he uses the word 'indubitable'.
But I have taken the liberty of coupling the two classes of
beliefs under the same designation, on grounds which should
become increasingly evident. With respect to the foregoing
distinguishing characteristics of Peirce's view the difference
between the two classes is only one of degree. On the first
point, the perceptual indubitables are less vague than the
social indubitables (as we may call them), but what is said
under (1) below applies equally; on the second point, we
shall find the important thing to be that the indubitables are
relative to a given mode of life, not necessarily a 'primitive'
one; and on the third point, the parity is evident. I have
not, however, neglected what Peirce would regard as significant differences between the two classes of indubitables, and
these appear in § 20.

(1) No statement or belief can be entirely free from vagueness, that is, perfectly definite; but the indubitable beliefs
are especially vague. When they are made more precise
they may, from being indubitable, be transformed into beliefs

that are dubitable, i.e. either doubtful or subject to doubt (cf. 6.496-499). A belief in the uniformity of nature may be indubitable in the sense that we can never act except in tacit accordance with it. Nevertheless, when the statement of this belief is expressed precisely, and a greater number of detailed consequences accordingly deducible, we may doubt it and even (as Peirce does, e.g. 6.100) brand it as false. This is perhaps even more clearly seen in the case of perceptual judgments. These cannot be doubted or criticized, try as we may. They are involuntary, not in the same sense that percepts are involuntary but in the sense that we do not choose to affirm just the judgment that we do; we affirm it as a fixed habit determined by our physiological constitution and linguistic conditioning. In this sense it is meaningless to say that perceptual judgments can be criticized (cf. 5.55). Such a judgment is "forced upon my acceptance" (5.157). But when we make it more precise it may no longer remain indubitable. Thus when we make precise just what is involved in judging something to be red, we may entertain real doubt as to whether what we judge to be so may not in fact be orange. But even if we do not actually doubt, one of the basic conditions making for indubitability has been removed, and it is now a question either of doubting or of not doubting, not of either being able to doubt or of not being able to doubt.

(2) A belief or habit upon which no new experience intrudes cannot be genuinely doubted. A set of beliefs that are not doubted implies a set of habits of action that are relatively fixed. A set of habits of action constitutes a mode of living; and according to Peirce the mode of living to which our traditional indubitable beliefs apply is of a 'primitive' character. A looser way of expressing this is to call such traditional beliefs 'instinctive' (5.445, 5.511). On the other hand, a better way of expressing Peirce's point is to say that indubitable beliefs in general are indubitable *relative to* a set of social and biological activities. In the history of the human race, thinks Peirce, "there is every reason to

suppose that belief came first, and the power of doubting long after" (5.512). As the sphere of human self-control is enlarged, new "occasions of action arise in relation to which the original beliefs, if stretched to cover them, have no sufficient authority. In other words, we outgrow the applicability of instinct—not altogether, by any manner of means, but in our highest activities" (5.511). The set of basic social activities seems not to have changed sufficiently to make it probable that the traditional indubitables have changed very greatly in human history (5.444). It may be pointed out that to make the indubitables dubitable by making them precise is nothing less than a way of altering the environment, so that (1) should, strictly, be subsumed under (2).

(3) The enlargement of the sphere of our activities and the elimination of vagueness (which is in general a consequence) thus show that what was once indubitable may become dubitable and be seen perhaps to be false. It is for this· reason that genuine doubt is to be constantly sought. We must provoke doubt and invent methods for attaining it. This cannot be done unless we realize that *any* of our beliefs *may* turn out to be false (cf. 5.451, 5.514). So that while there are certain beliefs which we do not, and cannot under our conditions of life, doubt, we nevertheless can *conceive* that they might be doubted under other conditions. There is nothing paradoxical in this view, and in fact it touches the crux of Peirce's critical common-sensism. For it calls attention to the distinction between indubitability and incorrigibility: Some of our beliefs are indubitable, but no belief is incorrigible. And it should now be clear that what Peirce meant by saying that the 'indubitables' are not 'inferential' is, not that they stand in no inferential relation to other beliefs (and are consequently. not of a hypothetical character), but that they are not conscious conclusions which are doubtful or drawn from doubtful premises.

20. **The Social and Perceptual Indubitables.** The body of opinion common to the mass of mankind comprises both the

social and the perceptual indubitables, and is what Santa-yana has called 'human orthodoxy'. "It is merely the current imagination and good sense of mankind—something traditional, conventional, incoherent, and largely erroneous, like the assumptions of a man who has never reflected, yet something ingenuous, practically acceptable, fundamentally sound" [1] and above all, capable of being corrected, both by itself and by the introduction of scientific abstraction. The two classes of indubitables fall under human orthodoxy or common sense, though it would seem that common sense as ordinarily understood comprises much more than these two classes of beliefs alone (cf. § 30 below). Although we have conjoined the perceptual and social beliefs as indubitables, it is necessary to stress the fact that they nevertheless play somewhat different rôles in Peirce.

(1) The social indubitables, the collection of opinions which spring from common sense and 'intuitive insight', and which people never question in the entire course of their everyday habits, have been felicitously designated by Dr. H. S. Leonard as the "social given".[2] The value of the social given lies in "the measure of direction that it may impart" to scientific investigation. "There must be some concept with which it [science] approaches the task of experimentation and the limits of whose application the experiment will indicate. . . . What shall we select? The social given operates to limit the field of choice to manage-able dimensions; by the analysis of its predicates, which the . . . social given assures us are true within a limited range, we find a starting point for our search for predicates worth the trouble of analysis and experimental testing."[3] It is a strong conviction of Peirce that the laws of empirical science are "but a development of original instinctive beliefs" (1.404), classical physics being uppermost in his mind whenever he reiterates it. He is impressed by the fact that out of number-

---

[1] *Obiter Scripta*, ed. Buchler and Schwartz, p. 95.
[2] In *Essays for Alfred North Whitehead*, p. 150.
[3] Review of Vols. V and VI of Peirce, *Philosophy of Science*, 1937, p. 118.

less possible hypotheses, successful ones should have been adopted (5.591), and he believes it impossible to explain this fact except on the assumption that science is an outgrowth of the social indubitables and of common sense in general. He believes that there is positive evidence for this view in the procedure and results of the classical physicists, Galileo having even made explicit appeal to common sense and *il lume naturale* (6.10-11; cf. 1.80, 6.567). The process of abduction, or adoption of a hypothesis to explain facts observed, is essentially a process of judicious guessing. These guesses would be utterly futile unless our indubitable beliefs served as a basis from which we could start, whence we go on to refinement of formulation as a result of experimental testing (cf. 1.80, 1.121 [1]). (Cf. § 38.)

(2) The perceptual indubitables are much less vague than the social indubitables. The latter initiate and facilitate the direction of scientific inquiry, but the perceptual statements can never be abandoned by science. ". . . Our perceptual judgments are the first premises of all our reasonings. . . ." (5.116). Science is a system of beliefs grounded on the perceptual beliefs, which are those most firmly established. Now to believe a statement is the same as believing it to be true (this being in fact tautologous; cf. 5.375). We shall see shortly that for Peirce the system of true beliefs is nothing more nor less than the system of empirical science, so that perceptual statements, which are essential to this system, are essential to the concept of truth: 'true' statements must be defined as statements based on them. (Cf. §§ 22 and 23.) Thus the essential difference between the social and perceptual indubitables is that the latter belong to the *system* of science. We may say that whereas the social indubitables are *replaced* by scientific hypotheses, the perceptual indubitables are *explained* by scientific hypotheses, though they are themselves, as we have seen, hypotheses of fundamentally the same character.

[1] Also, 1.118 ; 2.753, 776 ; 5.47, 173, 586, 591, 603-604 ; 6.418, 491, 500, 531 ; and many other places.

21. ' Theoretical ' and ' Practical ' Beliefs. It will presently become clear that it is necessary for Peirce to make
some distinction between two kinds of beliefs, since the
'beliefs' of science are not quite of the same character as
beliefs ordinarily understood. An unpublished ms. of Peirce
(5.538-545) makes an explicit attempt to distinguish beliefs
as 'practical' and 'theoretical'. It is obscure even for mss.
of Peirce, certain parts of it (e.g. 5.540) unusually so. I
want to restate it as intelligibly as possible.

We said, in somewhat different words, that a belief is a
"habit of deliberate behaviour" (5.538). We must now
modify this statement and confine it to the definition of
'practical' beliefs, for it is not adequate to define what Peirce
calls 'theoretical' beliefs. As an example of a practical
belief Peirce gives the belief that "anthracite is a convenient
fuel"; of a theoretical belief, that "the pole of the earth
describes an oval of a few rods' diameter". But in order to
embrace the difference between these kinds, we require a
more general definition: a belief is essentially an *expectation*.
The difference between practical and theoretical beliefs is
that they are expectative in different senses. A practical
belief is expectative of 'muscular feeling', of a 'sense of
effort' (in which the 'sense of duality' is 'specially prominent'). A theoretical belief is expectative of feeling that is
not muscular. But what do these distinctions mean? We
must first understand what it means for *any* belief to be
expectative. "Every belief is belief in a proposition" (542).
To believe a proposition is to believe that if it were true
something else would follow as a consequence (i.e., of course,
another proposition). Thus if I believe that something is
blue, I believe that that thing will have the properties which
would be revealed by a spectral analysis. And if I believe
that anthracite is a convenient fuel, what I believe is that
anthracite will have all the properties that convenient fuels
have. In other words, every belief is expectative in the
sense that from it we can 'expect' (deduce, predict) consequences. What, now, does it mean to say that a practical

belief is expectative of muscular feeling? It is not a *feeling* that we predict in a belief, for feelings cannot be (logical) consequences. What we mean is that the consequence we predict or 'expect' is one that involves muscular feeling in the *confirmation* of it. Thus, 'Anthracite is a convenient fuel' is a 'practical' belief because to believe this is to believe that anthracite will, for example, provoke a steady fire, entail less labour in handling, etc.—all these beliefs involving muscular feeling in their verification. The kinetic theory of gases, on the other hand, would be a theoretical belief, because while it would predict for the behaviour of gases experimental results in the confirmation of which sensible feeling would be involved, this would presumably be other than muscular feeling. It would seem that on Peirce's criterion of distinction, most perceptual judgments should be classed as theoretical beliefs. This would be quite satis-factory to his general scheme, since, as we have seen, the 'laws' of empirical science and the perceptual statements differ only in degree of generality.

But the ground of distinction here given between 'prac-tical' and 'theoretical' belief is unsatisfactory. In the first place, we cannot ask at all whether practical beliefs do in fact involve muscular feeling (in the sense explained); for Peirce *defines* a practical belief as one that does. Though it is thus a matter of nominal definition, Peirce himself does not seem to realize it. He seems to take it for granted that we can test his ascription of the distinguishing properties by examining practical and theoretical beliefs, unaware that we have no way of choosing examples except on the basis of the distinction. Secondly, it is not at all easily ascertainable just when a belief does or does not involve muscular feeling, so that the distinction itself is tenuous and in any case relatively unimportant. Peirce does not, once again, realize sufficiently that on any of the usual distinctions between practical and theoretical belief the difference is one of degree rather than of kind. This contrasts with his con-ception of difference in degree between scientific laws and perceptual statements, though even in that case he cannot always be said to be faithful to his best analysis.

As for the main point, however, namely that all beliefs are essentially expectative, it is nothing less than a highly compact statement of pragmatism, and we shall understand it better when we come to Part II and discuss the meaning of synthetic predications in general. The use of the terms 'practical' and 'theoretical' is in a way somewhat unfortunate; for as the statement of pragmatism will show, all beliefs are in a sense 'practical'—in fact, in the same sense that they are 'expectative'. Peirce perhaps recognizes the weakness of the terminology when he says that every theoretical belief is "at least indirectly" a practical belief (5.539).

22. **Doubt, Belief and Empirical Science.** To say that doubt encroaches upon beliefs that are indubitable means that the conditions of life surrounding, and the modes of expressing, these beliefs are widened, supplemented and refined. And this extension of the habits of life is synonymous with the growth of empirical science. Though science takes its start from the social indubitables and depends for its trustworthiness upon the perceptual indubitables, it nevertheless is the instrument by which both these classes of indubitables are made more precise, and by which the former is corrected and perhaps subsequently disbelieved. For despite the fact that science is an outgrowth of these social indubitables, they "are so mixed up with error that they can never be trusted till they have been corrected by experiment" (1.404). The perceptual indubitables, though they ground science, are explained by it. Science, generally speaking, is a formula which "is fitted to sum up and reconcile" the mass of perceptual judgments (5.607). We start scientific inquiry with certain principles, social and perceptual, which we cannot help accepting; from the perceptual principles, mainly, we draw new knowledge by abduction; we test this knowledge by further comparison with the percep-

tual principles (induction); but by means of our new knowledge all of our principles have become clearer and better
understood, and some of them ready to be discarded.

Now the enlargement of our knowledge is nothing more
than the enlargement of the sphere of our beliefs, and we
must consider in greater detail the relation of science to
belief. When doubt arises we seek to replace it by belief.
When we establish new beliefs, these remain secure until the
growth of our experience again awakens doubt; whereupon
the search for belief commences once more. We never can
be said to struggle to attain belief unless we doubt. This is
a profoundly important fact. For Peirce calls this struggle
to attain belief 'inquiry', and it follows that the *sole object*
of inquiry is to settle belief or opinion. From this it further
follows that in order to pursue inquiry it is not necessary, as
a great many philosophers imagined, to start from 'first
principles', whether these first principles be 'absolutely certain' (or 'self-evident') general principles or intuitive perceptual judgments. It is not even necessary, though to a
large extent it may in fact be the case, that we ground our
inquiry on indubitable propositions. All that is required is
that we start with propositions free from actual doubt.[1] "If
the premisses are not in fact doubted at all, they cannot be
more satisfactory than they are" (5.376). In other words,
because all empirical propositions are corrigible it does not
follow that we cannot make positive advances in empirical
inquiry; for an analysis of the nature of inquiry shows it to
consist essentially in the struggle to appease doubt. The
premisses of any inquiry are, after all, beliefs established by
the evidence of some prior inquiry, and in order that further
investigation should be capable of bearing fruit, we cannot
ask more than that we start from evidence which we honestly
accept.

[1] ' Start ' here means ' start logically ', not psychologically. Descartes
was one of those who thought that inquiry could be logically started
or grounded upon only ' self-evident ' premisses. Yet (according to
Peirce) he started psychologically, on the contrary, with complete
doubt.

What kind of inquiry is best fitted to help us attain stable beliefs, beliefs in which we shall be satisfied? Peirce distinguishes four methods of settling or 'fixing' belief, though only the last of these, perhaps, can properly be called 'inquiry'. These methods, described in one of Peirce's two best-known papers, are relatively familiar, and I shall confine myself to a brief summary of them. (1) The first is called by Peirce the 'method of tenacity'. It consists in the deliberate and wilful determination by the individual to retain those beliefs which satisfy him emotionally. A set of opinions is clung to tenaciously; whatever reinforces these opinions is welcomed, whatever threatens to change them by suggesting new evidence is avoided. ". . . The instinctive dislike of an undecided state of mind, exaggerated into a vague dread of doubt, makes men cling spasmodically to the views they already take." Such a form of belief is a species of faith.[1] It resembles somewhat the ostrich's burying his head in the sand when danger approaches. But this method of settling belief cannot be exclusively practised while men live in society. Mutual influence and adoption of opinion is inevitable, so that the method of tenacity is in any case inadequate. (Cf. 5.377-378.) (2) It thus comes about that belief is settled not by the individual alone, for himself, but for the whole community by the influence of a dominant power, exercising the 'method of authority'. This method has been historically associated with the state and the church. The doctrines decreed to be correct are endlessly reiterated and taught to the young, contrary doctrine is prevented from being spread in any way, the masses are kept in ignorance in order to avoid even the potentiality of heresy, prejudice and public passion is fostered, physical persecution is practised, and a dogmatic code is drawn up. This method Peirce regards as on the whole intellectually and morally superior to "self-mendacity, the most degraded of all intellectual conditions" (5.564). But the method of authority, which is after all intellectual slavery, is capable of

---

[1] See a letter to James, 1897, in Perry, *op. cit.*, I, p. 222.

settling opinion only on the most fundamental social issues, and the fact will remain that in the minds of a reflective minority doubts will arise.[1] (Cf. 5.379-381.) (3) The method that they will use is distinguished from wilful belief and arbitrary force in that it emphasizes the influence of 'natural preferences' in acting to settle belief. It adopts beliefs that are 'agreeable to reason'; a most apt expression, says Peirce, for "it does not mean that which agrees with experience, but that which we find ourselves inclined to believe". This method, which may be called the 'a priori method' and which is employed by those who confidently appeal to the 'self-evident', is best illustrated in the history of metaphysical philosophy. It fails because "it makes of inquiry something similar to the development of taste". Metaphysics, like taste, fluctuates in the manner of a fashion. The a priori method, like the other two, contains the element of accident and caprice in the settlement of belief. For at least one group of people, therefore, it does not suffice to eliminate real doubt on important issues. (Cf. 5.382-383.) A method is necessary according to which beliefs will be determined "by some external permanency" rather than by selfishness, rapacious interests or aesthetic considerations.

(4) This is the scientific—or as Peirce sometimes calls it (e.g. 5.406), the 'experiential'—method. The essential characteristic of this method is that it conceives of truth as something *public*, something which it seeks to ascertain by public methods.[2] Its fundamental assumption, according to Peirce, is: "There are Real things, whose characters are entirely independent of our opinions about them; those Reals affect our senses according to regular laws, and, though our sensations are as different as are our relations to the objects, yet, by taking advantage of the laws of perception,

---

[1] Peirce's view (in 1877) of the gullibility of the masses is, to say the least, dubious. " For the mass of mankind . . . there is perhaps no better method ", he thinks, than the method of authority. I would suggest that this is a classic example of a priorism, such as Peirce himself condemns.

[2] " Truth is public." Letter to James, 1907 (Perry, *op. cit.*, II, p. 437).

we can ascertain by reasoning how things really and truly are; and any man, if he have sufficient experience and he reason enough about it, will be led to the one True conclusion." In other words, science introduces the concept of empirical reality, and presupposes that the character of this reality is publicly ascertainable. That this concept and this presupposition are justified is shown, first, by the fact that all basic practice assumes them, whence they cannot be genuinely doubted. ("Everybody uses the scientific method about a great many things, and only ceases to use it when he does not know how to apply it.") Second, by the fact that the scientific method has been remarkably successful historically in the settlement of opinion. (Cf. 5.384-385.) Are the other methods inferior in every respect to the scientific? Not necessarily. Those who primarily pursue the method of tenacity develop a strong and determined will, that of the 'successful' man; those who primarily follow the method of authority, if intellectual slaves, may perhaps enjoy timid security; and the a priori method makes thought a comfortable and delightful process. But in one respect the method of science is alone possible, namely, in the determination of 'truth'. Properly speaking, science *introduces* the concept of truth. One who "wishes his opinions to coincide with the fact" has no other choice. The scientific method is the pursuit of evidence. (Cf. 5.386-387.)

It is interesting to consider the relation of the four methods of settling belief to the indubitable propositions. Peirce would probably say that these have become indubitable as a result of the interplay, largely unconscious, of the four methods. Social authority through the generations (conjoined with the physical environment), lifetime psychological habits resulting therefrom, the universal habit of adopting plausible and agreeable conclusions, and the evidence of hearsay and the senses,—all have combined to establish the indubitables, social and perceptual. The indubitables thus result from a combination of logical and extra-logical methods of obtaining evidence, the latter in the greater proportion. The scientific method seeks to establish belief solely on the basis of logical methods of obtaining evidence.[1]

Belief, then, is fixed or established by inquiry; and the form of inquiry best fitted to fix belief is the method of science. Further, not only does scientific inquiry in fact settle belief but this is its sole function. Here, however, we must have recourse to the distinction between practical and theoretical belief, though we found the particular statement of it by Peirce somewhat unsatisfactory. Science may indirectly determine practical belief, but its essential function is to settle only theoretical belief. Some years before Peirce makes his explicit practical-theoretical distinction he contrasts 'science' with 'practice': belief is something practical, in the sense that it means "willingness to risk a great deal upon a proposition"; and therefore belief "is no concern of science" (5.589). Even around the time that he makes the distinction, he still thinks of belief in practical terms: "Strictly speaking, *belief* is out of place in pure theoretical science, which has nothing nearer to it than the establishment of doctrines, and the provisional establishment of them, at that" (5.60). Science is interested, not in whether a hypothesis has received such a degree of confirmation that it will be a living thing in practical affairs, something on which we might stake interests that affect us, but in the process of selecting fruitful hypotheses and the process of marshalling evidence. We are interested only in 'pure retroductions' and inductions; hypotheses abduced and

[1] Though Peirce in 1877 has no theory of the social indubitables he seems to suggest that such beliefs and the results of the a priori method are similar in status, being based on the 'natural', 'instinctive' or agreeable. To this it may be replied that while the indubitables are in fact thus based, the a priorisms differ according as a priori philosophers conceive differently of the 'natural' or 'evident'. Both are, of course (cf. 5.386), refined by 'rough facts'. But again, the social indubitables reliably impart direction to science, while the varieties of a priorism impart such direction only accidentally.

subsequently confirmed to a certain degree are not "matters for belief" (5.589). Science simply regards these as "established truths, that is . . . propositions into which the economy of endeavour prescribes that, for the time being, further inquiry shall cease" (ib.).

Thus a distinction between practical and theoretical beliefs is necessary if Peirce's conception of the function of science is to be intelligible. If the propositions of science are beliefs, they are a special kind of beliefs. (It might at first sight seem that we could confine the term 'belief' to practical belief, which will continue to be defined as that "on which we are willing to act", the propositions of science not being beliefs at all. But this is open to two objections, the first of which is that the term 'act' is not precise enough to exclude the propositions of science from being in some sense opinions on which we are willing to 'act'. The second and more important objection is that we cannot without serious damage to Peirce's thought abandon the conception that the end of scientific inquiry is essentially the settlement of belief;—truth, for instance, is defined in terms of doubt and belief, 'truths' being 'true beliefs', established by the method of science;—so that we must regard the propositions of science as actually beliefs.) We have no difficulty if we recall that belief is essentially expectation, in the sense already defined. The purpose of a scientific hypothesis is "through subjection to the test of experiment, to lead to the avoidance of all surprise and to the establishment of a habit of positive expectation that shall not be disappointed" (5.197). That is, its purpose is to enable us to predict consequences which shall continually be confirmed and enable us to strengthen indefinitely our induction of it from these confirmations.[1] We can distinguish between practical and theoretical beliefs, which are both expectative, on the basis of applicability to human affairs, to 'practical matters' or 'actions' in the popular sense of the terms. Some such dis-

[1] Cf. above, § 14, where the 'formation of habit' is expressed as 'induction'.

tinction is acknowledged on all sides, and Peirce really intends no more (cf. 1.635-637). And perhaps we can be as exact as Peirce will allow us if we state the distinction, not in terms of expectation of muscular or non-muscular feeling, as in § 21, but rather as follows: A practical belief is *likely* to be associated with a habit of action as well as of expectation, while a theoretical belief is not likely to be associated with a habit of action as well as of expectation. But although the distinction in general is an acknowledged one, there is hardly unanimity on the viewpoint that Peirce chooses to adopt. For he dreads the introduction into scientific inquiry of moral or quasi-moral considerations. Once science is looked upon as a "guide to conduct" or "as an instrument for a practical end" (1.55), free inquiry is throttled. "True science is distinctively the study of useless things. For the useful things will get studied without the aid of scientific men" (1.76).[1] One cannot help feeling that while the practical-theoretical distinction is worthwhile and proper, Peirce nevertheless does not sufficiently stress (in fact he does not mention at all) the essential continuity of the practical and theoretical. The difference, after all, is in degree of precision and abstraction. Every synthetic proposition is properly to be considered a proposition of empirical science—this comes out clearly in pragmatism—though in actual inquiry it may play no part. The status of all such propositions, as hypotheses, we have seen, and will continue to find reinforced.

23. **The Meaning of 'Truth' and of 'Reality'.** 'Truth' and 'falsity' are properties of a certain class of signs, viz. propositions. A proposition, in fact, is partially defined as that sign which is said to have one or the other of these properties. We call a proposition 'false' if any proposition can be deduced from it which contradicts a 'direct perceptual judgment'; and a proposition is 'true' if it is not false (2.327; cf. 5.569). But we want to define truth in such

---

[1] See *Pop. Sci. Mo.* 1900-1901, pp. 296-301, for a more extended discussion by Peirce, in opposition to Pearson. Cf. also 1.618 ff.

a way that we can explain what we mean when we also call a perceptual judgment 'true'. According to Peirce, the instrument that ascertains truth (we continue, of course, to speak only of synthetic statements) is empirical science. Science regards a proposition as an 'established truth' if it is confirmed to a high degree, i.e. supported inductively by a large and diversified number of perceptual judgments that are among its possible consequences. Such a proposition regarded as an established truth is nothing more than a belief which cannot be doubted as long as the evidence for it is of the character mentioned. We cannot ask for a sounder guarantee of stable belief than science. Hence true beliefs, or 'truths', are the beliefs supported or established by science. Perceptual judgments, though all other beliefs depend upon them, may themselves be called true in the sense that they are indubitable. While beliefs of a more general kind cannot be doubted, in the sense that the method of science furnishes evidence for them based on the perceptual beliefs, the perceptual beliefs cannot be doubted in the sense we have explained. Now to say that a belief is 'true' is to say that it is in a certain sense "satisfactory" (5.556), though these two words are by no means synonymous. "Mr. Ferdinand C. S. Schiller informs us that he and James have made up their minds that the true is simply the satisfactory. No doubt; but to say 'satisfactory' is not to complete any predicate whatever. Satisfactory to what end?" (5.552). To this end: A true belief is satisfactory in the sense that doubt has been expelled from it by the method of science. A belief satisfactory in the sense that it is emotionally comfortable, or in any other sense than the one just stated, is not a 'true' belief. True beliefs are satisfactory in the sense that they have been established by a method superior to any other in collecting evidence to settle beliefs (cf. 6.485). To be satisfied in a belief is to be untroubled by doubt. In general, we need not speak at all of 'truths' if we do not wish to; we need only speak of beliefs settled by the best available method (cf. 5.416). Sometimes Peirce expresses this conception of truth in somewhat different terms: "The opinion which is fated to be ultimately agreed to by all who investigate, is what we mean by the truth, and the object represented in this opinion is the real" (5.407). This should be translated: All who investigate (by the scientific method) will attain a belief (i.e. be led to agree upon an opinion) which is what we call the 'truth'.—Sometimes also Peirce says something like this: ". . . By the True is meant that at which inquiry aims" (5.557). There is implied here a distinction between 'perfect' and 'approximate' truth, the relation between which we shall discuss (as well as that between analogous conceptions of 'reality') in Part II (§ 38). The justification, however, of the concept of 'approximate' truth is given by the principle of fallibilism (see § 24).

The best way of explaining what is meant by 'reality' is to say that it is what is represented in true statements,—in the class of true statements, if we use it as a collective term. The 'nature of reality', to put it otherwise, is described by true statements. From this it follows that the conception of reality, like that of truth, "essentially involves the notion of a *community*, without definite limits, and capable of a definite increase of knowledge" (5.311). What we understand by 'reality' is determined by the community, or rather the scientific sub-community which by its technique determines the beliefs of the community, in the sense that it agrees upon certain statements as 'representative of reality', i.e. the 'true' statements. This does not mean that reality derives its properties as a result of public collusion or arbitrary legislation, nor that reality is 'determined' in the sense that it is dependent upon human perception. In fact Peirce defines "the real as that whose characters are independent of what anybody may think them to be" (5.405). What is affirmed by him is simply that the character of the world is best described by science and experience in general, and that the character thus described is the 'real' character. The full justification of this view will appear in the discussion of pragmatism. But enough has already been said to

show why there is good ground for it. To deny that empirical science describes what is 'really' the case is to deny that
the statements of empirical science are true. But to deny
that they are true and to actually doubt them are two
different things. No one can doubt the perceptual judgments on which science is based, and no one who understands the general hypotheses that are systematically confirmed does doubt these. Not to doubt that the method of
science leads to true results and yet to hold that it does not
describe what is 'really' the case is, therefore, contradictory.
The discussion of pragmatism will, in fact, reveal that the
latter view is meaningless. What we can meaningfully hold
is that scientific accounts can be improved upon—for this
means that no scientific statement, no synthetic statement
whatever, is incorrigible or infallible, that is, *absolutely*
indubitable.

24. **The Principle of Fallibilism.** It is not exactly a secret
that scientific theories are in process of constant revision, and
that what are regarded as 'established truths' come to be
modified often to a considerable extent. How, then, can we
say that scientific inquiry issues in truth, and that it has
been historically successful? This question has been partially answered. It confuses the concepts of empirical truth
and incorrigibility. To found an inquiry on corrigible premisses, indeed to carry on inquiry at all times with corrigible
premisses, does not mean that such inquiry cannot be fruitful as a means of uncovering 'truths'. Such a view, we saw,
is based on a false conception of inquiry. Peirce's conception
of truth allows for the instability of theories, and even for
scientific disagreement on a given theory. It characterizes
scientific investigation as a communal or public process of
settling belief. A hypothesis may be called true and yet be
subject to refinement, for *beliefs are relative to evidence*. As
our method of uncovering new evidence grows, our beliefs
are corrected and restated.

Peirce's conception of the character of inquiry is dominated by a 'rule of reason', an informal rule but one carrying tremendous conviction with him and constituting a kind of ethics of inquiry. He understands by it "that in order to learn you must desire to learn, and in so desiring not be satisfied with what you already incline to think" (1.135). But it is the 'corollary' of this rule which is most often called attention to by Peirce in his writings: "Do not block the way of inquiry". Whatever the substance of a philosophy may be, its "one unpardonable offence in reasoning" is to violate this rule. The main hindrances to inquiry are certain forms of both scepticism and dogmatism (cf. 5.416). One form of scepticism, which questions the trustworthiness of the scientific method in general, we have mentioned. Another form of scepticism, while upholding the value of science, *sets limits* to its possible progress even within its proper domain. It consists in maintaining that "this, that, and the other never can be known" (1.138). Peirce cites, as an instance of the stultifying character of such an assertion, Comte's specification of the chemical composition of the fixed stars as a matter of fact "to the knowledge of which no man could by any possibility attain". Of course the discovery of the spectroscope soon afterward transformed what was 'absolutely unknowable' into a matter progressively ascertained. The dogmatic hindrance to inquiry, like the sceptical, is of a more and a less general form. Some of the claims of dogmatism in its more general form we have likewise mentioned—the claim, for instance, that direct or immediate experience is an infallible source of knowledge, confusing knowledge with ineffable, incommunicable feeling. Another form of dogmatism is religious revelation, which, whether it assumes the form of an imposition of belief not to be questioned (the method of authority), or of private mysticism (a form of the method of tenacity: (5.384)), bases its claim to infallibility on extra-mundane sources of evidence, thus excluding possible test by free public inquiry. But the form of dogmatism most noxious to the pursuit and progress of science is the dogmatism within science itself. History shows science to have been practised by many who were in the habit of "over-confident assertion" (1.137), these being for the most part, says Peirce, men more concerned with teaching than with learning. Science itself has not been free from a priorism and the belief in 'self-evident' truths, a characterization which, Peirce quotes W. K. Clifford, really means no more than "we do not know how to prove" (1.38). The most important hindrance to scientific investigation, however—since it is most easily likely to occur—is the view "that this or that law or truth has found its last and most perfect formulation" (1.140). It is chiefly with this last form of dogmatism in mind that Peirce enunciates his conception of fallibilism.[1]

The principle of fallibilism in its widest implications we have already virtually expressed, for it is the principle that no synthetic statement can be regarded as finally verified and beyond question (1.149; cf. 2.663, 1.404). All thought, all inquiry is inferential, and all reasoning about positive fact "is of the nature of judging the proportion of something in a whole collection by the proportion found in a sample" (1.141). This statement is a little narrow, applying strictly to induction and neglecting the other kind of positive reasoning, abduction; but it serves to emphasize Peirce's point. Which is, that since every one of the statements of empirical science and common experience is related inferentially to other statements, "there are three things to which we can never hope to attain . . . namely, absolute certainty, absolute exactitude, absolute universality" (*ib.*). Empirical science is the instrument which attempts constantly to come closer to these ideals. The set of opinions to which science approximates by making its own statements more certain, exact and universal, lies indefinitely in the future. Peirce goes so far as to say that the confession of a statement's defection in each of these three properties is "an essential ingredient of truth" (5.565; he does not specify the three

[1] With respect to the scepticism of the 'unknowable', see 1.139, 5.254 ff., 5.265, 5.310.

properties). The body of opinions which science regards as established cannot be regarded as permanently established (cf. 6.3); the "economy of endeavor prescribes that, *for the time being*, further inquiry shall cease" (5.589; my ital.). Accordingly the body of opinions of science is not to be regarded as a body of dogma; nor is it even a body of "organized knowledge" (1.44, 6.428, 6.450), so much as a process of continually trying to find out, a hungry attempt to increase and correct knowledge indefinitely. This, after all, is what is implied in the word 'inquiry', and Peirce's systematic use of it is no accident.

The principle of fallibilism is a principle of radicalism in science and in all thought. Conservatism in thought means "a dread of consequences" (1.148), this dread of consequences characterizing the scepticisms, so-called, as well as the dogmatisms.[1] The radicalism of science is the "radicalism that tries experiments", that carries "consequences to their extremes". It is hardly in the spirit of the scientist to fear consequences lest they change established opinions, but it is easily understandable why traditional religion and morality should be hostile to fallibilism. Fallibilism is inseparable from the scientific *method*, which implies eternally free inquiry; hence it is repugnant to authority and established interests. It is most readily embraced by those who are primarily learners and only secondarily teachers; by those who understand that "the first step toward *finding out* is to acknowledge you do not satisfactorily know already" (1.13). Peirce's own insatiable interest in so many branches of inquiry, his constant attempt to refine and reformulate his convictions, illustrated in what to superficial examination seems mere repetition and redundancy, is permeated by this spirit. ". . . Out of a contrite fallibilism, combined with a high faith in the reality of knowledge, and an intense desire

[1] " I applaud scepticism with all my heart, provided it have four qualities : first, that it be sincere and real doubt ; second, that it be aggressive ; third, that it push inquiry ; and fourth, that it stand ready to acknowledge what it now doubts, as soon as the doubted element comes clearly to light " (1.344).

to find things out, all my philosophy has always seemed to me to grow. . . ." (1.14).

25. **Peirce and the ' Cartesian Tradition '.** Perhaps we are now in a position to see why as far back as 1868 Peirce considered his views collectively as a break with the Cartesian tradition in philosophy. Cartesianism, says Peirce, "teaches that philosophy must begin with universal doubt", and that "the ultimate test of certainty is to be found in the individual consciousness" (5.264). This initial scepticism is "a mere self-deception, and not real doubt" (5.265). The prerogatives of philosophy to the contrary notwithstanding, "we cannot begin with complete doubt. We must begin with all the prejudices which we actually have when we enter upon the study of philosophy. . . . Let us not pretend to doubt in philosophy what we do not doubt in our hearts" (*ib.*). As a result of the naïve introspectionism which it takes for granted (cf. 5.391), and which enables it to discern whether the contents of the mind are clear or not clear, the Cartesian philosophy formulates its criterion of truth: "Whatever I am clearly convinced of, is true" (5.265). This intuitive criterion makes the individual the absolute judge of truth, and the method of ascertaining it becomes the a priori method. Truth becomes a private rather than a social matter. The metaphysicians agree on nothing but that metaphysics is certain. Unlike the method of the sciences, in which different fields of investigation yield results that support each other, and which seeks always to widen these fields of investigation, the Cartesian method imposes the requirement of self-evident first principles as the premisses of investigation. These logical foundations are arrived at psychologically, that is, in the actual pursuit of philosophy, by the individual's gradual self-liberation from thoroughgoing doubt.

Peirce feels that Descartes is truly the father of modern philosophy, most modern philosophers having been, at least 'in effect', Cartesians. This judgment may or may not be true, but it is worth remarking that the manner in which

Descartes has been maligned by subsequent philosophers probably is an index of the debt they owe to him. Like Peirce, Reid (and of course others before him, notably Leibniz), speaking of Descartes' method and his maxim 'Cogito ergo sum,' says: ". . . It is evident he was in his senses all the time, and never seriously doubted of his existence".[1] Yet Reid, surely enough, proceeds no differently from Descartes. His criticism boils down to a criticism of Descartes' results, not of his method; Descartes no less than he attempts to refute scepticism; his real grievance is that his predecessor's attempt was not successful. But it is especially with respect to Peirce's criticism that the cudgels can be taken up for Descartes. The 'spirit of Cartesianism' perhaps, but not Descartes, teaches that "philosophy must begin with universal doubt". Quite like Peirce he aims to show that complete doubt is impossible, that certain principles, the 'self-evident' principles, as he believed, force themselves upon the mind. The *procedure* of the First Meditation amounts, not to an inauguration of complete doubt, but to a proposal that all opinions should (tentatively) be looked upon as corrigible; and it is subsequently shown that this proposal was illegitimate, that our 'doubts' were not real. This procedure is analogous to a *reductio ad absurdum* proof. At the end of the Sixth Meditation the original 'doubts' are revealed by Descartes to be 'hyperbolical'. Curiously enough, Peirce himself in 1878, ten years after his criticism, observes that Leibniz "missed the most essential point of the Cartesian philosophy, which is, that to accept propositions which seem perfectly evident to us is a thing which, whether it be logical or illogical, we cannot help doing" (5.392; cf. also 5.391). But more curious still is the fact that he continues, even in very late years, to reaffirm the original criticism of the 'Cartesian error'.

26. The Meaning of ' Common Sense ' and of ' Experience '. We have used the terms 'common sense' and 'experience'

---

[1] Hamilton's Reid, p. 100.

without first explicitly defining them. It would have meant
little to have done so, for these terms are best understood in
the light of the foregoing opinions. By 'common sense'
Peirce means "those ideas and beliefs that man's situation
absolutely forces upon him" (1.129). Clearly the two classes
of indubitable beliefs fall under 'common sense'. But
common sense is a *kind* of beliefs primarily, and it is not the
status alone of these beliefs that is to be emphasized. Beliefs
that are adopted and soon discarded, empirical generalizations that may or may not endure, all are built up out of
what we call the 'ideas' of common sense, and they are no
less a part of it than the indubitables. So that, more
generally, common sense "is the resultant of the traditional
experience of mankind" (cf. Santayana, § 20); it "witnesses
unequivocally that the heart is more than the head, and is
in fact everything in our highest concerns . . ."; "the dicta
of common sense are objective facts . . . what the healthy,
natural, normal democracy thinks" (1.654).

Thus 'critical common-sensism', covering the whole of this
Part, according to the sense in which we have used it, is
roughly comprised of two more specific parts: §§ 17-27 stress
'common-sense', its nature, importance and fundamental
soundness; §§ 1-16, epitomized in the principle of fallibilism, stress the critique of common sense; and the whole of
critical common-sensism is therefore a refined, or as Peirce
would say, a 'precided', common-sensism. ". . . The
difficulty is to determine what really is and what is not the
authoritative decision of common sense. . . ." (1.129).

What is 'experience', of which common sense is said by
Peirce to be the 'resultant'? By and large, we understand
fairly well what is meant when it is said that science and
common sense are based on experience, and that the scientific method is the 'experiential method'. But even in
ordinary usage the word 'experience' has more than one
sense, and in Peirce at least five senses can be found. By
stressing one of these, I believe a definition of 'experience'
can be stated which is general enough to embrace all five.

Roughly, in one of the senses ((4) below) 'experience' means that which we obtain from a certain source; in another (1) it means the source from which we obtain what we do; in another (3) it means the 'operation' by which we obtain what we do; in still another (2) it means a certain way in which the source acts upon us; and finally (5) it means 'feeling'.

(1) Peirce, in the first sense, accepts Locke's characterization of experience. He quotes: "Whence has [the mind] all the materials of reason and knowledge? To this I answer, in one word, from *experience*: in that all our knowledge is founded; and from that it ultimately derives itself. Our observation employed either, about external sensible objects, or about the internal operations of our minds perceived and reflected on by ourselves, is that which supplies our understanding with all the materials of thinking."[1] This definition, says Peirce, "should be accepted as definite and as a landmark that it would be a crime to displace or disturb" (5.611).[2] In this sense of 'experience' we ordinarily say that science 'resorts' to experience, that experience is the 'source' of scientific knowledge, and that experience 'decides' scientific questions. But this sense is hardly made precise yet; for both Locke and Peirce use 'experience' in this sense to mean (a) the *method of investigation*—to which science 'resorts', which is the 'source' of its knowledge, and which 'decides' its questions; and (b) the *reality or permanency* (the external world)—to which science likewise may be said to 'resort', which is the 'source' of its knowledge, and which 'decides' its questions. A difference between Locke and Peirce is that Locke regards 'observation' (the method) as including, each with equal status, external perception and reflection (introspection), the loci of observation being the external world and the mind; whereas Peirce, as we saw, regards even introspection as a process of inference from external perception.

[1] *Essay*, II, i, 2.
[2] In 5.11 Peirce speaks of Locke's " clean definitions ".

(2) In the second sense, 'experience' is "the influence of the world of fact" (upon us); and this influence is a "forcible modification of our ways of thinking" (1.321). Experience cannot be "summoned up at pleasure" (5.524). "It is the compulsion, the absolute constraint upon us to think otherwise than we have been thinking that constitutes experience" (1.336). (Cf. e.g. 2.138, 2.784.)

(3) In the third sense, 'experience' denotes a mental process, an operation. We are said to 'experience', and this 'experiencing' is a cognitive process. What kind of cognition is it? According to Peirce, it is to be distinguished from 'perception'. The concept of experience is "broader than that of perception, and includes much that is not, strictly speaking, an object of perception" (1.336). It is not accurate to say that we 'perceive' events; we 'experience' events. An 'event' here seems to mean a 'change of perception': "It is the special field of experience to acquaint us with events, with changes of perception" (ib.). Change produces shock in us (cf. 6.19, § 16), and this produces a sense of resistance or effort. ". . . Resistance is effort opposing change. Therefore there must be an element of effort in experience; and it is this which gives it its peculiar character" (ib.). Now experience in this third sense is the mental process under which the influence or compulsion by fact, which is experience in the second sense, is exercised. An experience in this third sense may be regarded as an instance of such compulsion, and is presumably to be identified by the 'sense of effort' associated with it. But is the sense of effort sufficient to distinguish 'experiencing' from 'perceiving' (assuming that Peirce is not confusing perception as cognitive with feeling, which sometimes in 1.336 is doubtful)? For perception too, in fact all cognition, as we have seen, involves the 'sense of duality'; and Peirce elsewhere (5.539) tells us that the sense of effort is simply an "especially prominent" manifestation of the sense of duality. Moreover, he says that often in an 'experience' we are hardly aware of the sense of effort, and know of its presence

only "through the axiom that there can be no force where there is no resistance or inertia" (1.336); so that the sense of effort is not necessarily even an 'especially prominent' case of the sense of duality. But if we do not speak of the sense of effort as a differentia of experience, and confine ourselves merely to saying that after all 'experience', unlike 'perception', is of 'events' or 'changes of perception', this still is unconvincing, for what constitutes an 'event' or 'change of perception' is not something of a hard and fast character: perceptual cognition is likewise cognition of 'changes of perception', only in a lesser degree. It is also possible that if experiential cognition is to be defined in the present sense as the mental process involved in experience understood in the second sense, then this definition does not exclude perceptual cognition; for perceptual judgments are also in a certain sense 'forced' upon us (cf. 2.141, 5.55). But I believe that what Peirce intends as the essential difference between experiencing and perceiving is a feeling of 'surprise' or unexpectedness associated with the former (cf. 5.51-52). We shall say something more of surprise in a moment, though of the cognition-as-content which it produces rather than of the cognitive process involving it. The relations of 'experience' in the second, third and fourth senses are: A forcible action by the world of fact upon us (2), involves a cognitive process distinctive for the feeling of surprise associated with it (3), which in turn involves cognitive content (4).

(4) 'Experience' as cognitive content is synonymous with 'information' (cf. 1.537). It comprises that "of a cognitive nature which the history of our lives has forced upon us" (5.539); and this means cognition no matter from where derived, not merely that derived from sense or scientific inquiry. "By experience must be understood the entire mental product", including "hallucinations, delusions, superstitious imaginations and fallacies of all kinds" (6.492). It is in this sense that we speak of our 'fund' of experience. Experience comprises anything derived from some source,

provided it is cognitive. It is important to stress that experience in this sense is not to be understood as meaning simply a collection of cognitions. It is not amount of cognition that is essential, even though actually we cannot speak of our cognitions as constituting 'experience' except as taken collectively. What is essential is that experience in this sense emphasizes cognitive content rather than cognitive process.

(5) 'Experience' in Peirce sometimes means mere immediate feeling, of any kind, though when it has this meaning it is usually qualified as 'direct experience' or 'immediate experience' (e.g. 1.145). Experience in all the other senses obviously involves direct experience. Probably the usage of the word in this sense is the most popular (or perhaps the fourth sense is, in so far as it is a 'fund' or 'collection'); but 'experience' as used to emphasize this sense alone is comparatively rare in Peirce. Thus he combines this sense with sense (2) when he says, "The percepts . . . constitute experience proper, that which I am forced to accept" (2.142).

'Common sense', to return for a moment, is the name of a body of beliefs (experience in 4th sense), a certain part of which is obtained, as a result of external compulsion (experience in 2nd sense), from experience (in 1st sense), by a psychological process (experience in 3rd sense). The sense of 'experience' which is most common in Peirce and which he regards as most important is the second. On the basis of this, 'experience' can be defined in a way that does justice to all the senses. I think it would not be an unwarranted interpretation of Peirce to define it as a *relation*, between (roughly) ourselves and a portion of the external world. By stressing the external world, and not simply any source of influence, we modify somewhat the conception of experience in the fourth sense; but on the other hand we give greater prominence, as Peirce would wish, to experience in the second. Let us state more precisely what the experience-relation, as we may call it, entails.

The terms of this relation are ourselves and the external world. But we may describe the relation itself best in terms of two elements that go to constitute it. The first consists of experience in the second sense, the other, of experience in the four remaining senses. On the one hand, there is the element of compulsion and forcible modification of our opinions, which "cannot be summoned up at pleasure". But "how does this action . . . take place? It takes place by a series of surprises" (5.51). Now what are the results, so to speak, of these surprises? The results, forming our cognitive experiential content, are hypotheses.[1] This leads us to the other element of the experience-relation. We cannot speak of the forcible action of the external world upon us, of surprise, unless there is a certain receptivity on our part: we cannot react to or be influenced by surprise unless a definite mental attitude and a previous cognitive content made us capable of being surprised. So that while we could not adopt hypotheses unless we *encountered* something 'surprising', that same thing would not be surprising unless we were *capable* of adopting some sort of explanation or hypothesis. If we consider those instances where the first element of the experience-relation plays the biggest rôle, we get the indubitable beliefs; if we consider those where the second plays the biggest rôle, we get experimental science. But while compulsion and surprise predominate in the formation of the indubitable beliefs, the element of prior intelligence is not absent in determining these beliefs. And while the element of prior intelligence and knowledge, in the form of deliberate experiment to test hypothesis, predominates in science, the element of unexpectedness and surprise is far from absent in determining the character of science: for if all experiment turned out as anticipated, without unexpected results occurring, hypotheses would never be modified, new hypotheses would never be suggested, and consequently knowledge would never be promoted. Purposive experimentation and external compulsion are each, in some degree, necessary for the experience-relation. But so far as science is concerned,

---

[1] Cf. 5.189—"The surprising fact, C, is observed . . ." etc., whereupon we adopt a hypothesis to explain this fact.

the former is most important. "Instead of waiting for experience to come at untoward times, [man] provokes it when it can do no harm and changes the government of his internal world accordingly" (1.321). Scientific experiment is the most refined form of 'provocation' of experience. The scientist 'provokes experience' (as, in accordance with our account, we may interpret Peirce) in the sense that he deliberately, on the basis of a hypothesis or theoretical belief, establishes *one of the conditions* of the experience-relation. It is as a result of this preparation or provocation that he can profit most from the experience-relation when its other condition, unexpectedness or surprise, occurs.

Perhaps as a result of this definition we can better understand what was meant when we asserted that the reinforcement or the doubt of our beliefs is due to experience.

27. Peirce and Contemporary Logical Empiricism. It is possible to make any number of instructive comparisons between the views of Peirce and present-day opinion. I believe, however, that a comparison of the foregoing with one aspect—or rather one *tendency*, since the views of this movement change and develop so rapidly—of contemporary logical empiricism is the most impressive index of Peirce's modernity.

We have said that for Peirce a proposition is called 'true' if it is confirmed to a certain degree. To what degree? That regarded as sufficient by the scientific community. Now philosophers will not object to the view that the 'laws' of empirical science can never be regarded as more than 'probable', i.e. as other than 'probable' inferences from statements confirmed perceptually. But how about the perceptual statements themselves? Must not they be 'certainly' true; does not the principle of fallibilism, which insists on the corrigibility even of perceptual statements, destroy empiricism? For, it may be said, if the perceptual statements too are corrigible, then there is no genuine foundation of empirical knowledge. We cannot be said to 'know' unless we 'know certainly', that is, unless what we know is 'really' the case.   This is, of course, the argument for intuitive judgments in another guise.   The argument insists that there must be first principles—empirical first principles, intuitively established—in order that we should be able to call our scientific knowledge empirical.   We have given the reasons why Peirce does not subscribe to such a view.[1]   It has been advanced by the so-called 'right wing' of logical empiricism, and for purposes of comparison with Peirce I want to state in the briefest possible way some theses characterizing the two wings of this school, especially with respect to the concept of truth.[2]

The view of the left wing (R. Carnap, O. Neurath, etc.) is essentially that of Peirce with, of course, certain refinements. Empirical science is a system of hypotheses.   The general hypotheses are regarded as 'true' if supported by basic statements, called 'protocol statements' or 'protocols'. Protocol statements do not necessarily have to be perceptual statements; which statements will be regarded as basic depends upon the context of investigation.   In certain limited fields of investigation general hypotheses will be taken as the basic confirming statements, in others singular statements;   and for empirical science in general, the

[1] Peirce sometimes does speak as if 'knowledge' meant the possession of incorrigible propositions, and that therefore (since he does not believe in the latter) science, properly speaking, cannot be called knowledge but only a process leading up to that ideal (1.8, 1.44; cf. § 24).   Such instances are to be interpreted liberally, however; Peirce would call the body of science 'knowledge' in the sense that he calls it 'true': knowledge is none the less knowledge for the fact that it is subject to correction. (Cf. 1.37 : ". . . there is a world of difference between fallible knowledge and no knowledge.")

[2] I follow, to a certain extent, the scheme of C. G. Hempel's account of "The Logical Positivists' Theory of Truth", *Analysis*, II, 4 (1935). For the most comprehensive and up-to-date account of logical empiricism in general, see E. Nagel, "Impressions and Appraisals of Analytic Philosophy in Europe", *Journal of Philosophy*, 1936, nos. 1 and 2.

Reports at this writing have it that the 'left wing' view is in process of considerable modification.   But whether or not what is set forth above retains its original proponents, it remains a well-defined view, and this is all that matters for our purpose.

observation or perceptual statements. (Let us confine ourselves, in speaking of 'protocols', to the perceptual protocols.) The general hypotheses of science, then, are true because their consequences agree with the protocols. Protocols are themselves essentially hypotheses, and belong equally to the system of science. They can never be said to be verified conclusively, but are always subject to possible alteration.

Against this view the late M. Schlick made the following objection: It is all right to say that a statement of science is called 'true' if its consequences coincide with perceptual statements, but only if these protocols are true unquestionably. For if not, then it is conceivable that scientific systems should be constructed with a different set of protocols, supporting different hypotheses, possibly hypotheses incompatible with those which we now accept. We should then have contrary systems of 'true' statements. What is to distinguish true from false statements, if not protocols known certainly to be true (*Konstatierungen*, translated as 'constatations' or ostensive statements) by empirical intuition? The reply to this from the opposing wing is that true protocols are distinguished from false ones by the fact that the scientific community, which represents all mankind, adopts them. But, then, would it not be possible for a division of opinion to arise and for groups to differ on the protocols which they adopt? To which the reply is, once more, that this possibility is not realized, because the universal adoption of protocols is due to conditioning, to lifelong habits of linguistic response (Carnap). That is to say, under certain circumstances, e.g. when a light flashes, our conditioning is such as to make us judge, 'This light is blue', or whatever the case may be. This statement is a hypothesis, standing in logical relation to other statements. We could, if we wished, make further investigations, indefinitely, to test this statement. But the process must stop somewhere, and we stop with such protocols. We do not *have to* stop there; we do it only as a matter of utmost expedience. In this sense the protocol statements are conventional. By the tacit consent of the scientific community, they serve as the confirmatory or basic or foundation statements of science.[1]

The moot point in the controversy under consideration is thus the character of the protocols. It is impossible to enter here in detail into the views of those who (Popper, Carnap, etc.) have studied the conventional character of the protocols. Nor, perhaps, can full justice be done to the opposing arguments, advanced for intuitive protocols. But I hardly think it inaccurate to say that the points of difference are essentially the same as those between Peirce and Reid.

Schlick himself states the moot question in the form: Can statements be compared (i.e. for the purpose of immediate or intuitive verification) with 'reality', with 'facts'?[2] He maintains that hypotheses are compared mediately with facts or reality, via the protocols, which are not hypotheses but are compared directly with the facts they express. Thus the statement 'I see blue now' is a protocol, because it is immediately verifiable. It is interesting to compare the following passage, by another advocate of this view, with quotation (4), § 15 above, of Reid. ". . . In gewissem Sinne kann man sagen, dass Konstatierungen gar keiner Verifikation bedürfen. In dem Sinne nämlich, dass wir im Augenblick, wo wir Konstatierungen gewonnen haben—weil eben Gewinnung und Verifikation dieser Sätze zusammenfallen— schon auch ihren Wahrheitswert kennen, d.h. im Augenblick wo wir sie verstehen, wissen wir auch schon, ob sie wahr oder falsch sind."[3] According to the opposing view, a statement cannot be compared with a 'fact'; to say that it can is actually a corruption of proper usage. Statements can only be compared, in a logical relationship, with other statements. But for Schlick not only is this proper usage: the very concept of empirical science rests upon it. Science

---

[1] For a discussion of the conventional element in Peirce, see § 38; with respect to conventionalism in logic, §§ 45, 46, and 48.

[2] " Facts and Propositions ", *Analysis*, II, 5 (1935).

[3] B. Juhos, in *Erkenntnis*, VI, 1 (1936), p. 45.

depends for its truth upon a set of statements not having the property of being habitual with scientists but having the property of being testable by 'reality' itself. The reason why a man trusts the scientists and calls the system of science 'true', according to Schlick, is that in his own experience he can test the consequences of that system. "If all the scientists in the world told me that under certain experimental conditions I must see three black spots, and if under those conditions I saw only one spot, no power in the universe could induce me to think that the statement 'there is now only one black spot in the field of vision' is false." [1]

In this controversy, each of the two wings of logical empiricism finds metaphysical elements in the other. Schlick regards the view that a statement cannot be directly tested by reality as a tendency of traditional rationalism—a non-empirical 'coherence' explanation of truth. The opposing wing, on the other hand, regards the concept of the ostensive sentence as a metaphysical form of absolutism. It claims that the view of the system of science as a system of hypotheses is based on and justified by a logical ('syntactical') analysis of that system. It is impossible, as I have said, to even sketch this syntactical apparatus here; but it may be mentioned that according to it, only analytic statements can be called 'certain', and precisely because these statements do not refer to any matter of fact, the symbols out of which they are constructed being arranged in such a way that they are necessarily true when materially interpreted. It may also be said that both wings of logical empiricism in common espouse the application of syntactical or logical analysis to the formulation of the empirical point of view; and it is partly because of this fact that the movement generally, as opposed to positivistic or sensational empiricism, is known as logical empiricism.

It is now scarcely necessary to point out the similarity, on the matters mentioned, in the views of Peirce and one of the wings, which is perhaps the dominant one, of contemporary

[1] *Loc. cit.*, p. 70.

logical empiricism. We may merely call attention to some particular aspects of this similarity. Peirce's destructive arguments against intuitive cognition and his view that every cognition stands in a logical relation to some other, is another, and well-grounded, way of holding that statements can be compared only with one another and not with 'facts'.[1] His explanation of perceptual judgments as associationally inferred is also another way of explaining them on the basis of conditioning. His account of the nature of indubitables, when confined to perceptual indubitables, explains the circumstances governing the adoption of a set of basic statements for empirical science. The homologue in Peirce of the concept of protocol levels is his view that the sole condition for inquiry to proceed is that the statements upon which we build be not actually doubted: they need not be 'first principles' in a traditional sense, nor even indubitables. In more modern language this view is: any field of scientific inquiry constitutes a system in which it is required only that certain statements regarded as 'established' be taken as the basic confirming statements. The distinction we have seen in Peirce between perceptual indubitables as a foundation for all empirical science and statements not actually doubted as a foundation for any given field of inquiry, corresponds to the distinction between observational protocols and protocols of a general kind serving as foundation statements. Peirce, perhaps, would not place so great an emphasis on the sense in which the perceptual statements are conventional. He likes to look upon these statements as forcing themselves upon our minds despite their corrigibility, as forcing us to arbitrate empirical questions by their help. The recognition of the rôle of these statements is the recognition of the rôle

---

[1] ". . . You look at an object and say ' That is red '. I ask you how you prove that. You tell me you see it. Yes, you see *something* ; but you do not see *that it is red* ; because *that it is red* is a proposition ; and you do not see a proposition. What you see is an image and has no resemblance to a proposition, and there is no logic in saying that your proposition is proved by the image. For a proposition can only be logically based on a premiss and a premiss is a proposition " (6.95).

of experience in questions of fact. Our system is guaranteed to be experiential without our describing it in terms of ultimately confronting statements by facts. We *do* come directly into contact with the external world, but by means of non-cognitive percepts and the sense of duality involved in cognition. The notion of *Konstatierung*, Peirce would say, confuses percept and perceptual judgment, the 'material quality' of cognition and cognition proper.

PART II

PRAGMATISM

PEIRCE speaks on one occasion of critical common-sensism as a "consequence" of pragmatism (5.439), and says, on another, that "a pragmaticist, to be consistent, is obliged to embrace" critical common-sensism (5.499); he says also, on the other hand, "I have myself called pragmatism 'critical common-sensism'; but, of course, I do not mean this for a strict definition" (5.494). If we remember that 'critical common-sensism' in Peirce may be understood in a broad and a narrow sense, we should interpret these statements loosely, bearing in mind only that between critical common-sensism as understood in Part I and pragmatism as it emerges from the considerations to follow there is an intimate connection.[1] One might say that to accept common sense as the fundamental basis of knowledge is to accept a pragmatic analysis of meaning, but one might with equal justification say that to accept such an analysis is to accept common sense. We could say that the argument against purely demonstrative names, which underlies the argument against intuitive knowledge, depends to a certain extent on the pragmatic criterion of the meaning of these names; but from another point of view it might be sounder to say that the formulation of the pragmatic criterion is based on the nature of knowledge in general, and its communication in signs, and that an examination of the nature of knowledge refutes by itself the notion of purely demonstrative names. (Cf. above, p. 35.)

---

[1] ". . . Pragmaticism . . . implies faith in common sense and in instinct, though only as they issue from the cupel-furnace of measured criticism " (6.480).

28. **Origin of Pragmatism.** The word 'pragmatism' seems to have been first publicly used by James in the lecture "Philosophical Conceptions and Practical Results" of 1898. He there speaks of "Peirce's principle", "the principle of practicalism—or pragmatism as he [Peirce] called it, when I first heard him enunciate it at Cambridge in the early 70's".[1] The occasion to which James refers was probably one of the meetings of the "half-ironically, half-defiantly" named "Metaphysical Club", formed by Peirce.[2] These meetings were attended by James, Chauncey Wright, Nicholas St. John Green, O. W. Holmes Jr., F. E. Abbot and John Fiske. It was at this Club that "I drew up," says Peirce, "a little paper expressing some of the opinions that I had been urging all along under the name of pragmatism" (5.13). The paper expanded, five or six years later, into the two papers "The Fixation of Belief" and "How to Make Our Ideas Clear", appearing in the November 1877 and January 1878 issues, respectively, of the *Popular Science Monthly*. Although what later became known as the 'maxim'[3] of pragmatism was stated in the second of these papers, the word 'pragmatism' was not used by Peirce himself in print until 1902, when he contributed an article on the subject to Baldwin's Dictionary. He says that as late as 1893 he could have inserted the word in the Century Dictionary (for which he wrote many definitions) but refrained out of uncertainty that the extent of the word's usage justified it, as well as out of over-modesty (5.13, 13 n.).

---

[1] *Collected Essays and Reviews*, p. 410.

[2] Peirce's accounts of the date at which the Metaphysical Club was started and pragmatism introduced vary. See 5.12, 6.482, 6.490, and *Journal of Philosophy*, 1916, p. 719.

[3] "Consider what effects, that might conceivably have practical bearings, we conceive the object of our conception to have. Then, our conception of these effects is the whole of our conception of the object" (5.402). It will be noticed that I make little reference to this maxim in what follows. As a statement made in 1878 it is justly famous; but it is a mistake to base a discussion of Peirce's pragmatism on it. Considered relatively to the whole of Peirce's writings it is one of a class of statements that are unprecise. (Cf. § 33.)

James continued to ascribe the origin both of the conception and the word to Peirce, notably in 1902 [1], 1904 [2] and 1907 [3]; and he quoted or referred to Peirce in various writings. Professor Perry holds it to be "clear that the idea that pragmatism originated with Peirce was originated by James". For "Peirce states explicitly, in his contribution to . . . the Dictionary of Philos. and Psychol. [Baldwin's], 1902, that he derived his view from Kant".[4]   Peirce does not, in fact, say that he "derived his view from Kant" but that he "was led to the maxim by reflection upon Kant's *Critic of the Pure Reason*" (5.3 or Baldwin's Dict., "Pragmatic and Pragmatism"), which is somewhat different. He repeatedly writes that of all philosophical classics he was virtually reared on that of Kant, and almost knew it by heart, in which case it would be small wonder that his reflections should take their point of departure from it. That his pragmatism was also positively influenced by Kant no one doubts, but then he himself says that the ancestry of pragmatism can be traced to Socrates; and if we are to take his words in such matters seriously, there is almost no classical philosopher by whom he has not been positively influenced.[5]   Professor Perry's opinion seems, therefore, to be correct only in the sense that pragmatism was not absolutely original with Peirce.   No important conception is absolutely original; as Peirce says, "Any philosophical doctrine that should be completely new could hardly fail to prove completely false" (5.11).   James's judgment, that Peirce "expressed in the form of an explicit maxim" what was implicit in certain previous philosophies, particularly in the "great English way of investigating a conception",[6] is

---

[1] *Varieties of Religious Experience*, p. 444.

[2] *Coll. Ess. and Rev.*, p. 448.

[3] *Pragmatism*, pp. 46-7.

[4] *Thought and Character of William James*, II, p. 407 n[6].

[5] One of Peirce's favourite classical ancestors of pragmatism is Berkeley (cf. 5.11, 6.482 ; Perry, II, p. 425).   But he regards Spinoza (!) too as a prominent ancestor (cf. 6.490, 5.412).

[6] *Coll. Ess. and Rev.*, p. 434.

probably correct, though Peirce's explicit contribution was in its totality far more profound than the maxim of which James was thinking.

The immediate ancestry of pragmatism Peirce ascribed to members of the Metaphysical Club. He emphasizes particularly the influence of Chauncey Wright (5.12, 5.64), and Green he calls the "grandfather of pragmatism", for "he often urged the importance of applying Bain's definition of belief, as 'that upon which a man is prepared to act'"',[1] from which definition "pragmatism is scarce more than a corollary" (5.12).

But already in the second of the 1868 papers Peirce says that the meaning or "intellectual value" of a thought "lies . . . in what this thought may be connected with in representation by subsequent thoughts; so that the meaning of a thought is altogether something virtual" (5.289). And in 1871, in his review of Campbell Fraser's edition of Berkeley's Works, he offers a "rule for avoiding the deceits of language": "Do things fulfil the same function practically? Then let them be signified by the same word. Do they not? Then let them be distinguished." [2] These passages are rudimentary, but they touch the core, respectively, of the doctrine and the purpose of pragmatism.

29. **The Purpose of Pragmatism.** What did Peirce intend to accomplish by the formulation of pragmatism? In 1878 he intended it as a principle making for the clarification of 'ideas', and to this essential purpose he clung always, expressing it more fully as the years passed. He emphasizes that the clearness of ideas which his pragmatic maxim, then unnamed, is designed to attain is not clearness in either the Cartesian or the Leibnizian senses, which he regards as the two 'grades of clearness' inferior to the pragmatic. The clearness which Descartes prescribed amounts to a psychological sense of agreeableness, derived from introspection,

---

[1] Cf. Bain, *The Emotions and the Will*, 3rd. ed. (1875), p. 505.
[2] *North American Review*, Vol. 113 (1871), p. 469.

and neglects the possibility that ideas which seem clear may in fact not be so. The 'distinctness' which Descartes further prescribed is intended to put ideas to the test of 'dialectic': they must remain clear when their consequences are examined, and in any context of discussion that they may enter. The Leibnizian criterion of distinctness emphasized the importance of abstract definitions. This requirement Peirce regards as important in setting beliefs "in order", order being "an essential element of intellectual economy, as of every other" (5.392). That Peirce himself was, incidentally, much concerned with this aspect of 'clearness' is shown by his considerable attention to the theory of terminology (cf. 2.219-226, 5.413, 5.611). But the criterion of suitable abstract definition is hardly sufficient to guarantee that the members of a linguistic group should know each with relative precision what he is talking about and communicate unequivocally. This the pragmatic criterion is designed to achieve. (Cf. 3.457, 5.206.)

Pragmatism "is, in itself, no doctrine of metaphysics, no attempt to determine any truth of things. It is merely a method of ascertaining the meanings of hard words and of abstract concepts" (5.464). The most important application of the pragmatic method is therefore to philosophical inquiry. Suppose that two philosophers are engaged in dispute. The question which they are disputing, let us further assume, cannot be settled by appeal to the observation of facts. Yet each philosopher claims that the other is wrong, and moreover, claims to prove it. In such a situation, "Pragmatism maintains that . . . the disputants must be at cross-purposes. They either attach different meanings to words, or else one side or the other (or both) uses a word without any definite meaning" (5.6). Plainly a method such as pragmatism is necessary "for ascertaining the real meaning of any concept, doctrine, proposition, word, or other sign" (ib.). Pragmatism "will serve to show that almost every proposition of ontological metaphysics is either meaningless gibberish . . . or else is downright absurd" (5.423). The

reason is that the words of traditional metaphysics derive
their meaning *merely* from abstract definition: a term is
defined by others, these by others still, without "any real
conception ever being reached" (*ib.*). Peirce's pragmatism,
then, is a criterion of the meaning of words and sentences.
It is not a criterion which simply legislates for the sake of
convenience or elegance what the meaning shall be, but
which is based on the way in which words and sentences are
actually used; Peirce intends to make precise the criterion
of meaning implicit in the linguistic intercourse of all men;
and by the use of this more precise and explicit criterion we
should be able to say, not only in actually doubtful cases
but in every case, whether a word or sentence is or is not
meaningful. ". . . After all," Peirce wrote to James in
1904, "pragmatism solves no real problem. It only shows
that supposed problems are not real problems."[1] It will be
observed that Peirce speaks sometimes of the meaning of
words or sentences and sometimes of the meaning of 'ideas'
or 'concepts'. It is more general, and at the same time
more accurate, to speak of pragmatism as a criterion of the
meaning of *signs*. For a sign may be either a purely linguistic sign, under which we may class such things as words,
algebraic notation and visual diagrams; or it may be a
thought, i.e. a mental sign, which is at least quasi-linguistic.[2]

Now there are two limitations to the kinds of signs the
meaning of which pragmatism professes to determine. The
first of these limitations is only implicit in Peirce, but the
second he emphasizes on more than one occasion. (1) So
far as words are concerned, pragmatism determines the
meaning only of non-logical words; that is to say, it applies
only to *descriptive* signs or *names* (whether of qualities or

---

[1] In Perry, *op. cit.*, II, p. 430.

[2] ". . . All thought whatsoever is a sign, and is mostly *of the nature
of language*" (5.421 ; my ital.). Also, ". . . The woof and warp of all
thought and all research is symbols, and the life of thought and science
is the life inherent in symbols ; so that it is wrong to say that a good
language is *important* to good thought, merely ; for it is of the essence
of it" (2.220).

relations) and does not apply to such logical words as 'and', 'not', 'if', etc. So far as sentences or propositions are concerned, pragmatism applies only to *synthetic* sentences. (2) Pragmatism, according to Peirce, ascertains the meaning only of "intellectual" signs, i.e. signs "upon the structure of which, arguments concerning objective fact may hinge" (5.467). Thus he says that pragmatism has nothing at all to do with the meaning of the names 'red' or 'blue', for "red and blue name mere subjective feelings only"; pragmatism has "nothing to do with qualities of feeling", and "could two qualities of feeling be everywhere interchanged, nothing but feelings could be affected" (*ib.*). Pragmatism indeed has nothing to do with qualities of feeling, which are incommunicable; but in excluding from its domain names like 'red' and 'blue', Peirce confuses a feeling with the name of a feeling, and he fails to see, moreover, that a name may be the name of a feeling and yet more than *merely* that. And not only does he exclude names like 'red' from pragmatic interpretation but also proper names "or other designation[s] of an individual object" (5.429). Here again he seems to confuse a proper name with a demonstrative pronoun (cf. 3.460), and would apparently regard the former as purely demonstrative if he so regarded the latter. (In contemporary terminology, he confuses a 'proper' name with a 'logically proper' name.)

If limitation (2) to the scope of pragmatic definability should not be a confusion, then it affects limitation (1), and the latter becomes a more drastic limitation. But even if it should not be confused in itself, i.e. as a separate point, it would at least be inconsistent with Peirce's fundamental opinions. For it would be a genuine limitation only if proper names and names like 'red' were purely demonstrative. In being a limitation to the scope of pragmatism it would really be contrary to pragmatism; for purely demonstrative names are repugnant (as we have already in some measure seen) to Peirce's conception of knowledge, on which pragmatism is in a sense based. I believe, however,

that not only on this point—i.e. the limitation of the pragmatic criterion to 'intellectual' signs—but on others Peirce
suffers from confusion rather than from serious internal
inconsistency. I shall return to it in §31 (and also, from a
somewhat different angle, in §41), after some considerations
which ought rightfully to precede.

30. **What is an Interpretant ?** We have seen (§ 2) that
something can be called a 'sign' only when it has an 'object'
and an 'interpretant'. But it must be pointed out that
Peirce's various definitions of 'sign' contain a number of
different emphases, depending upon what he has in mind in
the place of discussion. Consequently, the definitions of
'object' differ, and so do, especially, the definitions of 'interpretant'. What is the most general statement of the sign-
relation, the triadic relation of representation? We cannot
say, for instance, that by 'object' Peirce means the extension of a sign, since that is what he means (or can mean)
only in the case of names; nor can we say that by 'object'
he means the 'referend' (as it is called today), for while a
name or a map has a referend, we should ordinarily not say
that the sign 'the' or the sign which we call an analytical
inference has a referend. A case can easily be made out for
such 'signs' as the pointing of a finger or a weathervane as
having extension, namely, the thing pointed to or indicated.
But in general it seems clear that while perhaps every name,
including, if we must, the 'natural' signs and demonstratives,
has extension (Peirce prefers Hamilton's term 'breadth'
to 'extension'), not every sign has. Thus, contrary to
Peirce's analysis, which holds that every sign is part of a
triadic relation, it would seem that certain signs either do
not have an 'object' or have one in a rather strained sense.
If we turn to 'interpretant', the case would seem to be
different: 'interpretant' *would* always seem to mean
'depth'. According to Peirce, in order that a sign should
be a sign, it must have an explanation (2.230), a translation
(5.594, 5.427), an interpretation (5.569)—in brief, an inter-

pretant. It is rather important to emphasize that by 'interpretant' we mean 'possible interpretant'. "It is not necessary that the Interpretant should actually exist"; an interpretant "*in futuro* will suffice" (2.92). So that every term, logical or non-logical, every proposition, synthetic or analytic, every inference, would seem to have an interpretant, whether in the form of a definition (actual or possible) or a consequence (actual or possible). But if 'interpretant' as applied to all terms (and logical plus non-logical terms constitute, after all, the whole of any proposition or inference) is synonymous with 'depth', it follows that no sign is purely demonstrative. This is the internal evidence. We have yet to consider Peirce's explicit utterances on the matter. Deferring them to the next section, let us make certain points that will be useful.

(1) We may distinguish, in Peirce, between psychical signs and non-psychical (or non-mental) or 'external' (5.569) signs. A psychical sign is a thought or cognition; an external sign is a written word, gesture, or other physical instrument of representation. We may divide the external signs into linguistic signs on the one hand and 'natural' signs or 'physical symptoms' (3.361) on the other. Now Peirce holds, in many places, that the interpretant of a sign is 'mental'; or he often uses 'interpretant' as synonymous with 'thought' (e.g. 2.315, 2.274). Does he mean that every interpretant is a psychical sign, that is, an actual thought or cognition? May not the definition of a word be a linguistic formula, or the interpretant of a proposition another proposition? What Peirce means is that every sign must ultimately have significance for a mind (cf. 2.242, 2.274). And he sometimes speaks, not only of an interpretant but of an *interpreter* (e.g. 4.536). An interpretant implies an interpreter: every sign must ultimately have an interpretant that is a mental interpretant. Every sign, in other words, must have a translation or interpretation, which is meaningful only to some mind.

(2) The concepts of interpreter and interpretant are capable of generalization. We may regard the 'interpreter'

as the *system* in which a given set of signs occurs, the notion
of a system implying rules or conventions both for the number and type of signs that will be admissible, and for the
translation or transformation of a given sign into others.
We may regard the 'interpretant' as the definition or translation of any sign within the system. The interpretant of a
sentence is the class of its consequences, and any term is
definable by means of the primitive terms of the system;
the primitives too have an interpretant, both in the sense
that they *could* be defined and in the sense that they are
implicitly defined by the axioms in which they occur.
Peirce perhaps suggests this generalization by referring to
the interpreter as the 'quasi-mind' (4.536). But I believe
he would insist that however generally the notions of interpreter and interpretant are understood, we must ultimately
fall back, in order to give significance to the sign-relation,
upon an interpreter that is a mind and upon an interpretant
that is a thought in this mind.

(3) We saw that in so far as a sign is thought it is judicative, i.e. is a tacit assertion. In view of the fact that some
signs are merely linguistic, and are, moreover, mere terms,
does this require modification? It might seem that the
definiens of a definition could remain a non-assertive set of
signs, even if thought. But in fact, such a sign, when interpreted by a mind would, on the view of Peirce, be interpreted in an assertion. Most significant, however, is the fact
that Peirce regards every linguistic sign (and probably,
although on this I am not sure, every sign—cf. 2.264) as, if
not actually assertive, tacitly assertive, or 'rhematic'.
Peirce's term 'rheme' is the equivalent of what is now
called a 'propositional function'. (Cf. 2.340-341; 4.438,
4.354; 2.250, 2.264.) A rheme is an incomplete predication.
Ordinarily a proper name, for instance, is not regarded as
a predicate or propositional function. It is not a 'rheme'.
But it may nevertheless be regarded as *rhematic*, in the
sense that it must ultimately be interpreted as occurring in,
and forming a definite part of, some assertion.

(4) The interpretant of a sign, being always itself a sign, whether a psychical or linguistic translation, is also a sign of the same object and is translatable by another interpretant. This may in turn be regarded as a sign of the same object, etc. Thus every sign has an indefinite number of interpretations, each a sign of the same object. We saw this without difficulty in the case of psychical signs (§§ 2, 4).

Now our account of how 'interpretant' is to be understood would be altogether satisfactory if it were not for the fact that Peirce distinguishes *three kinds* of interpretants. Our account of the interpretant as being a translation in terms of signs, of signs which interpret a given sign, has taken no cognizance of two other 'kinds' of interpretants. We shall see shortly that this threefold distinction is what underlies the distinction between 'intellectual' signs, of which pragmatism defines the meaning, and non-intellectual signs, with which pragmatism supposedly has nothing to do.

To cover the following threefold distinction, the most general sense of 'interpretant' would have to be, not 'depth' or 'consequence', but 'significate effect' (5.475). There are three kinds of interpretants or significate effects which a sign may produce in the interpreter (cf. 5.475, 4.536). There is, first, the 'emotional interpretant', which consists in a feeling produced by the sign. Every sign, whatever else it produces in the interpreter, produces some sort of feeling. But in particular, "There is almost always a feeling which we come to interpret as evidence that we comprehend the proper effect of the sign. . . ." This feeling is, then, a kind of 'feeling of recognition'. In many cases this feeling or 'emotional interpretant' is the *only* 'significate effect' which the sign produces. "Thus, the performance of a piece of concerted music is a sign. It conveys, and is intended to convey, the composer's musical ideas; but these usually consist merely in a series of feelings." So that the sign known as a musical performance has only an emotional interpretant. A second kind of significate effect may be produced by a sign "through the mediation of the emotional interpretant, and such further effect will always involve an effort". Peirce calls this the 'energetic interpretant'. He instances the command "Ground arms!" as having an energetic interpretant. In this instance the effort excited by the sign is a muscular effort, but it may be and in fact usually is, he says, no more than a mental effort. The third kind of interpretant—which we have hitherto identified with 'interpretant' in general—is the 'logical interpretant'. The logical interpretant of a sign is not a feeling or effort excited by it but *another* sign, a thought, which is a translation in the proper sense of the word. 'Intellectual' signs alone, on the view of Peirce under consideration, have logical interpretants. (The quotations in this paragraph are all from 5.475.) [1]

31. **Peirce's 'Limitation' of Pragmatism; On Purely Demonstrative Signs.** The conception of other than logical interpretants appears in two of Peirce's writings, both of 1906. This is a very late date in his literary career, and one cannot help feeling that the crowded terminology with which the later papers are laden breeds confusion in his thought, making for views very unlike those earlier emphases we have encountered. But it is not necessary to rest with a mere conclusion that Peirce is inconsistent. On the contrary, the proper judgment should be that there are two emphases in Peirce, one fundamental, the other not. With respect to the concept of 'interpretant', it can be shown, I believe, that the great majority of Peirce's uses of this word regard it not as any 'significate effect' of a sign but as another sign interpreting or translating the first. [2] But more conclusive is the fact that upon this sense of interpretant depends Peirce's whole conception of the character of thought or knowledge.

---

[1] The three 'interpretants' are, in the only other place where they are distinguished (4.536), called 'immediate', 'dynamic' and 'final' interpretants, respectively. These terms are taken for granted in correspondence of 1909 with Lady Welby (printed in Ogden and Richards, *The Meaning of Meaning*, Appendix D, sec. 6).

[2] E.g. 1.542, 2.94, 2.228, 2.242, 2.303, 5.569.

While the distinction between three kinds of possible significate effects is a sound one in itself (for the distinction
between feeling, the sense of duality, and cognition, on
which it is based, is essentially sound), the terming of two
kinds of significate effects 'interpretants' is misleading and
infelicitous (just as it would be misleading to call 'feelings',
and instances of the 'sense of duality', 'kinds of cognition').
By 'interpretant' Peirce should have meant 'logical interpretant'; from which it follows that a sign which has *only*
an emotional (or energetic) 'interpretant' ought not to have
been called a 'sign'. ". . . A sign is not a sign unless it
translates itself into another sign in which it is more fully
developed. . . . Thought must live and grow in incessant
new and higher translations, or it proves itself not to be
genuine thought" (5.594).

Let us return to Peirce's opinion that the names 'red'
and 'blue' are not 'intellectual' signs. He says: ". . . The
qualities of hard and soft strikingly contrast with those of
red and blue; because while red and blue name mere subjective feelings only, hard and soft express the factual
behaviour of the thing under the pressure of a knife edge"
(5.467). 'Hard' is thus presumably an 'intellectual' sign,
with a logical interpretant, but 'red' is a sign the 'meaning'
of which is given by a feeling which the name suggests. In
order to explain what 'red' means we do not give an abstract
description but rather excite the feeling-quality which it
denotes. 'Red', therefore, has only an emotional interpretant; pragmatism cannot undertake or pretend to give
the meaning of such a sign. Does Peirce mean that 'red'
is purely demonstrative, that it has a denotation but no
depth? On the internal evidence, derived, as we said, from
Peirce's general theory of signs and of knowledge, there
should be no purely demonstrative signs. What are Peirce's
explicit statements on the matter?

Demonstrative pronouns, which are as likely to be purely
demonstrative as any linguistic sign, are classed by Peirce as
'indices', signs which have some physical relation or other

to their objects. Thus a demonstrative pronoun (or adjective) 'calls attention' to a physical object. An index may be
a non-linguistic (i.e. a 'natural') sign, for instance, a weathervane, a pointing finger, or fever as an index of illness. The
question is whether Peirce regards any sign as a *pure* index,
a sign purely denotative. We could, of course, make a
catalogue of every reference by Peirce to the word 'index',
but that would be futile and devoid of clarity. Let us choose
one or two references which we can be assured are deliberate
and fully conscious. In his definition of 'sign' for Baldwin's
Dictionary, Peirce says: "An index is a sign which would,
at once, lose the character which makes it a sign if its object
were removed, but would not lose that character if there
were no interpretant. Such, for instance, is a piece of mould
with a bullet-hole in it as sign of a shot; for without the
shot there would have been no hole; but there is a hole there,
whether anybody has the sense to attribute it to a shot or
not" (2.304). Is Peirce saying that an index may possibly
have no interpretant and thus be a pure index? Not at all.
He is not saying that an index may *function* as a sign without an interpretant, but that it would retain its *character as
an index*, its factual or physical connection with an object
(cf. 2.285-286, 2.299). (He is thinking here mainly of 'natural'
or non-linguistic indices.) The sign 'horse', which Peirce
calls a 'symbol', or sign in virtue of its establishment by
convention, would not retain its character as a symbol without an interpretant, though it would retain this character
even if its object did not exist. All this is clear from a
passage in another definition for Baldwin's: "Of course,
nothing is a sign unless it is interpreted as a sign; but the
character which causes it to be interpreted as referring to
its object may be one which might belong to it irrespective
of its object and though that object had never existed
[symbol], or it may be in a relation to its object which it
would have just the same whether it were interpreted as a
sign or not [index]" (2.308). And finally, in the definition
of 'index' for Baldwin's, Peirce says: ". . . It would be

difficult if not impossible, to instance an absolutely pure index. . . ." (2.306). As a kind of addendum, we should not overlook the fact that at least in his diagrammatic classification of all signs (cf. 2.264) Peirce regards every sign not actually assertive (i.e. not propositional or argumentative) as being rhematic, that is (as I believe Peirce's views imply), interpretable from the point of view of the position it would occupy in an assertion.

'Red', then, if indexical, is not purely indexical. Why Peirce should have considered 'hard' and 'soft' as expressing the factual behaviour of a thing, and 'red' and 'blue' as not, is a little difficult to understand. For on other occasions it must surely have been evident to him that 'hard' and 'soft' likewise *may* be regarded as denoting qualities of feeling—as in fact they commonly are. 'Red' and 'blue', 'hard' and 'soft', all of them do have feelings as significate effects, as have other signs in varying degrees. But 'red' and 'blue', if they are to be regarded as signs and not as mere causes producing mere effects, are pragmatically definable, in physical definitions, no less than 'hard' and 'soft'. And what of proper names? They certainly are not *ordinarily* defined pragmatically, and in fact even less commonly than 'red' and 'blue'. But they are pragmatically *definable*; and if they were not we should have no instrument by which to discriminate the use of a proper name like 'King Henry V' from the use of a name like 'The Absolute'. Peirce's conception of 'intellectual' signs is thus confused. All signs are definable, and only logical signs are exempt from the pragmatic criterion of meaning. Pragmatism does not pretend to deal with the *feeling* of red, nor with any feeling whatsoever, but it does deal with the *name* 'red', and lays down a rule for defining it as it does for all other names (descriptive signs). So that we may assume only the one limitation to pragmatism that we mentioned above. And we may repeat that Peirce is not radically inconsistent in this matter. He himself can be found to explicitly substantiate the foregoing interpretation: ". . . To say that a body is hard, *or* red, or heavy, or of a given weight, *or has any other property*, is to say that it is subject to law and therefore is a statement *referring to the future*" (5.545; my ital.).

In § 41 we shall return to the problem, and suggest, not that Peirce had in mind for certain signs an interpretation *different* from the pragmatic, but one *besides* the pragmatic.

32. General and Special Analyses of Meaning.

We may distinguish two kinds of usage of the word 'meaning' in Peirce. One is more general than the other. In the general sense 'meaning' is a relation, and none other than the sign-relation, which is triadic. This relation (to repeat what will bear repetition) involves a sign considered materially, its object, and thought (more accurately, some interpreter's mental interpretant, ultimately involved in all representation). We shall find (esp. § 40) that 'meaning' in the general sense, that is, the sign-situation, is an important presupposition of pragmatism. Signs cannot be said to have a meaning in a special sense apart from their relation to some interpreter's conception. In this general sense, then, we understand by 'meaning' the meaning-situation or -relation, or conditions under which a sign has meaning in a special sense to be explained.

Now many analyses of the "meaning of 'meaning'" fail to take into consideration the meaning-relation, and they are therefore inadequate; but they are not illegitimate, for they aim to define 'meaning' in a more special usage. We ordinarily, when we speak of the 'meaning of a sign', do not intend to speak of the meaning-relation even though we may be aware of it as underlying the use of signs. What we intend to speak of when we use the expression 'meaning of a sign' may, for example, be a referend; or it may be a definition, or whatnot. Peirce's pragmatism assumes that we refer to the definition when we speak of a sign's meaning; that is, to the logical interpretant. But, of course, anyone can say that by 'meaning' (in this special sense) we mean 'definition'; the question is, What *kind* of definition; and it is this which pragmatism answers. But before we go into detail we must convince ourselves that Peirce does use 'meaning', in the special sense, as logical interpretant. ('Logical interpretant', as we have indicated, is a wider term than 'definition', covering translations of propositions as well as of terms.) If we examine the actual text of Peirce we find not one but three special senses of 'meaning'.

(1) "A meaning is the associations of a word with images, its dream exciting power" (4.56). This statement, fraught with an emphasis against which Peirce himself inveighed repeatedly, may safely be considered a casual and unimportant one. He knew well that no word has the same image-associations for any two persons, and that such a view was unduly psychological. But in view of the fact that Peirce speaks of the emotional interpretant, the present statement is instructive in showing how in spite of himself he sometimes was tinged with a strain of pyschologism in matters logical.

(2) Two other passages in Peirce require explanation. (a) The first is 2.293, where he speaks of "the object of a symbol, that is to say, its meaning". (b) The second is 1.339, where he does nothing less than distinguish between the 'object' of a sign, its 'interpretant' and its 'meaning'; and calls the 'object' a 'representation'.

The most likely explanation of these passages—and by 'explanation' we mean primarily explication—is to be found in a distinction of Peirce between the 'immediate object' and the 'dynamic object' of a sign (4.536). The dynamic object of a sign is its object in the familiar sense: it is the actual thing or fact to which the sign applies, its referend, or what it denotes. The immediate object, on the other hand, is itself a sign. Peirce is very vague on the concept of 'immediate object' and says little about it.[1] An objection at once arises, namely, If the immediate object is a sign, then would not a sign and its immediate object be mutually translatable, and

[1] See correspondence in Ogden and Richards, *op. cit.*, p. 289; also, 2.293 n.

are not mutually translatable signs 'interpretants' of one
another? Peirce's own explanation of the immediate object
as "the Object as the Sign itself represents it, and whose
Being is thus dependent upon the Representation of it in
the Sign" (4.536), is too obscure to be speculated upon.
There are, however, two explanations which seem plausible.
(i) If we think of signs standing in temporal relation to one
another—in other words, of the series of cognitions—then a
cognition B which precedes a cognition C may be regarded
as the latter's immediate object (both having the same
dynamic object). B may in turn have an immediate object,
A, preceding it, and C would be its interpretant. And so on.
A distinction between interpretant and immediate object
would thus be based on temporal order; and it would be
accurate to say that relatively to different cognitions a given
cognition is both interpretant and immediate object. (Cf.
§§ 2, 5.) (ii) If we consider, not thoughts but linguistic signs
generally, 'immediate object' may still be regarded as a relative conception, understood, however, in terms of greater
specificity of translation rather than of temporal priority.
With respect to a term, the immediate object would be the
denotation expressed in signs. Thus, the immediate object
of 'man' would be 'Jones', 'Brown', etc., or in general, the
class of proper names whose dynamic objects are actual men.
This would be distinct from the interpretant, which would
be, e.g., 'bipedal animal, etc.'. But a proper name, which is
an immediate object relative to 'man', might itself be an
interpretant relative to a more specific spatio-temporal
designation. And so on. (The temporal series of thought-
signs would not seem to require preceding thoughts to be
more specific denotatively, though this is likely to be the case
when the series as a whole is young.)

To return, then, to passages (a) and (b), in (a) Peirce uses
'meaning' as *immediate* object; in (b) he uses 'object' as
immediate object, 'meaning' as the logical interpretant in so
far as it is the conventional (customary) linguistic definition
or translation, and 'interpretant' as the logical interpretant

in so far as it is a cognition or actual mental translation.[1]
Having made the senses of these usages clear, we can see
without much difficulty that 'meaning' is used loosely, in
contexts where it is not the main term and where no great
harm results from its being used synonymously with concepts like 'interpretant' and 'immediate object' that differ
only relatively.

(3) Peirce's real view is that 'meaning' in its special sense
is synonymous with 'logical interpretant'. ". . . 'Meaning' . . . is, in its primary acceptation, the translation of a
sign into another system of signs. . . ." (4.127). ". . . The
meaning of a sign is the sign it has to be translated into"
(4.132). ". . . By the *meaning* of a term, proposition or
argument, we understand the entire general intended interpretant. . . ." (5.179). The meaning of a proposition, for
instance, would be the class of its necessary consequences
(cf. 5.165).

The meaning of a sign is its logical interpretant. But we
only begin the problem. A logical interpretant, being
another sign, has itself a logical interpretant, and so on.
Which of these is the 'meaning' of a given sign? In the case
of a term, the logical interpretant may be nothing more than
an abstract definition, and we may never reach "any real
conception" (5.423) in this process of defining. And likewise
in the case of propositions, to say that the meaning of a
proposition is the set of its consequences is valuable only
"as the beginning of an analysis of what the meaning of the
word 'meaning' is" (5.165). For every proposition, whether
logical or synthetic, has consequences, deduced in accordance
with rules or leading principles. It is only a certain *kind* of
consequences that will distinguish a synthetic from a logical
proposition, and, most important for our purpose, a genuine
or meaningful synthetic proposition from one that is pseudo-

---

[1] Peirce says here (i.e. 1.339) that the series of objects of a sign (like
the series of its interpretants) is infinite. That is—I take it—there is no
limit to specificity in the successive series of signs called 'immediate
objects'.

synthetic or meaningless. Hence while the foregoing analysis of meaning as the logical interpretant has been necessary, "it is by no means sufficient to cut off all non-sense" (5.179). We require a formula for a certain *kind* of logical interpretant, and this is supplied by pragmatism.

33. **The Pragmatic Criterion of Meaning.** I believe it is desirable to separate Peirce's enunciations of pragmatism into two classes. On the one hand, we may extract from him a statement of pragmatism the language of which is modern and invites comparison with current discussion along similar lines. On the other hand, we shall consider (§ 40), though more briefly, a different kind of statement of pragmatism, less clear, motivated by the strong influence on Peirce of classical philosophic tradition as well as by his preoccupation with the mushroom pragmatism that sprang up in the neighbourhood of 1900. In this second class of utterances Peirce's pragmatism speaks, among other things, of an 'ultimate' logical interpretant as being the meaning, and states what this ultimate interpretant is. I do not believe that the notion of an 'ultimate' interpretant is required for a statement of Peirce's pragmatism. In such a statement we need only emphasize that the meaning of a term or proposition is given by a definite kind of logical interpretant, and specify what that is. In this and the next section I want to proceed with such a statement.

Consider any term.[1] The meaning of this term is given by an expression mentioning certain properties. This translating expression or logical interpretant will be equivalent to the original term. But the properties mentioned by it will not be any properties. They will be sensible properties. Pragmatism holds that a term has meaning if, for any statement in which it occurs, another statement about sensible properties is always substitutable. A term has meaning, in other words, if it is definable by other terms describing

---

[1] 'Term' will hereafter be understood to mean 'name'; 'proposition' to mean 'synthetic proposition'.

sensible properties. The way in which, genetically speaking, these other terms, which may not in turn be thus defined, acquire meaning, is by being *associated* or *correlated*, in their usage, according to empirical convention, with such properties. Thus the term 'hard' is a meaningful term because it is equivalent to the expression 'not scratchable by many other substances' (cf. 5.403). But it is somewhat misleading to speak merely of the meaning of terms, as if terms could have a meaning apart from their possible employment in a proposition. Let us continue, in the manner just suggested, to speak of the meaning of terms-occurring-in-statements. Then we may say that the term 'hard' is a meaningful term because the statement (e.g.) 'This is hard' is always interchangeable with the statement (e.g.) 'This will not be scratched by many other substances'. It may be held that by speaking of terms in this manner we can say *whether* a term *has* meaning or not, but not *what* the meaning of a term *is*. Such an objection, if not properly qualified, is likely to suggest a hypostatic conception of meaning that is not Peirce's, despite an impression sometimes given by his words. When we say that pragmatism 'gives the meaning' of terms and propositions, we should be understood as saying that pragmatism states the conditions under which a term or proposition can legitimately be called meaningful, not that pragmatism labels an entity 'the meaning'. If we do speak of 'the meaning' we refer to a logical interpretant of a certain kind (which we have just begun to describe); 'the meaning' of a proposition will be a certain kind of equivalent formula; 'the meaning' of a term will be an equivalent expression. Pragmatism will be the view that terms or propositions are meaningful if they have logical interpretants of a certain character; or in the other way of stating the matter—not objectionable if we remember the caution against hypostasis —the view that 'the meaning' of terms or propositions 'consists in' a certain kind of logical interpretant.

We were saying that the statement containing the translating expression of a term occurring in a given statement was one that asserted something about 'sensible properties'. This is not specific enough, and although we cannot be as clear as we should like until we speak of the meaning of propositions in addition to that of terms, we may nevertheless move another step forward. Suppose we ask, to choose a good example of Peirce, What is meant by 'lithium'? An ordinary definition might say, It is that element which has an atomic weight of nearly 7. But according to pragmatism, the meaning of 'lithium' is given in some such statement as the following:

". . . If you search among minerals that are vitreous, translucent, grey or white, very hard, brittle, and insoluble, for one which imparts a crimson tinge to an unluminous flame, this mineral being triturated with lime or witherite rats-bane, and then fused, can be partly dissolved in muriatic acid; and if this solution be evaporated, and the residue be extracted with sulphuric acid, and duly purified, it can be converted by ordinary methods into a chloride, which being obtained in the solid state, fused, and electrolyzed with half a dozen powerful cells, will yield a globule of a pinkish silvery metal that will float on gasolene; and the material of *that* is a specimen of lithium" (2.330).

This is not an abstract definition, or *mere* interpretant. It is, as Peirce says, a 'precept'. ". . . It tells you what the word lithium denotes by prescribing what you are to *do* in order to gain a perceptual acquaintance with the object of the word" (*ib.*). The pragmatic criterion holds that to predicate any term of some object "is equivalent to declaring that a certain operation, . . . if performed upon that object, would . . . be followed by a result of a definite general description" (5.483). We can now be a little clearer as to what kind of reference to sensible properties is contained in the logical interpretant of 'lithium' or of 'hard': it is a reference to a definite *operation* leading to a definite *sensible result*. A predicate is a meaningful predicate if (and only if) it is definable in terms of a type of sensible result following a type of operation upon that of which it is predicated. And any statement that contains a meaningful predicate is nothing less than a kind of *rule*. For the statement to which it is equivalent asserts that when a definite operation is performed, a definite sensible result follows. This is nothing but a rule or formula or 'precept' for gaining 'perceptual acquaintance'.

Peirce's emphasis on 'precept' and 'operation' is in effect an emphasis that meaning is something *public*. We properly explain the meaning of a term to someone not by eloquently attempting to evoke familiar images in his mind but by prescribing how he can 'gain perceptual acquaintance' with what the word denotes. The appeal is not primarily to imagination but to tests that can be undertaken by everybody. All sorts of images and feelings are associated with any term or proposition thought about, but we must not "mistake a mere sensation accompanying the thought for a part of the thought itself" (5.401). Thought can be expressed only in language; and since language (understood as inclusive of 'natural' signs) is the instrument of social communication, it is successful to the degree that what it conveys is publicly intelligible. And we employ it successfully if we define our terms on the basis of publicly observable operations. The meanings of our words, that is to say, are established by correlating these words with what is repeatable and universally observable. But it must be emphasized that it is not the correlation of a term with the sensible merely as sensible on which Peirce's pragmatism insists. It is with the sensible in so far as it is public, and this is why we speak of the sensible in so far as it is the result of operations. Such a sensible result is 'of a definite general description'; the merely sensible (or 'sensuous'), on the other hand, is private, variable and of a particular quality. James, who preached that terms must have sensible import, neglected (perhaps intentionally) this consideration. His purpose was simply an appeal to the concrete as a wholesome influence in philosophy, and the distinctions implicit in Peirce's pragmatism could never win his interest or seem to him very important. But for Peirce these distinctions were necessitated by his analysis of knowledge, which convinced him that in a criterion of meaning it was not sufficient to turn merely to the concrete but to the concrete in so far as it is public.[1]

From the pragmatic analysis of terms to that of propositions it is evidently no great step, and we have remarked that to deal with the meaning of terms is at least tacitly to deal with that of propositions. In Peirce there is virtually no stress on a distinct treatment of the two; he does not say explicitly that the pragmatic analysis of propositions is subordinate to that of terms in some such respect, for instance, as this: a proposition is a genuine synthetic proposition because all of its (non-logical) terms are conventionally associated with empirical properties. But something of the sort is implied by his analysis. For he wants to say that a proposition has meaning only if its necessary consequences, which constitute its logical equivalent, can be experimentally investigated. A proposition of metaphysics also has a set of necessary consequences, none of which may be thus investigable. That a proposition does have experimental consequences is due to the fact that the descriptive terms occurring in it satisfy the pragmatic criterion.

34. **The Criterion with Respect to Sentences.** Any synthetic proposition is "admissible", according to Peirce, ". . . provided it be capable of experimental verification, and only in so far as it is capable of such verification. This is approximately the doctrine of pragmatism" (5.197). The pragmatic method is, after all, "no other than that experimental method by which all the successful sciences (in which number nobody in his senses would include metaphysics) have reached the degrees of certainty that are severally proper to them today" (5.465). What is it to say that a proposition is 'admissible' or 'inadmissible'? Since pragmatism is a

---

[1] ". . . Man is not whole as long as he is single . . . he is essentially a possible member of society. Especially, one man's experience is nothing, if it stands alone. If he sees what others cannot, we call it hallucination. It is not ' my ' experience, but ' our ' experience that has to be thought of ; and this ' us ' has indefinite possibilities " (5.402 n.).

theory of meaning, an 'inadmissible' proposition is a meaningless proposition. So that by the statement just mentioned, correctly termed   approximate', since we must
explain more fully the sense of 'verify', a meaningless
proposition is one that is unverifiable. Every sentence must
have, not merely consequences, but consequences the truth
or falsity of which can be examined by experimental methods.
The pragmatic criterion of meaning is implicit in the method
of science. Any sentence means, to the scientific investigator, "that if a given prescription for an experiment ever
can be and ever is carried out in act, an experience *of a given
description* will result. . . ." (5.411; my ital.). A proposition, then, is meaningful if it is verifiable. Roughly we
could say that according to pragmatism every synthetic
proposition must be understood in terms of experience.
But 'experience' is a treacherous word, and the pragmatic
criterion might easily be abused to such an extent that any
proposition of traditional metaphysics would be forced into
harmony with it. If pragmatism is to be explained by means
of the word, it must be public experience that we speak of,
consisting of public operations, and public in the sense that
scientific experiment is. With this qualification of the meaning of 'experience', the argument that propositions of transcendental metaphysics are 'experiential', though not in the
sense of the word assumed by natural science, could not
arise.[1]

What is it that Peirce does not intend to imply by his
pragmatic criterion of verifiability for propositions? By
'verifiable', first of all, he does not mean 'conclusively
verifiable'. The pragmatic criterion does not assert that in
order for a proposition to be meaningful it must be possible
to either verify or refute that proposition once for all. If
only those propositions were deemed meaningful which could
be known conclusively to be either true or false, then by the
principle of fallibilism no proposition at all would be meaningful, and certainly not the general hypotheses of natural

[1] See § 39.

science. No experiment by which we gather evidence for (or against) a hypothesis is isolated and completely independent. When we speak of 'an experiment' we mean not literally a single experiment but a *collective* experiment, consisting in fact of a series of operations connected with one another (5.424). Pragmatism holds that a statement is meaningful if it is possible to gather evidence for or against it, not, if we can know definitely and precisely under what conditions it is true and under what conditions it is false. A conclusively verifiable sentence would be an atomic or intuitive sentence, and most of the sentences that we use are more general than perceptual judgments, which alone might be deemed atomic. But pragmatism does not even require all statements to be ultimately resolvable into atomic statements, or as we should say today, to be truth-functions of atomic statements.[1]

The proposition which gives the meaning of another, i.e. the logical interpretant which pragmatism calls the meaning, is *general*. It is a formula, stating that *whenever* certain operations are performed certain results follow, and these are definite operations and definite results. The meaning of 'This stone is hard' is: 'Whenever I attempt to scratch this stone with a sharp edge and a standard pressure, I fail'. The meaning is in terms, not of a specific operation and a specific result—which would be merely in terms of a particular sense experience—but of a kind of operation and a kind of result. The meaning is thus given in a 'conditional' proposition. A statement is meaningful because it is possible to say what the operations and results are in terms of which it is understood. The conditional statement which gives the meaning of any proposition is "the general description of all the experimental phenomena which the assertion of the proposition virtually predicts" (5.427). Peirce intends

---

[1] In 1901 Peirce says, ". . . It can hardly be maintained that, when Poincaré says that there is no physical law whatever which will not be rendered more certain by every new confirmatory experiment, he is depriving those laws of all meaning as propositions " (6.370).

to say that the conditional translation which gives the meaning is a *prescription* for attaining definite experimental results upon definite experimental operations. Clearly there is no limit to the prediction (or prescription) of experimental consequences involved in any synthetic sentence. "To call the stone *hard* is to predict that no matter how often you try the experiment, it will fail every time. That innumerable series of conditional predictions is involved in the meaning of this lowly adjective" (1.615). This limitless reference, involved in any sentence, to the prediction of experimental results, is what Peirce means by his declaration that "the rational meaning of every proposition lies in the future" (5.427). Every synthetic sentence involves, in its very meaning, an infinite series of experimental confirmations. The pragmatic analysis, by its translation of any synthetic sentence, shows such a sentence to be general, and therefore to be incapable of final confirmation. Far, then, from construing every sentence ultimately in terms of intuitive or atomic sentences, pragmatism is actually one form of the argument against intuition or incorrigible verification. It may be regarded as a bulwark of fallibilism.

If we wanted to state pragmatism concisely, we could do it somewhat as follows. Every statement has consequences; but only those statements are genuinely synthetic which have sensible or experimental, i.e. confirmable, consequences. Each consequence of a statement is a logical interpretant of that statement. Any single interpretant, however, or any finite class of interpretants, is only a partial translation, and cannot be said to be the 'meaning' of the statement. As the meaning of a given statement we require another statement that is general, and this statement will be a definite kind of logical interpretant, which we may conveniently call the 'pragmatic interpretant'. It will be, in effect, a *formula for the entire class of confirmable consequences* of a statement; it will illuminate the statement, so to speak, by revealing its logical equivalent. Pragmatism is the doctrine that the meaning of a synthetic sentence is its pragmatic inter-

pretant; or in other words, that no synthetic sentence has
meaning unless it has a pragmatic interpretant.

In the succeeding sections I propose to dwell on the scope
and implications of pragmatism. It is desirable to consider
pragmatism's relation to other essentially empirical views
which on certain points share common ground with it. One
of these is positivism, another is the pragmatism of James.
In the case of positivism I shall not to the least extent enter
into a discussion of the views of those men generally known
as positivists, but consider only Peirce's attitude toward
them and the movement they represent, regardless of
whether or not he understood them perfectly; it is sufficient
for us that this attitude makes clearer his own pragmatism.
In the case of James, whose enunciation of pragmatism has
been better known and more influential than that of Peirce,
it seems profitable to consider the relation of his pragmatism
to Peirce's both in the latter's eyes and in fact. What we say
concerning Peirce and positivism is contained in the next
four sections, and concerning James in § 42.

35. **Pragmatism and Positivism.** Peirce disposes of the
possible suggestion that his pragmatism can be called a
"thorough-going phenomenalism" (5.428). Phenomenalism
lays emphasis on the phenomenal interpretation of signs,
that is, on a sensuous interpretation. Peirce admits that a
"thorough-going phenomenalism" would be a "kind of
pragmatism." But we have seen enough to understand why,
far from being a mere method of sensuously interpreting
signs, pragmatism "on the contrary, eliminates their sential
element, and endeavours to define the rational purport. . . ."
(*ib.*). We must once again recall the distinction between the
material quality of cognition (the sensuous) and cognition;
between that which is inseparable from thought yet insufficient, and thought properly speaking, which has the character of representation; between meaning as the set of
images associated with a sign, and as the formula for the
publicly ascertainable definition or confirmation of a sign.

What Peirce always calls the 'rational purport' or 'rational meaning' is expressed by the pragmatic interpretant in public, communicable, cognitive terms.[1]

Although Peirce finds a pragmatic strain in a number of preceding philosophers, he credits Comte with perhaps a predominant share (cf. 5.11, 2.7, 6.273). In Peirce's words, Comte formulated the maxim that "no hypothesis ought to be admitted, even as a hypothesis, any further than its truth or falsity is *capable* of being directly perceived" (5.198). Comte was correct in condemning hypotheses that were not 'verifiable'; but the important thing, in Peirce's opinion, is to understand the proper import of this word. The positivistic conception of verifiability is perhaps the chief point of distinction between positivism and pragmatism. Comte's works, says Peirce,

" are *warm* (as they say in Hide and Seek) to living truths, although these are invariably most inaccurately analyzed and formulated. For example, nothing can be truer than that a hypothesis is good for nothing unless it is, as Comte says, 'vérifiable', provided this means that the hypothesis is of such a nature that, if true, it will lead to correct anticipations as to the characters of percepts and diminish the number of surprises; but Comte's definition, that a verifiable hypothesis is one whose substance is of such a nature as to be capable of being itself directly perceived, makes his maxim an arbitrary and indefensible limitation of useful knowledge. The past, for example, is of its nature incapable of being directly perceived, and therefore, according to Comte (too literally taken), we ought not to believe at all that there ever was any past, and, as

[1] " Suppose two men, one deaf, the other blind. One hears a man declare he means to kill another, hears the report of the pistol, and hears the victim cry ; the other sees the murder done. Their sensations are affected in the highest degree with their individual peculiarities. The first information that their sensations will give them, their first inferences, will be more nearly alike, but still different ; the one having, for example, the idea of a man shouting, the other of a man with a threatening aspect ; but their final conclusions, the thought the remotest from sense, will be identical and free from the one-sidedness of their idiosyncrasies " (Review of Fraser's ed. of Berkeley, *N. Amer. Review*, Vol. 113, 1871, p. 455).

he proposes to give up the use of the word 'cause' altogether,
so he ought to have given up the preterit definite and indefinite of all verbs." [1]

The important thing, after all, is the proper analysis and
formulation of pragmatism, not merely its adumbration;
and Peirce may be justified in taking Comte's words literally
if by so doing he can reveal the inadequacy of analysis and
lack of rigour of formulation inherent in it. He attributes the
feebleness of Comte's analysis (in a characteristic charge
which he makes against many others) to a pleasant but
unfortunate habit, that of "cherishing contempt for the
close study of logic" (5.11). But Peirce finds a similar
conception of verifiable hypotheses in others to whom he
would not attribute such a vice—for instance, Poincaré,
Mach and Karl Pearson. The positivistic conception of verifiability, on Peirce's view, springs from a failure to grasp
thoroughly the distinction between the cognitive and the
merely perceptual, that is, from a failure to understand the
character of knowledge. [2] A proper understanding of the
character of knowledge penetrates to the fallibility of all
knowledge, to the impossibility of finality in verification.

The sensationalistic atomism of the positivists regards the
'real' as consisting in the 'first impressions of sense'; what
Peirce regards as the genuinely cognitive it labels 'ficti-
tious' or 'subjective'. All the complex intellectual operations are conceptual devices or instruments whose sole
purpose is to subserve the reception of sense-impressions. But
for Peirce these so-called 'first impressions of sense' are not
such at all: there are no purely specific and isolated sense-
impressions; there are only relatively complex percepts, this
complexity being always discoverable on subsequent (i.e.
retrospective) analysis (cf. § 10). And moreover, even these
percepts are a necessary but insufficient constituent of
knowledge. Sometimes (in other language, no longer speak-

---

[1] Review of L. Lévy-Bruhl's *The Philosophy of August Comte*, in *Nation*,
Vol. 78 (1904), p. 336. Cf. 2.511 n.
[2] Cf. 5.597, and review of Pearson, *Pop. Sci. Mo.*, Vol. 58.

ing of either 'impressions' or 'percepts'), the view of Peirce is set over, by positivists, against empiricism, which is said to appeal, as its cardinal tenet, to the authority of 'immediate experience' (cf. § 27). But "as for *immediate* experience, . . . it is known to us as immediate only inferentially."[1] The "method of prediction and experimentation has proved the master-key to science; and yet . . . Professor Pearson tries to persuade us that prediction is no part of science, which must only describe sense-impressions."[2] On the contrary, to say that a hypothesis ought to be verifiable is to say that "it ought to be little more than a ligament of numberless possible predictions concerning future experience, so that if they fail, it fails" (5.597). On Peirce's judgment of the positivists, their analysis fails to understand that it is the predictive character of a hypothesis which makes it a *meaningful* statement in the first place.

36. **Peirce's Realism.** Against the nominalistic view of the positivists, that genuine cognition consists in the reception of sense-impressions and that the intellectual processes are merely convenient devices for the organization and ordering of these sense-impressions, Peirce opposed his realism. He says that a "strenuous insistence upon the truth of scholastic realism, or a close approximation to that . . ." is one important characteristic distinguishing his pragmatism from positivism (5.423). Often he calls himself a follower of Duns Scotus in this matter (e.g. 4.50).[3] Perhaps no theme is so recurrent and so vehemently reiterated as this belief in realism. Whatever Peirce finds susceptible of criticism in another thinker he is sooner or later likely to brand 'nominalistic', often with remote relevancy. In spite of this voluminousness it is amazing that a clear or concise statement of his realism is not to be found in his writings. Very

[1] Review of English trans. of Mach's *The Science of Mechanics* ; *Nation,* Vol. 57 (1893), p. 252.

[2] Review of Pearson, *loc. cit.,* p. 305.

[3] But cf. 1.560, where Scotus is said to "incline too much toward nominalism". (Cf. also *N. Amer. Rev.,* 1871, Vol. 113.)

significant, however, are his remarks that the view which he holds is "well-stated by the late Dr. Francis Ellingwood Abbot in the Introduction to his *Scientific Theism*" (5.423); and that this book "has so clearly and with such admirable simplicity shown that modern science is realistic that it is perhaps injudicious for me to attempt to add anything on the subject" (4.1). He says also that he himself had formerly "acknowledged that the tendency of science has been toward nominalism", but that Abbot had convinced him of the superficiality of the nominalistic aspects he had pointed out, and that science had in fact been and must always be realistic (1.20; cf. 4.50). In view of the long digression that a thorough discussion of Peirce's own pronouncements on realism would involve, I am going to take his statements about Abbot literally and adopt the unorthodox procedure of considering only the latter's formulation of realism for the purpose of attributing it to him.

Abbot calls his realism 'relationism'. It "carefully shuns the great error of scholastic realism, i.e. the hypostatization of universals as substances, entities, or things; it teaches that genera and species exist objectively, but only as relations, and that things and relations constitute two great, distinct orders of objective reality, inseparable in existence, yet distinguishable in thought."[1] He points out, as did Peirce in 1877, that the scientific method presupposes the existence of an objective order; but he emphasizes clearly that the supposition of real or independently existing things entails the view that there exist real relations among these things; that the conception of distinct things as not standing in relation to one another is senseless, or that the logical consequence of such a supposition is solipsism. He holds that the objective reality of relations explains the character of knowledge; for "all knowledge consists in the seizure of the relations of things".[2] And the propositions of science are formulations of these relations.[3] Abbot's account of

---

[1] *Scientific Theism* (1885), p. 28.
[2] *Ibid.*, p. 42. [3] Cf. *Ibid.*, pp. 59-65.

'objective reality' has much in common with Peirce's (§ 23): "The known objectivity of a relation is simply the known objective truth of the proposition which states it. But the relation itself was objectively real before the proposition which states it was conceived; it determined the proposition, not the proposition it." [1] It is a great temptation to quote at length from this book of Abbot, whom Peirce called "one of the strongest thinkers I ever encountered"; [2] and it is a nice question just how much Peirce was influenced by both the writings and conversation of his old friend of the Metaphysical Club.

It is precisely because of the fact that names—and positive knowledge consists of assertions or tacit assertions in which names occur—are on Peirce's view names not of atomic, independent things or properties but of properties-in-*relation*, that knowledge is fallible, for we can never attain a perfectly complete account of all of a thing's relations; and the view that names are names of properties-in-relation is nothing less than a highly condensed way of stating the pragmatic criterion of their meaning. "Generality", says Peirce in a manner reminiscent of Abbot, "is . . . an indispensable ingredient of reality; for mere individual existence or actuality without any regularity whatever is a nullity" (5.431). [3] If we accept the realism just outlined as essentially the view of Peirce, we can appreciate the force of his belief that it is an important feature distinguishing pragmatism from positivism. The sensationalistic atomism which he had in mind presupposes a world of things analyzed (and known) in terms of individual sense-impressions. Mach and Pearson explain the alleged 'relations among things'—the most important of which are the so-called natural laws—as fictions created by science to organize these sense-impressions. And not merely the system of physical science but all mental

---

[1] *Ibid.*, p. 63.

[2] Letter to James, 1904 (in Perry, *op. cit.*, II, p. 431).

[3] In 1871 Peirce says : ". . . General conceptions enter into all judgments, and therefore into true opinions. Consequently a thing in the general is as real as in the concrete" (*N. Am. Rev.*, Vol. 113, p. 457).

processes in any degree abstract, are not a reflection of real relations but a mental device subserving an account of the succession of sense-impressions. It is therefore not the abstract or predicative or judicative element of thought that makes it genuinely cognitive but the element of immediate feeling. This view of the judicative element of thought as fictive in character Peirce attributes to the influence of the "pre-scientific sensationalists", those who, like Hobbes and Locke, held that generalization and abstraction were matters of convenience. "Mach pushes this idea so far as to see no value in science except as an economy. 'The end of science', he says, 'is to *save* experiences by the reproduction and anticipation of facts in thought.' He does not make it quite clear why he should wish to save experiences, unless they are disagreeable, nor how he can save experiences except by slumbering." [1]

Peirce, then, believes in the objective reality of law. Scientific formulae do not create these laws but attempt to represent them, and by so doing to predict what will be confirmed or discredited by experiment. And not only scientific formulae but knowledge in general reflects real relations and is not merely a device superimposed upon the phenomenally given. In Peirce's review of Pearson's *Grammar of Science* there is a little burlesque of positivist nominalism which, since it reveals clearly the tenor of his criticism, is worth quoting in full:

"An ignorant sailor on a desert island lights in some way upon the idea of the parallelogram of forces, and sets to work making experiments to see whether the actions of bodies conform to that formula. He finds that they do so, as nearly as he can observe, in many trials invariably.

[1] Review of Mach, *loc. cit.*, p. 252. Peirce is elsewhere more sympathetic yet not sufficiently liberal in interpretation. He says (5.601), "Mach . . . has done the most to show the importance in logic of the consideration of Economy. . . ." But he holds that "Mach goes altogether too far. For he allows thought no other value than that of economizing experiences. This cannot for an instant be admitted. Sensation, to my thinking, has no value whatever except as a vehicle of thought."

He wonders why inanimate things should thus conform to
a widely general intellectual formula. Just then, a disciple of Professor Pearson lands on the island and the
sailor asks him what he thinks about it. 'It is very
simple', says the disciple, 'you see you made the formula
and then you projected it into the phenomena.' *Sailor:*
What are the phenomena? *Pearsonist:* The motions of
the stones you experimented with. *Sailor:* But I could
not tell until afterward whether the stones had acted
according to the rule or not. *Pearsonist:* That makes no
difference. You made the rule by looking at some stones,
and all stones are alike. *Sailor:* But those I used were
very unlike, and I want to know what made them all move
exactly according to one rule. *Pearsonist:* Well, maybe
your mind is not in time, and so you made all the things
behave the same way at all times. Mind, I don't say it
is so; but it may be. *Sailor:* Is that all you know about
it? Why not say the stones are made to move as they do
by something *like* my mind?

"When the disciple gets home, he consults Dr. Pearson.
'Why', says Dr. Pearson, 'you must not deny that the
facts are really concatenated; only there is no rationality
about that.' 'Dear me', says the disciple, 'then there
really is a concatenation that makes all the component
accelerations of all the bodies scattered through space
conform to the formula that Newton, or Lami, or Varignon
invented?' 'Well, the formula is the device of one of
those men, and it conforms to the facts.' 'To the facts
its inventor knew, and also to those he only predicted?'
'As for prediction, it is unscientific business.' 'Still the prediction and the facts predicted agree.' 'Yes.' 'Then', says
the disciple, 'it appears to me that there really is in nature
something extremely like action in conformity with a highly
general intellectual principle.' 'Perhaps so', I suppose
Dr. Pearson would say, 'but nothing in the least like rationality.' 'Oh', says the disciple, 'I thought rationality was
conformity to a widely general principle.'" [1]

Let us remember that according to the pragmatic criterion
of meaning any judgment of fact is an implicit prediction, a
reference to the future. Now ". . . a prediction is essen-

[1] *Loc cit.*, p. 305.

tially of a general nature, and cannot ever be completely fulfilled. To say that a prediction has a decided tendency to be fulfilled is to say that the future events are in a measure really governed by a law. . . . If the prediction has a tendency to be fulfilled, it must be that future events have a tendency to conform to a general rule" (1.26). In a universe devoid of law knowledge would be impossible; the very meaning of the thought-signs which constitute it is such that they involve prediction.

37. **On Hypotheses.** Peirce declares, in his "Lectures on Pragmatism" of 1903, that pragmatism is "the logic of abduction". It is a rule "as to the admissibility of hypotheses to rank as hypotheses" (5.196). Now we have employed, up to this point, a definite sense of 'hypothesis', according to which the word characterized any synthetic statement whatever, a synthetic statement being a hypothesis in the sense that it is not intuitive, i.e. in the sense that it is theoretically capable of further confirmation. But we must now examine in more thorough fashion Peirce's use of 'hypothesis', because on the matter of 'scientific hypotheses' pragmatism differs from positivism. Let us consider (1) What the positivist view which Peirce sets over against his own is; (2) What Peirce's fundamental views on 'hypothesis' are; (3) What the pragmatist view which Peirce opposes to positivism is.

(1) The view which we find Peirce opposing to his own holds, on account of, or as expressive of, its underlying nominalism, that the propositions of science should properly describe sense-impressions, and hence that no proposition is admissible in science which is not at least capable of being conclusively verified by direct perception. Positivists, of course, differ; we ought not, if we were exact, to speak of Comte and Mach as positivists in the same sense. We have agreed not to enter into such discrimination so long as we succeed in clarifying Peirce's own view. Nevertheless it may not be irrelevant to point out that with respect to Comte in

particular—in Peirce's brief references to positivism he is given comparatively the most attention—Peirce's interpretation (p. 121 above) may not be so questionable as it appears. Chauncey Wright, as early as 1865, did take it for granted, it is true, that the positivists accepted hypotheses that were 'indirectly' verifiable: ". . . the value of these theories can only be tested, say the positivists, by an appeal to sensible experience, by deductions from them of consequences which we can confirm by the undoubted testimony of the senses".[1] If Comte admitted 'indirect' confirmation, at least the consequences of a hypothesis would have to be directly, and conclusively, confirmed. But that he did admit it is doubtful. He accepts the distinction, much older than his positivism, between 'hypotheses' and empirical laws; and it would seem that his radicalism consisted in stressing not merely verification but verification by direct observation. Empirical laws presumably *are* verified by direct perception; hypotheses, to be admissible, must be *capable* of such verification.[2] Regardless of their actual differences,

---

[1] "The Philosophy of Herbert Spencer", *N. Amer. Rev.*, 1865 (Rep. in *Philosophical Discussions*, ed. C. E. Norton, p. 47).

[2] Comte seems to use ' hypothesis ' in two senses.

(1) First, it means an initial conjecture necessarily preceding the formulation of any law. (" Il ne peut exister que deux moyens généraux propres à nous dévoiler, d'une manière directe entièrement rationelle, la loi réelle d'un phénomène quelconque, . . . l'induction ou la déduction. Or l'une et l'autre voie seraient certainement insuffisantes, même à l'égard des plus simples phénomènes, . . . si l'on ne commençait souvent par anticiper sur les résultats en faisant une supposition provisoire, d'abord essentiellement conjecturale, quant à quelques-unes des notions mêmes qui constituent l'objet final de la recherche. De là, l'introduction, strictement indispensable, des hypothèses en philosophie naturelle. Sans cet heureux détour, . . . la découverte effective des lois naturelles serait évidemment impossible. . . ."—*Cours de Philosophie Positive*, 28me leçon, p. 298 in Vol. 2 of 1877 ed.)

(2) Second, ' hypothesis ' means a proposition not an empirical law, in which case he divides hypotheses into two classes, admissible and chimerical, only the former meeting the above-mentioned criterion. From the *System of Positive Polity*, 1851, Vol. 1, pp. 421-2, it would seem that a molecular hypothesis is admissible (atoms being potentially capable of direct observation) ; the supposition of an ether, inadmissible. (". . . l'emploi de ce puissant artifice [i.e. hypothesis] doit être con-

all positivists seem to agree upon Newton as the main source
of the distinction between 'hypothesis' and 'empirical law';
in particular his assertion at the end of the *Principia*, "I
frame no hypotheses." Newton meant by 'hypothesis' a
proposition arrived at in a definite way. The laws proper to
'experimental philosophy' he believed should be framed by
'induction' from 'particular propositions' 'inferred from the
phenomena'. By 'hypothesis' he accordingly meant a proposition not arrived at in this way: ". . . whatever is not
deduced from the phenomena is to be called an hypothesis".
The law of gravitation is "deduced from the phenomena",
but a proposition about the "cause of those properties of
gravity" which Newton declares he had been unable to
deduce from phenomena would be a hypothesis.[1] Newton
thus apparently meant by 'hypothesis' not merely a proposition inferred in a certain way, but also (consequently)
one asserting something about properties not directly
observable.

(2) In Peirce there are to be found two fundamentally
different views of the meaning of 'hypothesis'. When I say
'fundamentally different' I do not mean 'wholly incon-

stamment assujetti à une condition fondamentale. . . . Cette condition,
jusqu'ici vaguement analysée, consiste à ne jamais imaginer que des
hypothèses susceptibles, par leur nature, d'une vérification positive, plus
ou moins éloignée, mais toujours clairement inévitable. . . ."—*Cours*,
pp. 298-299. ". . . Toute hypothèse scientifique, afin d'être réelement
jugeable, doit exclusivement porter sur les lois des phénomènes, et jamais
sur leurs modes de production"—*ibid.*, p. 312.)

[1] The entire relevant passage is: ". . . Hitherto I have not been
able to discover the cause of those properties of gravity from phenomena,
and I frame no hypotheses ; for whatever is not deduced from the phenomena is to be called an hypothesis ; and hypotheses, whether metaphysical
or physical, whether of occult qualities or mechanical, have no place in
experimental philosophy. In this philosophy particular propositions are
inferred from the phenomena, and afterwards rendered general by induction. Thus it was that the impenetrability, the mobility, and the
impulsive force of bodies, and the laws of motion and of gravitation, were
discovered. And to us it is enough that gravity does really exist, and act
according to the laws which we have explained, and abundantly serves
to account for all the motions of the celestial bodies, and of our sea."
(*Principia*, penultimate paragraph.)

sistent', for they are not. What I mean will be clear if we consider the two views as concerning not the meaning of 'hypothesis' alone but the relation between abduction and induction. An examination of Peirce's writings will reveal that the two views, which we may call (a) and (b), are respectively earlier and later, the first prevailing almost up to 1900, the second after 1900. It should be strongly emphasized at the outset that common to both views is the conception of a hypothesis as the conclusion of an inference, namely, abduction. This type of inference is always conceived by Peirce in the same way, as of a form in which the conclusion is obtained by 'affirming the consequent' (cf. 5.189, p. 37 above; 6.472, 2.623, 2.706, 2.712; p. 40 above [1]). The points on which the two views differ are, first, the nature of the conclusion of an abduction, i.e. the nature of 'hypothesis'; second, the relation between abduction and induction, which involves views on the purpose and function of each.

(a) On this view, abduction and induction are two kinds of inference, each of which is independent of the other. By induction we discover (conclude) 'laws', by abduction we discover 'causes' (i.e. conclude 'hypotheses'). Peirce recognized that he was following Newton's usage, if not his views (2.707). In induction "we conclude that facts, similar to observed facts, are true in cases not examined"; in abduction "we conclude the existence of a fact quite different from anything observed" (2.636). Induction is thus "reasoning from particulars to the general law; [abduction], from effect to cause. The former classifies, the latter explains" (ib.). This conception of a hypothesis as a statement 'quite different' from an observed fact from which it is abduced (and which, with other observed facts, it is able to predict) is quite broad, and, to judge from Peirce's examples, comprises three sub-classes of statements.

(i) A hypothesis may, in the first place, be a statement of a fact not observed when the abduction is made but which

[1] See also Century Dictionary, " Hypothesis ", usage no. 4.

is nevertheless capable of subsequent direct observation. For example, if I see some white beans, and I happen to know that if these beans come from a given bag then they must be white, I may conclude that the beans I saw do come from this bag (cf. 2.623). This hypothesis, like any other, would 'explain' the whiteness of the observed beans, would state the 'cause' of the beans being white. It is itself, however, capable of direct observation. (ii) A hypothesis may be not capable of direct observation because it refers to the past (cf. 2.642); as for instance when we abduce the hypothesis that the sea once covered the land, in order to explain piscivorous fossils observed, or when we abduce the hypothesis of the existence of Napoleon, in order to explain the presence of documents (2.625); and these hypotheses may, more properly than those of the first class (as Peirce apparently failed to see), be called statements of 'causes'. (iii) Finally, a hypothesis may be a 'scientific' hypothesis, a 'theory' (excluding historical theories, which belong to the second class), in which case it would be a statement about what has never been observed, e.g. atoms, luminiferous ether, etc. (cf. 5.589). Statements of this third class would be most properly called statements of 'causes'. On the present view, they 'explain' empirical laws or formulae, which are the result of induction or generalization from facts directly observable.

These three classes of hypotheses, then, are all statements of facts 'quite different' from the observed facts from which they are abduced.[1] They all infer "from facts of one kind to facts of another", while induction "infers from one set of facts another set of similar facts" (2.642). The conclusions of inductions, as opposed to these conclusions of abduction, are 'generalizations'. In induction "we find a certain thing to be true of a certain proportion of cases and infer that it is true of the same proportion of the whole class"; in abduction we observe some fact or circumstance "which would be

---

[1] The perceptual judgment as hypothesis would be the most extreme case of the first of these classes.

explained by the supposition that it was a case of a certain general rule, and thereupon adopt that supposition" (2.624).[1] The present view will be most clearly seen to differ from (*b*) if we consider the following passage, which appears in "A Theory of Probable Inference" of 1883 and is used almost verbatim by Peirce as part of his definition of "Hypothesis" for the Century Dictionary in 1889:

". . . The conclusions of Hypothetic Inference *cannot be arrived at inductively*, because their truth is not susceptible of direct observation in single cases. *Nor can* the conclusions of Inductions, on account of their generality, *be*

---

[1] Cf. p. 37 above : " The surprising fact, C, is observed ; but if A were true, C would be a matter of course ; hence, there is reason to suspect that A is true " (5.189). The second of these (" if A were true, C would be a matter of course ") is the ' general rule ', the third is the hypothesis. The observed fact is explained in the sense that it follows deductively (is ' predicted '), together with other facts, from the hypothesis taken together with the general rule. Now in 2.636 Peirce says : " By hypothesis [abduction], we conclude the existence of a fact quite different from anything observed, from which, according to *known laws*, something observed would necessarily result " (my ital.). In the Century Dictionary (" Hypothesis ") similarly a hypothesis is a " proposition held to be probably true because its consequences, according to *known general principles*, are found to be true " (my ital.).

The specification that the general rule must be a known rule is objectionable. If we wish to explain fish fossils on land, we do have to know the general rule that when the sea washes over land such fossils are likely to remain, in order to adopt the hypothesis that the sea did wash over the land. But if we want to explain the observed behaviour of gases by the kinetic theory, it is not the case that we adopt this theory because of a known law that a molecular constitution of a gas results in such behaviour ; for if this were already a known law the kinetic theory would have been suggested ipso facto. Thus in general, as I felt free to interpret Peirce on p. 37 above, the perception that " if A were true, C would follow in fact " is actually *part* of the hypothesis or supposition A. The hypothesis is adopted because the ' general rule ' suggests a connection that will be confirmed. Let C_1 be a particular observed fact. Then from the premiss that the hypothesis is true, and the premiss that an observable fact of the kind C is connected with some circumstance asserted by the hypothesis (this is the general rule), the particular fact C_1 is rigidly predicted. The second premiss thus already asserts something about the hypothesis. Peirce justifies this interpretation when he says (5.189) that the hypothesis A cannot be " abductively inferred . . . until its entire content is already present in the premiss ' If A were true, C would be a matter of course '."

reached by hypothetic inference. For instance, any historical fact, as that Napoleon Bonaparte once lived, is a hypothesis; we believe the fact, because its effects—I mean current tradition, the histories, the monuments, etc.—are observed. But no mere generalization of observed facts could ever teach us that Napoleon lived. So we inductively infer that every particle of matter gravitates toward every other. Hypothesis might lead to this result for any given pair of particles, but it never could show that the law was universal" (2.714, my ital.; cf. Cent. Dict.).

(*b*) On Peirce's later view, which we take to be definitive and have already assumed throughout Part I, abduction and induction are different types of inference, but they are not independent, and the conclusion of any induction is identical with that of some abduction, that is, it is some hypothesis. *Any* synthetic proposition, in so far as it is for the first time entertained as possibly true, must be the result of an abduction. Whether the proposition be a statement about non-observable entities or a generalization (so-called) or a perceptual judgment, it is a hypothesis arrived at by abduction. Peirce calls abduction the "First Stage of Inquiry" (6.469). On this view, however, not only is every synthetic proposition a hypothesis in so far as it is first suggested to the mind as true, but every proposition remains a 'hypothesis' in so far as it is synthetic; and in a moment we shall repeat somewhat more precisely the reason which we gave in Part I. What is induction? "Induction is the experimental testing of a theory. . . . It sets out with a theory and it measures the degree of concordance of that theory with fact" (5.145); "Induction consists in starting from a theory, deducing from it predictions of phenomena, and observing those phenomena in order to see *how nearly* they agree with the theory" (5.170); Induction "consists in testing a hypothesis *already recommended* by the retroductive procedure. . . ." (2.755; my ital.); "Induction takes place when the reasoner already holds a theory. . . ." (2.775). But perhaps the clearest statement is: "Induction is an Argument which sets out from a hypothesis, resulting from a previous Abduction, and from virtual predictions, drawn by Deduction, of the results of possible experiments, and having performed the experiments, concludes that the hypothesis is true in the measure in which those predictions are verified. . . ." (2.96 ; cf. 6.472, 5.590-591). The conclusion of an induction consists in "extending a certain confidence to the hypothesis" (6.526; cf. 6.527, 2.777). The conclusion of an induction, then, is always some hypothesis previously abduced. An induction concludes a hypothesis by 'generalization' from the confirmed consequences of that hypothesis; and the more numerous, diverse and random these confirmed consequences are, the stronger the induction and consequently the sounder the confirmation of the hypothesis. And the reason why every synthetic proposition remains a hypothesis is that it is always further confirmable by induction. I want to quote further in support of the point that any statement, of whatever generality, may be concluded by an abduction.

> "All our knowledge may be said to rest upon *observed facts* (6.522; P.'s ital.). . . . Knowledge must involve additions to the facts observed (6.523). . . . *Any* proposition added to observed facts, tending to make them applicable *in any way* to other circumstances than those under which they were observed, may be called a hypothesis (6.524; my ital.). . . . By a hypothesis, I mean, not merely a supposition about an observed object, as when I suppose that a man is a Catholic priest because that would explain his dress [etc.], but also *any other* supposed truth from which would result such facts as have been observed, as when van't Hoff, having remarked that the osmotic pressure of one per cent solutions of a number of chemical substances was inversely proportional to their atomic weights, thought that perhaps the same relation would be found to exist between the same properties of any other chemical substance" (6.525; my ital.).

On view (*a*) this last example of an abduction would have been called a 'generalization' which could only be the result of induction, abduction being unable to conclude anything of such generality (cf. 2.714, quoted above). On the present view any such generalization is *suggested* by abduction, and only *confirmed* by induction. Clearly, contrary to (*a*), a generalization, no less than any other proposition conjectured (abduced), goes beyond actually observed facts; we have seen, in § 14, that even perceptual judgments in a sense do. On the present view abduction alone can introduce anything new in knowledge (e.g. 5.171, 5.145, 2.777); induction "never can originate any idea whatever" (5.145), for it simply confirms what has already been tentatively contributed to knowledge.[1]

In contrasting views (*a*) and (*b*), I do not wish to suggest that Peirce held one view until 1900 and suddenly abandoned it after that date; for the roots of the later view go further back, and it is only the case that they become explicit after 1900. In 1893 the view that induction properly occurs only after a previous abduction was virtually expressed when Peirce said, reflecting the "views of Whewell", that "progress in science depends upon the observation of the right facts by minds *furnished with appropriate ideas*" (6.604).

(3) We are now better able to understand the difference between the views of Peirce and the positivists who, meaning primarily by 'hypothesis' something opposed to an empirical formula, make it secondary or instrumental to the latter, and even then impose a radical condition on its admissibility. Peirce's opposition of hypotheses and empirical formulae on his earlier view was not this kind of opposition. It was concerned primarily with different types of inference; and whereas for the positivists 'hypotheses' were statements about assumed entities (subdivided into admissibly and fictitiously assumed entities), for Peirce a statement about assumed entities was only one kind of hypothesis.

---

[1] Peirce sometimes takes the view that inductive confirmation also is an "ampliation of our positive knowledge" (2.96). This, of course, is not incompatible with the sense in which abduction alone increases knowledge. Ordinarily, both abduction and induction are called by him 'ampliative' inferences; and this term may be retained in the sense that both are distinguished from explicative or analytic inference (cf. 2.623).

A fortiori, his later view is even further from that of the positivists, understanding by a 'hypothesis' any synthetic statement whatsoever. He specifically rejects the way in which 'hypothesis' is "ordinarily used" (under positivist influence), as that which "carries with it a suggestion of uncertainty, and of something to be superseded"; this sense "does not belong at all to my use of it" (2.707). Hypotheses are indeed 'provisional' or 'probational' (e.g. 1.68, 2.96), but in the sense that they are not perfectly certain, not in the positivist sense of something resorted to for lack of anything better, and instrumental in any event to what is purely descriptive (see 5.276 n. usage 8; Cent. Dict. usage 5; 2.642).

The reason why Peirce can safely ignore various considerations concerning the kinds of hypotheses and remain free from error or superficiality is that the ultimate test of any statement's admissibility is for him the pragmatic criterion. The class of hypotheses is identical with that of synthetic statements, and a hypothesis is admissible if it is meaningful. His full support of hypotheses which posit unobserved properties or entities [1] is based on his examination of the actual procedure of science and his long experience as professional physicist. In his review of the first volume of James's *Principles of Psychology* he takes issue with the dictum in James's Preface that "all attempts to *explain* [the] phenomenally given . . . as products of deeper-lying entities . . . are metaphysical". James had also said that "in this strictly positivistic point of view consists the only feature of [the book] for which I feel tempted to claim originality". Pointing out that the application of the epithet 'metaphysical' is too easy a way of eliminating from science a procedure for which one happens to have a distaste, and that the above

[1] Peirce makes no distinction between unobserved and unobservable, or between a hypothesis in science " adopted as a probable representation of a state of things which may really exist though imperceptible to the senses " [an ' objective ' hypothesis] and one adopted " merely as a convenient means of expressing the laws of phenomena " [a ' subjective ' hypothesis] (Rankine, *Miscellaneous Scientific Papers*, p. 210).

dictum cannot by itself suffice for such an elimination, Peirce says: "Nor is it in the least true that physicists confine themselves to such a 'strictly positivistic point of view'. Students of heat are not deterred by the impossibility of directly observing molecules from considering and accepting the kinetical theory; students of light do not brand speculations on the luminiferous ether as metaphysical. . . . All these are 'attempts to explain phenomenally given elements as products of deeper-lying entities'. In fact, this phrase describes, as well as loose language can, the general character of scientific hypotheses." [1] The important consideration is that hypotheses of this kind do have observable consequences and may be confirmed by the confirmation of a great many of these. *Any* statement is meaningful if it is capable of confirmation, and any statement is acceptable as established in science if it is actually confirmed. In a review of a translation of Spinoza's *Ethics*, Peirce calls attention to the fact that the procedure of Galileo, who appealed to both common sense and *il lume naturale* (cf. 1.80, 6.10), and Spinoza, are of precisely the same kind. "But what he [Spinoza] and all his school fail to remark is that the conclusions of the students of mechanics are sure to be brought to the test of experiment in various ways. . . . It is just that quiet verification that makes all the difference in the world. A hypothesis *of any kind* has no positive support until it has predicted something capable of being observed and that prediction has been verified" (my ital.).[2] Probably the protest that Peirce would on other occasions have made against the exclusion of hypotheses positing assumed entities is that it blocks the way of inquiry. To make strictures on such hypotheses is to discourage conjectural explanations whose immediate justification is not evident. Not only does it contradict the historical achievements of classical science, but it violates the freedom which lies at the basis of scientific method. All hypotheses are essentially the same in that

[1] *Nation*, Vol. 53 (1891), p. 15.
[2] *Ibid.*, Vol. 59 (1894), p. 345.

all are adopted to explain, or in general 'add to' (6.523-524), what is observed; and even the hypotheses concerning assumed entities are in principle no different from hypotheses about the past (cf. 5.597, 2.511 n.; p. 132 above). Especially can this be seen in historical philology, in, for example, the translation of the cuneiform inscriptions (5.589), where conjectures were multiplied one on another, until mutual confirmation of the readings, together with confirmation from accepted history and the facts of linguistics, established the theory.

Perhaps the statement we originally considered, that pragmatism is the 'logic of abduction', will now be clearer. For after all, abduction must on the whole "cover all the operations by which theories and conceptions are engendered" (5.590).

38. **The Element of Conventionalism in Peirce.** Peirce's satire of Mach's view that science is a device of "saving experiences by the reproduction and anticipation of facts in thought" is unduly attentive to the letter and hardly to the spirit, which differs not very greatly from that of Peirce himself. For he regards the purpose of a scientific hypothesis as being "to lead to the avoidance of all surprise and to the establishment of a habit of positive expectation that shall not be disappointed" (5.197). But granted the differences we have mentioned, we may ask whether it follows from Peirce's realistic interpretation of hypotheses that he excludes altogether the element of convention stressed by the positivists. Although his writings on this subject are scanty, it is possible to distinguish three forms in which conventionalism enters his views; first, with respect to the choice of hypotheses in science; second, with respect to the language of science; third, with respect to the results of science, i.e. with respect to the concepts of truth and reality. These divisions are closely related, and might in fact be regarded as the same set of opinions looked at from three different points of view. But if so, then at least it will be plain that the conventionalism regarded from the third point

of view is much more prominent than that regarded from the first.

(1) According to Peirce there is an "arbitrary element" in scientific theories; but as these theories progress, they "become more and more purified from the dross of subjectivity" (5.589). Just what this statement implies is not clear, for he does not expatiate. Very likely he has no more in mind than that the arbitrary element arises from the possibility of employing different hypotheses to explain the same set of facts, or fundamentally different interpretations —e.g. mechanical or non-mechanical—for a given branch of science, or more pervasive formulae in place of narrower ones. Peirce undoubtedly realized that, especially in the case of hypotheses concerning assumed entities, the replacement of one by another is not to be regarded simply as an advance toward 'objective truth' (5.589) but also as a change in formulation or expression for some reason of expedience. He would, however, hold that such a change ultimately constitutes a link in the progress toward 'objective truth' (as he defines it—cf. (3) below); that one of the two differently formulated hypotheses could ultimately be shown to be the 'truer'. Now the only point, discussed in a number of places by Peirce, that possibly bears on the matter of conventional choice among hypotheses, is the question of 'simplicity'. Peirce accepts Ockham's razor, which he states: ". . . Before you try a complicated hypothesis, you should make quite sure that no simplification of it will explain the facts equally well" (5.60); or as follows: "Try the theory of fewest elements first; and only complicate it as such complication proves indispensable for the ascertainment of truth" (4.35).[1] Peirce regards this principle as basic to scientific procedure and not nominalistic (4.1). His acceptance of it raises two questions: (a) What does he mean by one hypothesis being

---

[1] Other statements : " A hypothesis should be stripped of every feature which is in no wise called for to furnish an explanation of observed facts " (5.26) ; " A hypothesis ought not to introduce complications not requisite to explain the facts " (4.1). (Cf. 6.24, 6.535.)

'simpler' than another? (*b*) In what sense is the simple hypothesis preferable to the complicated one, i.e. what are the implications of the principle?

(*a*) One of the statements of the principle implies that the 'simpler' hypothesis is the one containing the 'fewest elements', or better, fewest concepts. But what kind of concepts? We must make some distinction here. For Peirce says that by the 'simpler' hypothesis he does not mean the 'logically simpler', which he defines as "the one that adds the least to what has been observed", but rather "the one that instinct suggests" (6.477). By saying, then, that the simpler hypothesis is the one containing the 'fewest elements' he does not mean the one asserting something about the fewest unobservable entities. A simple hypothesis is rather one "composed of a few conceptions natural to our minds" (6.10). So that in the first place, simple hypotheses contain numerically fewer concepts; and secondly, of two hypotheses with the same number of concepts, the simpler is not that with the least number of unobserved or unobservable 'elements' but that with the greatest number of instinctive' or 'natural' or 'familiar' (2.740) elements. The criterion of fewer unobservable entities is the positivist and nominalist criterion, going back to Ockham himself. Peirce's own sense of 'simple' he takes to be that of Galileo.

"That truly inspired prophet had said that, of two hypotheses, the *simpler* is to be preferred; but I was formerly one of those who, in our dull self-conceit fancying ourselves more sly than he, twisted the maxim to mean the *logically* simpler, the one that adds the least to what has been observed, in spite of three obvious objections: first, that so there was no support for any hypothesis; secondly, that by the same token we ought to content ourselves with simply formulating the special observations actually made; and thirdly, that every advance of science . . . discloses a world of unexpected complications. It was not until long experience forced me to realize that subsequent discoveries were every time showing I had been wrong, while those who understood the maxim as Galileo had done, early

unlocked the secret, that the scales fell from my eyes and
my mind awoke to the broad and flaming daylight that it
is the simpler Hypothesis in the sense of the more facile
and natural, the one that instinct suggests, that must be
preferred; for the reason that, unless man have a natural
bent in accordance with nature's, he has no chance of
understanding nature at all" (6.477).[1]

(b) Peirce's acceptance of the principle that the simpler
hypothesis is the preferable one does not imply his acceptance
of the view that a simple hypothesis is in every case the best.
He holds that in general there is no guarantee of the simpler
being the 'truer' hypothesis and that the evidence is often
to the contrary.   Nevertheless he believes that the more
familiar hypothesis should be 'tried first' (cf. 4.1, 5.598,
6.532). The reason appears to be twofold: First, hypotheses
that are simpler in this sense are more readily eliminable, and
the necessity of quick elimination is vital in scientific economy, since science is confronted with a tremendous number
of possible choices.[2] Secondly, it is Peirce's view that science

---

[1] There are some striking similarities in the views of Mach and Peirce
on the question of ' instinctive knowledge ' and its relation to science.
Mach points out that " an *instinctive*, irreflective knowledge of the processes of nature will doubtless always precede the scientific, conscious
apprehension, or *investigation*, of phenomena " (*Science of Mechanics*, p. 1).
It is in the history of mechanics that Mach, like Peirce, finds best witness
to the weight of instinct. Distinguishing between mechanical experience
and mechanical science, he says that prehistoric remnants reveal abundant
mechanical knowledge in the former sense. As Peirce's favourite historical
example is Galileo, his is Stevinus, whose investigation of the mechanics
of the inclined plane he believes to be a model illustration of scientific
growth from an instinctive starting-point. He emphasizes that instinctive
knowledge is essentially of a *guiding* character, that it is to a large extent
fallible, and that the combination of " the strongest instinct with the
greatest power of abstract formulation alone constitutes the great natural
inquirer " (*ibid.*, p. 27). Instinctive knowledge is a product acquired in
the development of the race. Far from being a priori or natural to individual minds prior to all experience, it consists of the " most familiar
experiences, the most thoroughly tested rules " (*ibid.*, p. 80). (See *ibid.*,
pp. 1-7, 24-31, 80-85.) These views were held independently by Peirce
and Mach. The *Mechanics* was first published in 1883, and the views
already appear in an 1878 paper of Peirce (see 6.418).

[2] Cf. also : ". . . Good scientific economy will usually prescribe that
simple hypotheses shall be thoroughly tested before resorting to com-

could not hitherto have been so successful unless there were a kind of affinity between man as a biological animal and the world he attempts to explain (cf. 5.604). For the overwhelming number of possible hypotheses could not have been manipulated if appropriate conjectures could not have been made on the basis of instinctive knowledge.[1] While it may not, on Peirce's view, be the case that the simpler or instinctive hypothesis is the correct one, it is the best to start out with for the reason that if our ultimate result is a complicated hypothesis, it is probably a complication *of* the simple one originally tried. So that 'instinctive beliefs', even if they do not furnish the central idea, at least furnish the main direction.[2] (Cf. p. 60 above.[3])

Peirce's belief that Ockham's razor, in the foregoing sense, is not nominalistic, thus appears to indicate that he regarded the difference between simple and complicated hypotheses not in terms of the more and the less convenient but in terms of greater and lesser approximation to 'objective truth'. He apparently did not consider very seriously the view that in any given case a 'complicated' hypothesis may be regarded as no less true than a 'simple' one, or vice versa. The ultimate consideration for him was in terms of truth: Try the 'simple' hypothesis first, both as good economy and as an

plicated ones. This is the truth in Ockham's razor. But it is very far from being true, in questions concerning any science of life—psychology, physiology, and the like—that the true hypothesis is likely to be simple. On the contrary, the history of discovery in those departments shows many more examples of the old theory being found to be too simple than of its being found to be too complex " (*Nation*, Vol. 73, 1901, p. 267).

[1] ". . . Our minds having been formed under the influence of phenomena governed by the laws of mechanics, certain conceptions entering into those laws become implanted in our minds, so that we readily guess at what the laws are. Without such a natural prompting, having to search blindfold for a law which would suit the phenomena, our chance of finding it would be as one to infinity " (6.10).

[2] Cf. 1.634 : ". . . We are driven oftentimes in science to try the suggestions of instinct ; but we only *try* them, we compare them with experience, we hold ourselves ready to throw them overboard at a moment's notice from experience." (Cf. also 1.404.)

[3] See an interesting essay by Peirce, " Guessing ", printed in *The Hound and Horn*, Vol. 2 (1929), pp. 267-282.

approximation toward the truth, but ultimately choose the 'truer' one in any event (cf. 4.1, 4.35, 5.26).

(2) Peirce recognized, as a result of the pragmatic criterion, that certain problems of traditional philosophy were verbal problems, soluble by more precise formulation. If the opposing answers to a problem do not differ in the observational properties consequent upon the truth of each, they are either both meaningless or both assert the same thing. However, not only in traditional metaphysics but in physics do pseudo-problems arise. For instance, it is a pseudo-problem to ask whether force *is* an acceleration or whether it *causes* acceleration (5.404). The adoption of one or the other 'view' is a convention of language, not a matter to be decided empirically. For the application of the pragmatic criterion shows the meaning of the two expressions to be identical. Similarly in the case of such questions as whether a diamond could be said to be 'hard' if it were not pressed, or whether a stone could be called 'brilliant' if it lay in darkness at the bottom of the sea. These "concern much more the arrangement of our language than they do the meaning of our ideas" (5.409). Peirce means that the proper question is not whether the diamond *is* hard when we are unable to press it (for this, by its very formulation, and by the pragmatic definition of the predicate, precludes our giving an answer, and is therefore, strictly speaking, meaningless), but whether we wish to *call* the diamond hard under such conditions. We may or may not do so, with impunity.[1]

(3) Concerning the results of science, the 'established truths', Peirce's conventionalism is much more outstanding.

---

[1] Peirce later (5.453, 457) calls attention to the fact that he expressed himself badly in the diamond illustration of 1878. He had implied by his words that the diamond could be called, indifferently, hard or not hard, when not *actually* pressed. This, he points out, was contrary to his basic realism, which must hold that the diamond is *really* hard even when not actually pressed. What he meant was that the diamond might indifferently be called hard or not hard if it *could* not be pressed. For " we must dismiss the idea that the occult state of things . . . which constitutes the reality of a diamond's hardness can possibly consist in anything but in the truth of a general conditional proposition " (5.457).

What is to be regarded as an established truth in science depends upon the degree of confirmation determined by the scientific community. Since no scientific result is ever conclusive, the concept of confirmation is a relative one, and is determined conventionally—yet not arbitrarily. We said in § 23 that for Peirce a statement is true if it is accepted by the community which practises the scientific method for the purpose of attaining its beliefs; and we said also that the real is that which is represented in true statements. If a true statement is one confirmed to a certain degree, and if what constitutes confirmation is determined ultimately by agreement, then, strictly, 'truth' is determined ultimately by agreement. This is not in the least strange or awkward. For this agreement is not arbitrary agreement. It is determined by profound considerations, truth being belief *compelled* by scientific inquiry. In § 23 we did not, however, stress at any length what was implied by the statement, "The opinion which is fated to be ultimately agreed to by all who investigate, is what we mean by the truth, and the object represented in this opinion is the real" (5.407). Is there a difference here between two views, one seeming to make truth consist in the opinion which science at a certain stage arrives at, the other (as reflected by the statement just quoted) to make truth consist in an ideal opinion which science indefinitely approaches? and in the case of reality, the one view making it consist in what is described by statements accepted as true, the other making it consist in what would be described by the ideal opinion?

Two points must be made in answer. (i) The statement of 5.407 just quoted does not, in itself, intend a distinction between 'perfect' and 'approximate' truth, and to assert that the latter approaches the former. It asserts merely: All who adopt the scientific method are sure to agree on an opinion which, since science is the best method of establishing opinion, is to be called the truth. The emphasis here is on the compulsive power of science, on the fact that scientific investigation (which for Peirce is synonymous merely with 'investigation') promotes unanimity. (ii) Nevertheless Peirce *does* intend to distinguish between approximate and perfect truth, and elsewhere, for instance, he defines truth as "that to a belief in which belief would tend if it were to tend indefinitely toward absolute fixity" (5.416).[1] The distinction is not a hard and fast one, but rather a distinction of two complementary elements in the general conception of truth. The notion of truth depends both upon the actual practice of science and on a goal which it seeks to attain. The notion of a perfectly true opinion has no meaning apart from the notion of opinions which correct themselves; and conversely, we cannot speak of opinions as approximately true unless we conceive of some limit to which they approximate. In spite of this interdependence, it is well to point out that it is the approximately true which represents what is ordinarily understood by 'true', and justifiably so. The 'true' is the 'confirmed'. The perfectly true would be that which theoretically required no alteration, or that which, no matter how far investigation were carried, would be uninfluenced in its status. It is no more than a limit or standard for increase of perfection; if it alone is regarded as synonymous with 'true', and existing opinion branded as therefore representative only of 'appearance' and not 'reality', inquiry is stifled in favour of an anti-pragmatic metaphysics. Peirce teaches that truth in general is relative to investigation; that the purpose of investigation is to destroy doubt and establish belief; and that science, being the best method of achieving this purpose, is the instrument of truth.

The sense in which truth is conventional is analogous to the sense in which 'reality' is conventional. ". . . Reality is only the object of the final opinion to which sufficient investigation would lead" (2.693). Peirce speaks of his "social theory of reality" (6.610), according to which the concept of reality "involves the notion of a community" (5.311). ". . . The real is the idea in which the community ulti-

[1] Cf. also : " I suppose that by the True is meant that at which inquiry aims " (5.557).

mately settles down" (6.610); "reality consists in the agreement that the whole community would eventually come to" (5.331). Corresponding to the two aspects of truth, is the distinction between the real as the object known in the final opinion and the real as that known in statements ordinarily called 'true'. And although the former appears to be emphasized in the statements just quoted, the latter is in fact what is emphasized by the spirit of Peirce's thought. We do know 'reality' (cf. 5.384), though of course not with perfect precision and completeness. Reality in the perfect and complete sense is "something which is constituted by an event indefinitely future" (5.331).

Now it is a statement recurrent time and again in Peirce that "that is *real* which has such and such characters, whether anybody thinks it to have those characters or not" (5.430); and in fact, "we may define the real as that whose characters are independent of what anybody may think them to be" (5.405). How does this—which Peirce calls the "abstract definition" [1] of reality—square with the other statements we emphasized, according to which the real is that which is represented in an opinion? Are these two views contradictory? Clearly not, once we elucidate the sense of the latter definition, which is in fact the pragmatic definition. It does not imply that reality is created by thought, that it comes into being because we happen to have opinions. It states that what reality is (i.e. what its character is), is given in a true opinion. But it goes further. It implies that if by reality as something independent of thought is meant something which cannot be known by thought, then the word is meaningless. For let us apply the pragmatic criterion. We then find that 'real' can mean nothing unless definable in terms of sensible operations; and no statement which is said to be about reality or some phase of it is a meaningful statement unless it is capable of confirmation. Reality, then, is that which can only be represented in confirmable statements. It would be senseless to

[1] I.e. its ' verbal ' or nominal definition (cf. 5.525).

say that a statement which could not possibly be verified 'describes' reality. But the opinions which we adopt as our truths or true beliefs are simply those which have been to a reasonable degree confirmed; and this is why the real can only be that which is represented in such opinions, though doubtless 'reality' in the perfect and complete sense would be that which is represented by the perfectly true opinion. If reality were held to be other than what is described by true opinions, that would be the same as saying that it was unknowable; and we cannot, by the pragmatic criterion, speak meaningfully of what is unknowable (cf. 5.310). Thus to speak of the 'nature of reality' is to speak of that about which we ultimately agree, of that described in our true opinions; and of anything else we cannot significantly speak. This is what is meant by a statement like the following: ". . . The reality of that which is real does depend on the real fact that investigation is destined to lead, at last, if continued long enough, to a belief in it" (5.408).

Truth, we said, is for Peirce the opinion on which the community agrees, not arbitrarily but as "the irresistible effect of inquiry" (5.494); it is the opinion which is "ultimately agreed to by all who investigate". But we must guard against misunderstanding. Peirce does not mean that on any given question the community will *in fact* always arrive at the truth (i.e. be compelled to agreement by inquiry) (6.610, 5.565). Certain questions have been settled, at least for the time being, and science therefore possesses a body of 'established truths'; but there is no guarantee that a given question will actually be settled. Peirce's point is that it is unwarranted "to suppose that, with regard to any given question (which has any clear meaning), investigation would not bring forth a solution of it, if it were carried far enough" (5.409). In other words, if a question is a meaningful question it is an answerable question, it is decidable: the truth or falsity of the answers to it must be capable of positive investigation. But to say that a question is answerable and that it will in fact be answered are clearly different. (With respect to certain questions there is *no* truth at all; i.e. the question may be meaningless.) Any assertion that a given question's truth will in fact be eventually decided, can be no more than a 'hope', based, perhaps with good reason, on the history of science (cf. 6.610, 5.407, 5.565, 2.654).

39. **" Purified Philosophy "**.   Peirce emphasizes (5.423) that his pragmatism condemns the bulk of traditional meta-physics as meaningless,[1] and in this respect he calls it a "species of prope-positivism" (*ib.*), meaning by the prefix "a broad and rather indefinite extension" (5.413) of that doctrine. But he holds that his pragmatism is distinguished even from prope-positivism, not merely by its realism but by its "retention of a purified philosophy" (5.423). When pragmatism disposes of traditional pseudo-problems, "what will remain of philosophy will be a series of problems capable of investigation by the observational methods of the true sciences" (*ib.*).   Philosophy Peirce understands to be a science of fact, a positive science (e.g. 5.120), and moreover, "the highest of the positive sciences" (5.423). But he speaks primarily (in 423) of metaphysics, and says that instead of discarding it, pragmatism "extracts from it a precious essence ".   I cannot enter into the whole of Peirce's archi-tectonic, which is a lengthy subject.[2] I wish only to consider

[1] Cf. 5.539, 5.410, 5.510, and letter to C. Ladd-Franklin in *Journal of Philosophy*, 1916, pp. 717, 720. " Verily, metaphysics is the Paris of the intellect : no sooner do the most scrupulously severe reasoners find their feet on this ground than they give the loosest reins of license to their logic." (Review of Sylvester's collected mathematical papers, *Nation*, Vol. 79, 1904, p. 203.)

[2] All science, in so far as it is ' science of discovery ', is divided by Peirce into three divisions : Mathematics, Philosophy and Idioscopy (Bentham's term).   Idioscopy branches into the Physical Sciences and the " Psychical, or Human Sciences " ; Philosophy into Phenomenology, Normative Science and Metaphysics.   There are further subdivisions, resulting in a fairly complex classification (see 1.180-202). "Mathematics studies what is and what is not logically possible, without making itself responsible for its actual existence. Philosophy is *positive science*, in the sense of discovering what really is true ; but it limits itself to so much of truth as can be inferred from common experience. Idioscopy embraces all the special sciences, which are principally occupied with the accumula-

briefly what 'metaphysics' means for Peirce, since he
believes that its retention is compatible with pragmatism.
James once said, "Every philosopher (W. J., e.g.) pretends
that all the others are metaphysicians against whom he is
simply defending the rights of common sense."[1]   Peirce
defended not only common sense but metaphysics as
well.[2]

He divides metaphysics into three branches (1.192):
Ontology (General Metaphysics); Psychical or Religious
Metaphysics, concerned chiefly with the questions of God,
Freedom and Immortality; and Physical Metaphysics,
"which discusses the real nature of time, space, laws of
nature, matter, etc."   As typical problems of metaphysics
he cites, for instance (6.6): "Whether there be any strictly
individual existence"; "What general explanation or
account can be given of the different qualities of feeling
and their apparent connection with determinations of mass,
space and time?"   "What external reality do the qualities
of sense represent, in general?"   ". . . What is the nature
of the reality that [time] represents?"   "Are time and space
continuous?"   "What is consciousness or mind like?"   "Is
there . . . any general tendency in the course of events
. . . ?"   These problems Peirce holds to be soluble problems,
capable of determination by the methods of science.   Metaphysics is an 'observational science' to which hypothesis and
induction are applicable precisely as in physics (6.5).   The
present unsatisfactory state of metaphysics is due to its
practice largely by theologians rather than men with the
scientific spirit, not to any difficulty in the character of its
problems.   But may it not be objected that the hypotheses

tion of new facts" (1.184) ; (cf. 1.241, and an important review of
Titchener's translation of Wundt's *Principles of Physiol. Psych.*, in *Nation*,
Vol. 81, 1905, pp. 56-7, and *New York Post*, July 21, 1905, p. 4).

[1] Letter to T. S. Perry, 1905 (in *Letters of Wm. James*, ed. H. James,
Vol. II, pp. 232-3).   Perhaps, also, every philosopher says *this*.

[2] In the Baldwin article, pragmatism is actually called "the opinion
that metaphysics is to be largely cleared up by the application of the . . .
maxim . . ." (5.2), thus apparently making the clarification of metaphysics
a primary purpose of the doctrine.

of metaphysics are unconfirmable because the 'objects' of
metaphysics are not open to observation?

> "The things that any science discovers are beyond the
> reach of direct observation. We cannot see energy, nor
> the attraction of gravitation . . . nor the forests of the
> carbonaceous era, nor the explosions in nerve-cells. It is
> only the premisses of science, not its conclusions, which
> are directly observed. But metaphysics, even bad meta-
> physics, really rests on observations. . . . It rests upon
> kinds of phenomena with which every man's experience is
> so saturated that he usually pays no particular attention
> to them. The data of metaphysics are not less open to
> observation, but immeasurably more so, than the data,
> say, of the very highly developed science of astronomy. . . .
> (6.2).

Metaphysics for Peirce is an 'explanation' of the universe,
"the function of which, like that of every logical explanation,
is to unify its observed variety" (1.487). He usually regards
it as something which underlies natural science, a set of
opinions of one sort or another assumed by the latter (cf.
5.521). It gives "life and light to cosmology and physics"
(5.423); and in fact a metaphysics is and must be maintained
tacitly by everyone (1.129).[1]

It is not clear in Peirce just where the line is to be drawn
between natural science and metaphysics so far as their
observational foundations are concerned. He holds that
metaphysics "is mainly distinguished" from natural science
"by its confining itself to such parts of physics and of
psychics as can be established without *special means* of
observation. But these are very peculiar parts, extremely
unlike the rest" (1.282; my ital.). What these 'peculiar
parts' are we never find expatiated in Peirce. As an instance
of a metaphysical presupposition of science, a "general
principle" that "cannot be proved or disproved by [its]

---

[1] " It has been made manifest that positive psychology cannot escape
taking for granted a metaphysics of one kind or another in no inconsiderable
measure " (Review of M. Maher's *Psychology* [*etc.*], in *Nation*, Vol. 73,
1901, p. 267).

ordinary methods of work", Peirce offers the assumption that the laws of mechanics hold good for the smallest corpuscles (1.129). If this assumption is not adopted some other would have to be. He regards also as a metaphysical presupposition an answer to such a question as whether "every single fact in the universe is precisely determined by law" (6.36). And of the view that "all laws are results of evolution", he says that it is "a hypothesis capable of being tested by experiment" (6.101).

Whether or not one wishes to controvert Peirce's belief that metaphysical inquiry is compatible with pragmatism, it is difficult to do so, for the simple reason that he is so vague and inadequate on the nature of metaphysical verifiability. One can only raise questions on the assertions that he actually makes. If metaphysics is an observational science, is the difference between it and natural science (as ordinarily understood) one of generality, so that the contrast is analogous to that between physics and physiology? Does the opinion of physicists on whether 'every single fact in the universe is precisely determined by law' affect the results of physics? if not, in what way *is* this metaphysical problem connected with the so-called presuppositions of physics? The same question applies to the problems of time and space. Further, does the assumption that the laws of mechanics hold (or not) for the smallest corpuscles affect the results of mechanics? if so, how does it differ from the other hypotheses of mechanics? Would it not seem that the criterion of verifiability in metaphysics cannot be very different from that of natural science, since the maxim of pragmatism lays down only one such criterion, influenced essentially by the procedure of the latter? (cf. 5.465). Undoubtedly, Peirce's own writings on matters metaphysical ought not to be judged in place of his programmatic pronouncements where the latter are not adequate enough for us to estimate the relations between pragmatism and metaphysics. But it is worthwhile venturing the opinion that a metaphysics consistent with pragmatism will not intentionally be filled with statements like "Active law is efficient reasonableness, or in other words is truly reasonable reasonableness. Reasonable reasonableness is Thirdness as Thirdness" (5.121).

One or two of Peirce's utterances on metaphysics do not accord very well with the view we just found him to hold. He says that "metaphysical conceptions are primarily and at bottom thoughts about words, or thoughts about thoughts" (i.e. in general, about signs) (5.294). And he says also that "metaphysical conceptions, as I need not waste words to show, are merely adapted from those of formal logic, and therefore can only be apprehended in the light of a minutely accurate and thoroughgoing system of formal logic" (1.625). It is regrettable, though altogether common in Peirce, that he regards as evident something even the meaning of which is not clear. If the first of these two passages means what it seems to mean, then metaphysical statements are statements about signs and metaphysics is consequently a branch of logic.[1] But I am hardly sure that it does mean this; and even if it did, we should possess nothing more than an isolated statement made in 1868.

40. **The Second Kind of Utterance on Pragmatism.** We said (§ 33) that in his attempt to set forth the exposition of pragmatism, Peirce makes statements couched in different terms than the statements on which we dwelt. Whereas the first type of statement employs such terms as 'sensible', 'operation', and 'verification', the second type speaks of 'conduct', 'practical', 'self-control', 'habit', and 'purpose'. I suggest that had we not stated the essentials of pragmatism in the way that we have, a statement like the following would have remained obscure despite interpretation: ". . . The true meaning of any product of the intellect lies in whatever unitary determination it would impart to practical conduct under any and every conceivable circumstance, supposing such conduct to be guided by reflexion carried to an ultimate limit" (6.490). And how much could have been

[1] Cf. § 44.

made of the following answer given by Peirce to his own question, What is the form of the proposition giving the meaning of a given proposition? "It is, according to the pragmaticist, that form in which the proposition becomes applicable to human conduct, not in these or those special circumstances, nor when one entertains this or that special design, but that form which is most directly applicable to self-control under every situation and to every purpose" (5.427). Except for one particular point, I do not propose to go into the details of this second mode of statement, for the reason that, in so far as pragmatism according to its primary purpose is a theory of meaning, I regard the second mode of statement as clarified by and translatable into the first. Peirce would probably not have been led into the vaguer statement of pragmatism had not James's gift of popularization given birth to an army of 'pragmatists' in Europe and America. In response to the different variations of pragmatism created by James and these philosophers, Peirce attempted to restate his view in their terms. The result was that pragmatism even in his own discussions became a doctrine of ethics and metaphysics; though, unconscious of this, he continued to reiterate the purpose of the maxim. This change becomes clearly perceptible after 1898, when James delivered his lecture "Philosophical Conceptions and Practical Results"; it is not to be found between 1878, when he formulated the then unnamed view, and that year. In the 1905 *Monist* article "What Pragmatism Is" (5.411-437), which is Peirce's best and most complete single account of the doctrine, there is a curious mixture of the two types of statement, one eye being toward the restatement in his own terms of the original maxim, the other toward the expression of the maxim in the current terminology.

But it seems to me that there is another reason why Peirce saw fit to continue employing the vaguer expression of pragmatism, once he had begun to use it. Whether it did seem to him vaguer than the other mode of expression is doubtful. But it must have occurred to him that in such terms pragmatism could best be, not stated, but *justified*. The precise statement of the pragmatic criterion and the justification of *a* pragmatic criterion are two different considerations. Perhaps we can indicate why, with respect to this latter consideration, the emphasis is naturally on the *practical* and on *conduct*, which are essentially human, social and biological terms.

What, we may ask, is the justification of pragmatism; what guarantee is there that a pragmatic criterion is the best criterion of 'meaning'? The answer depends upon the nature of our communication with one another and upon recognition of the fact that we ought not to call anything 'meaningful' which is not communicable—whatever else we may wish to call it. We communicate by means of signs, and no sign-situation is a genuine sign-situation unless we can distinguish in it the thing which functions as the sign-instrument, something to which the sign refers, and some possible translation necessarily dependent upon a mind that employs the sign. Minds communicate by employing the same set of signs in accordance with the rules of the language-community to which they belong. To employ the same signs is to employ the same translations; and it is important to stress this, for unless the members of a group were able to manipulate their signs according to a definite rule, there could never be public agreement on a sign's reference. Thus the use of signs, the very concept of a sign, involves a mind, and a mind in communication with other minds, all of whom must to a conventional extent agree on the translation of the signs constituting their language. Now pragmatism is a rule, applying to names and factual sentences, *delimiting* the possible translations of these signs to a definite kind. The translation according to pragmatism is such that it aids us in distinguishing two signs that are likely to be confused, and in identifying two signs that for no clear reason are likely to be distinguished. The fact that pragmatism is a rule which *promotes the success* of the sign-situation (i.e. of communication) proves that it is the best criterion of meaning. But does it in fact promote communication? Plainly, the insistence that the class of legitimate translations be limited to a formula for sensible operations (in the case of names) or a formula for confirmation (in the case of sentences) is an insistence on the facilitation of public agreement. These formulae enable us to determine publicly whether the meanings of given names and sentences are to be distinguished or identified.

The justification of the pragmatic criterion can be stated in somewhat other terms. The pragmatic criterion is a criterion natural to human thinking and communication. "Our idea of anything *is* our idea of its sensible effects; and if we fancy that we have any other we deceive ourselves. . . . It is absurd to say that thought has any meaning unrelated to its only function" (5.401). Thought cannot entertain conceptions (other than those purely formal or linguistic) which are not sensibly interpretable. One who is unable to explain his use of names and sentences in concrete terms will be acknowledged to mean nothing. We cannot—to speak more loosely—genuinely think of anything except in so far as it has practical bearings. This is not to base the concept of meaning on a psychological principle, as Peirce at one time (5.28) believed he had mistakenly done. It is rather to base this concept on social and biological considerations, to realize that it is a concept relative to individuals of a common biological character (with all the limitations and potentialities peculiar to that character) communicating in a society. ". . . Man is so completely hemmed in by the bounds of his possible practical experience, his mind is so restricted to being the instrument of his needs, that he cannot, in the least, *mean* anything that transcends those limits" (5.536).[1]

---

[1] Continuing, "The strict consequence of this is, that it is all nonsense to tell him that he must not think in this or that way because to do so would be to transcend the limits of a possible experience. For let him try ever so hard to think anything about what is beyond that limit, it simply cannot be done. You might as well pass a law that no man shall jump over the moon; it wouldn't forbid him to jump just as high as he possibly could."

Cf. also 5.532 : ". . . It is precisely the pragmatist's contention that symbols, owing their origin (on one side) to human conventions, cannot transcend conceivable human occasions."

Consider, in combination, these two statements : (i) 5.254 : A sign

Perhaps the foregoing explains, then, why Peirce clung to that type of statement in which the pragmatic maxim would be expressed, for instance, as being that "a conception can have no logical effect or import differing from that of a second conception except so far as, taken in connection with other conceptions and intentions, it might conceivably modify our practical conduct differently from that second conception" (5.196). Peirce understood that the general vindication of pragmatism was not less important than its precise statement—for James it was of far greater importance. Peirce was eager to show that the very concept of meaning implied the pragmatic criterion; that this rule for the meaning of signs was determined by the sign-relation in general. The sign- or meaning-relation is a human, social and biological fact.[1] To emphasize this, and accordingly how faithful to it pragmatism was, Peirce employed human, social and biological terms. In the natural state of things, the meaning of a sign is definable for the common man in terms of 'conduct'; only when we formulate the criterion of meaning do we speak rather in terms of 'operations'.

I want to consider now the particular point in the second mode of statement on pragmatism which I excepted from the proposal of not entering into detail. It involves, not merely a verbal variation in the statement of pragmatism, but an important element in its definition. Peirce says (5.491) that the "final" or "ultimate" logical interpretant cannot be another term or another proposition; for any sign has itself a logical interpretant, and so on ad infinitum. The "real meaning" of a term or proposition must therefore be, not

cannot have meaning "if by its definition it is the sign of something absolutely incognizable"; (ii) 6.344: Signs are "the only things with which a human being can, without derogation, consent to have any transaction".

[1] Thus James, when intentionally paraphrasing Peirce, says of any statement (or thought) that "conduct is *for us* its sole significance" (*Pragmatism*, p. 46; my ital.); and also, that "meaning, other than practical, there is *for us* none" (*Ibid.*, p. 48; my ital.).

another sign but a "habit". And "the most perfect account of a concept that words can convey will consist in a description of the habit which that concept is calculated to produce". To thus describe the habit is to describe "the kind of action to which it gives rise". The meaning "*is* that habit; the verbal formulation merely expresses it". It is the habit which is "the living definition, the veritable and final logical interpretant". Now if all that Peirce meant were that the essential condition for terms having meaning is their being associated, by some habit or convention, with sensible properties (whence all such terms would be translated by one another), there would be no room for objection and he would simply be emphasizing a truth already implicit in his statements of the pragmatic criterion. But he clearly intends much more. He intends that a 'habit' should be an 'interpretant', and that it should be the 'final' interpretant, because "a concept, proposition, or argument . . . cannot be the final logical interpretant . . ." (5. 491); they cannot be "the *ultimate* logical interpretant. . . ." (5.476).

There seem to be two possible interpretations of what Peirce means by 'habit' here. (1) The habit which is the 'meaning' of, say, 'This is hard', is not the verbal translating formula, nor the confirming operations considered as physical performances, but what is described by this formula. It is a rule, considered not as a statement but, realistically, as that which the statement enunciates (cf. 5.426, 427, 429). Synthetic statements do not simply express 'facts'; they express rules or 'habits'. The rule or habit is a kind of being *in futuro* (cf. 5.32, 2.86). (2) On the second interpretation, 'habit' would mean 'habit of usage'. The habit as the meaning of, say, a term, would be the class of all actual instances in which a term has been and continues to be operationally understood. 'Habit' in this sense would call attention to the fact that as social communication and the linguistic usages employed in it developed with the history of the human species, a technique of definition in sensible terms became crystallized, until now we are obliged to define pragmatically if we wish to do justice to the 'meaning', based on man's activity as a social and biological animal; this meaning consisting in the 'habit' developed out of such activity. The linguistic interpretant that would 'express' the habit would express something different from a realistic rule. On this interpretation 'habit' would be used somewhat as in physiological psychology; a habit would consist in the fact that under certain conditions certain definite responses occur (the conditions and responses here being usages and sensible definitions, respectively).

If we ask which of these is the correct interpretation, the answer is, I believe, a combination of both. In the second interpretation, the class of instances constituting the (pragmatic) habit must be extended to include instances that *might* arise; and in the first interpretation, any suggestion of hypostasis must be eliminated. The 'habit' will then be a *type* of operations-leading-to-specified-results, expressed by a linguistic interpretant. Such a habit is originally correlated with a term by social convention, but later becomes, by the requirements of social intercourse, the 'meaning' of the term. The 'meaning' of a sentence is thus the habit of going about confirming it, and this is described by a conditional formula.

If this be, as I think it is, a correct interpretation of Peirce (making him, at any rate, less vague than his own words do, and charitably discounting hypostasis), it represents a grossly unsatisfactory modification of the pragmatic view previously stated. In the first place, it is not clear in what sense a habit can be a logical interpretant. "The habit alone . . . is not a sign in that way in which that sign of which it is the logical interpretant is the sign"; but "it may", Peirce lamely says, "be a sign in some other way" (5.491). In the second place, is it a genuine objection on Peirce's part to say that the 'final' logical interpretant must be other than a sign for the reason that every sign has itself a logical interpretant? This objection really is that any ordinary pragmatic interpretant is constituted by signs which are each pragmatically interpretable, and so on ad infinitum; so that only a 'habit', to which this objection does not apply, can be the 'final' meaning, or 'real' meaning. But if the 'habit' is 'described' or 'expressed' by a verbal formula, which formula is it? If there is no final linguistic translation, what status has "the description of the kind of action to which it [the habit] gives rise"? If it is a perfectly faithful description, it is not open to the objection of being further refinable, so that here would be a 'final' translation; if it is not a perfectly faithful description, it is merely *a* description, not 'the' description, of the 'habit'. The fact is that Peirce's argument against a verbal translation as the pragmatic interpretant is weak. It is not necessary to assume a *final* translation in the form of a habit simply because every translation other than a habit is further translatable pragmatically.[1] The formula which we choose to call the 'pragmatic' translation is a *relatively* final translation or interpretant. It is distinguished, not by the specificity of its terms, but by the *kind* of formula it is. The formula in so far as it is prescriptive or conditional is what interests us essentially, not the fact of to what degree its own terms can be pragmatically refined.

It therefore would seem desirable, on the few occasions where the meaning is called a 'habit', to substitute for it 'formula for confirmation' or 'pragmatic interpretant', in accordance with the analysis we have found to be justified as basic in Peirce.

---

[1] I cannot agree with the view expressed by Prof. H. S. Leonard on this point. He holds "that pragmatism will be a doctrine vitiated by an infinite progressus unless it recognizes that there is *some* . . . category of propositions" which it construes "as atomic, i.e. as not requiring analysis of the sort proposed by the pragmatic doctrine"; and further, that "it [pragmatism] is not satisfactorily applicable until some such category is actually specified" (Review of Vols. V and VI of Collected Papers, *Philosophy of Science*, 1937, p. 116). I do not see why pragmatism is not 'satisfactorily applicable', nor why, granted the 'infinite progressus', pragmatism should be 'vitiated' by it. Such an argument is analogous to the one which holds that knowledge cannot be genuine or 'true' knowledge as long as it is fallible.

41. **Sentences about Feelings.** We saw (§ 31) that in several places Peirce limits the scope of pragmatism to 'intellectual signs', contrasted with signs like 'red' which "name mere subjective feelings only". We said that this was opposed to the spirit of pragmatism as reflected by more detailed and authoritative accounts, and by explicit statement to the contrary, e.g. 5.545: ". . . to say that a body is hard, or red, . . . or has any other property . . . is a statement referring to the future". We indicated, and now propose to expand on the point, that while pragmatism may allow Peirce to say that 'red' names a 'subjective feeling', it is contrary to pragmatism to say that it names a feeling *only* and is indefinable. According to pragmatism every name is definable, since it is the name of a property with an indefinite number of relations. We saw also that on certain occasions Peirce is inclined to exclude proper names from the scope of pragmatic definability, on the grounds that they are mere 'designations of an individual object'. On our account no name at all should, strictly, *be* a 'designation of an individual object'. For to hold that there are designations of purely individual things divorced from all relations implies a nominalistic atomism repugnant to Peirce's fundamental views.

If we turn now to the question of the relation between synthetic statements containing names like 'red' and synthetic statements in general, we find that there are four possibilities with respect to the view of Peirce. (i) All synthetic statements admit of only a pragmatic interpretation; (ii) some admit of both a pragmatic and non-pragmatic interpretation, others of only a non-pragmatic interpretation; (iii) some admit of both a pragmatic and non-pragmatic interpretation, others of only a pragmatic interpretation; (iv) all admit of both a pragmatic and non-pragmatic interpretation. Which of these is the view of Peirce; and if he holds that certain statements are non-pragmatically interpretable, what kind of interpretation is it that these statements have?

According to Peirce, the pragmatic interpretation, the "reasonable purport", is not "the only kind of meaning there is" (5.434; cf. 5.8). We cannot brush this statement aside, despite the fact that a great many other statements in which 'pragmatic purport' and 'meaning' are synonymous could be opposed to it. In § 30 we found that whereas 'intellectual' signs had logical interpretants, certain other signs had 'emotional interpretants'. Just what is this emotional interpretant? It is the feeling—a 'feeling of recognition'—aroused or suggested by, or associated with, a sign. Thus 'red' presumably has an emotional interpretant in the sense that it arouses a feeling which is what we would ordinarily say it 'means'. This feeling or emotional interpretant "we come to interpret as evidence that we comprehend the proper effect of the sign" (5.475). Sometimes, says Peirce, the emotional interpretant "may amount to much more than that feeling of recognition"; but "in some cases, it is the only proper significate effect that the sign produces" (*ib.*). We thus find two suggestions as to the nature of the emotional interpretant: on the one hand it may be a mere feeling, and on the other, it may be "much more than that"; but whether a mere feeling or more than a feeling, it "comes to be interpreted".[1] What the import of this last phrase is, is uncertain. But we saw, at any rate, that if the emotional interpretant consists in a mere feeling, it is, like the 'energetic' ('dynamic') interpretant, not really an interpretant but a mere causal effect; for an interpretant, as the name implies, interprets, and must therefore be another thought or

[1] Elsewhere (4.536) Peirce calls the emotional interpretant the "immediate" interpretant, which, he says, is "ordinarily" called the "meaning" of a sign. This is undoubtedly the case. But 'immediate interpretant' is used confusedly. For instance, Peirce says that pragmatism is the view "that the immediate interpretant of all thought proper is conduct" (4.539). Here (a) 'conduct' is called an immediate interpretant, which is supposed to be synonymous with 'emotional interpretant'; (b) pragmatism is thus defined in terms of a certain kind of emotional interpretant instead of a certain kind of logical interpretant. Peirce often tried to say the same thing in so many different ways that he inevitably became ambiguous.

sign. The statement having such an emotional interpretant would be purely demonstrative. Any statement, then, if no statements are purely demonstrative, must have a logical interpretant, another sign interpreting it, "in which it is more fully developed" (5.594).

Does this mean, then, that Peirce has no legitimate distinction in mind between a pragmatic and a non-pragmatic interpretation of statements? I believe that he has, but that the distinction is not to be expressed, as he confusedly attempts to express it, in terms of certain statements having 'emotional' as opposed to logical interpretants. All statements have logical interpretants. But whereas statements interpreted pragmatically have one kind of logical interpretant, statements not interpreted pragmatically have another kind, and the question is, What kind?

Peirce has in mind, as being non-pragmatically interpretable, statements in which names of relatively simple qualities, or, as he would say, 'subjective feelings', occur. Consider 'I see red', or better, 'I have the feeling red'. This statement, we may imagine Peirce to say, is about a feeling which an individual has. It cannot be translated as a prescription for public operations, for 'red' is the name of a sense-quality, and the only one who knows whether he has the sense-quality is the asserter of the statement. He alone is the authority on the truth of the predication. So that here, presumably, is a statement which is a meaningful statement and yet is not verifiable in terms of public operations.

The chief question which one who holds this view must answer is, How do we explain the fact that a statement of this kind is commonly understood? For if, when A makes the statement 'I have the feeling red' he alone knows whether it is true or false, in what way do others know what he means? In other words, how can the meaning of such a statement be communicated? Or we might ask, how does one person know that the quality which he names 'red' is the same as that which another person names 'red'? Peirce in one place (1.314-316) partially considers a question of this last form. He holds that "the evidence is ample that they [sense-qualities] are common to all beings whose senses are sufficiently developed", and even, "I am confident that a bull and I feel much alike at the sight of a red rag". Just what this evidence is, he does not make clear (cf. 5.506). And in general it cannot be pretended that Peirce has a satisfactory explicit answer to the questions just asked. But fairness to a philosopher requires that we apply what we accept as his fundamental analysis to those places where he is least clear. If this were done in the case of Peirce, the result would be somewhat as follows.

What, we may ask, do we mean by the word 'same' when we say: "The sense-quality which A feels and calls 'red' is the same as the sense-quality which B feels and calls 'red'"? Clearly, *this* statement *is* to be interpreted pragmatically. On the pragmatic interpretation, the felt qualities in the two cases will be defined as the 'same' when the publicly observable concomitants of each are the same. If the objects to which A and B apply the name 'red' are physically analyzed with a single result in both cases, then it is assumed that each feels the same way; and this is the only sense that we can give to 'same', for two individuals cannot examine each other's feelings. This pragmatic definition of 'same' at once answers the foregoing questions. Statements of the kind under discussion can be commonly understood because, and only in so far as, each sense-quality named is correlated with something publicly observable, i.e. something on which there will always be agreement.

These considerations would lead Peirce to a view like the following. There are two types of statements, public statements and private statements. The public statements are those whose meaning is given by the pragmatic criterion; and *all* statements must be *at least* public statements, if they are to be regarded as commonly understood. The private statements are those which, though in so far as they are communicable or publicly understandable are public, i.e. pragmatically interpretable, have in addition a 'meaning' that is private and incommunicable. 'I see red' or 'I feel tooth-ache' or 'I feel sad' can be said to mean the same for all only because of the fact that the feelings named can be correlated with physical concomitants observable by all. But to the asserters of these sentences, they 'mean' something in *another* way: what the sentences denote affects them in a way to which the physical defining criteria are not faithful. Peirce would say that we have here different 'kinds of meaning'. It might be desirable to employ another word for cases where there is other than pragmatic 'meaning', but whether we employ a special word or speak of a 'kind' of meaning is a linguistic question.[1]

If this be the view of Peirce on the matter in question, then he holds to the third of the four above-mentioned possible views; namely, that all synthetic statements are pragmatically interpretable and some are in addition non-pragmatically interpretable. If 'red', 'sad', etc., are regarded as used with the same meaning by everybody, they must be pragmatically definable—the statements in which they occur must be sentences 'referring to the future' —though for each individual they denote an incommunicable sense-quality. This is not to say, however, that in so far as sentences about feelings are privately interpretable they are purely demonstrative. They are not; for they are in *some* way translatable still, namely by means of other signs which are privately interpretable. Privately interpretable state-ments are not the less fallible for their status of private inter-pretability. For regardless of how a statement is interpreted, it remains a hypothesis in the stream of thoughts (cf. § 14).

---

[1] See a paper in *Analysis*, Vol. III (1935-6), where I have suggested that ' meaning ' be restricted to publicly confirmable statements, and that private (privately confirmable) statements be called ' significant ' or ' significantly confirmable '. Considered as an assertion about a feeling, a statement is significant for the asserter alone ; in so far as it is to be called ' meaningful ' it should be meaningful for everyone, i.e. publicly verifiable. (In this case the need for two distinct names is greater than in the case of Peirce, for it is also suggested that there are statements which are meaningless, i.e. incommunicable, yet which are significant or privately confirmable.)

The possibility of pragmatic translation is only a guarantee, so to speak, of a statement's hypothetical character.

42. Peirce and James. I do not want to compare Peirce and James on any matter but (1) their conception of the purpose of pragmatism, and (2) their statement of what pragmatism essentially is. The reason for this is not merely that a complete comparison would require for itself too great an amount of space, but that it would be unjust to James without having first given an account of the background of his views as well as those of Peirce.

That James's pragmatism was influenced chiefly by Peirce can hardly be doubted. The evidence lies in the content of his opinions, his references to Peirce in public print, and his acknowledgments in personal correspondence; though of course, as everyone knows, James was sometimes too generous. Peirce is first referred to in the 1884 essay on "The Function of Cognition",[1] which James calls "the *fons et origo* of all *my* pragmatism".[2] On the whole, throughout the literary career of both, James was less inclined than Peirce to regard the differences between them as fundamental; but I am not sure that Professor Perry is justified in holding that "perhaps it would be correct, and just to all parties, to say that the modern movement known as pragmatism is largely the result of James's misunderstanding of Peirce".[3] For although, as we shall see presently, there is an element of misunderstanding of Peirce in his work, James seems to have been quite aware that he was not *merely* interpreting Peirce in his original statement of pragmatism. For in the 1898 lecture "Philosophical Conceptions and Practical Results", where the term 'pragmatism' was publicly introduced by him, he says of the doctrine it represents, "I think myself that it should be expressed more broadly than Mr. Peirce expresses it",[4] and proceeds with such an expression.

---

[1] Rep. in *The Meaning of Truth*, 1909.
[2] Perry, *op. cit.*, II, p. 450.
[3] *Op cit.*, II, p. 409.   [4] *Coll. Essays and Reviews*, p. 412.

Peirce's opinions on the relation between his view and that of James are not always the same, varying from frank dissatisfaction with James to expression of belief in their basic community. His real opinion seems, however, to have been that James originally misunderstood the intent and implications of his maxim, and that consequently a fundamental difference remained, despite an equally fundamental similarity. So far as his written words are concerned, on the one hand he says that "there is a most essential difference between his pragmatism and mine",[1] that James "pushed this method [the pragmatic] to such extremes as must tend to give us pause" (5.3), that he "transmogrified it into a doctrine of philosophy, some parts of which I highly approved, while other and more prominent parts I regarded, and still [1908] regard, as opposed to sound logic" (6.482). James's short piece in Baldwin's Dictionary, printed along with his own article, he later calls "an exegesis, not very deep" (5.13 n.). In 1905 he introduces the term 'pragmaticism' to distinguish his own pragmatism from that of others, including James.[2] But on the other hand, he says that James's "'radical empiricism' substantially answered to the writer's definition of pragmatism, albeit with a certain difference in the point of view" (5.414), that "I am inclined to think that the discrepancies reside in other than the pragmatistic ingredients of our thought" (5.466), and that "practically, his view and mine must, I think, coincide, except where he allows considerations not at all pragmatic to have weight" (5.494).

(1) With respect to the differences of James and himself on the purpose and scope of pragmatism, Peirce's judgment is quite sound. We saw in § 29 what his own conception of this purpose was. There is evidence here too that James's difference was a conscious one. He says, for instance, that "the word pragmatism has come to be used in a still wider

---

[1] Letter to C. Ladd-Franklin, printed in *Jour. of Philos.*, 1916, p. 718.

[2] Writing to James in 1904 he says, " You and Schiller carry pragmatism too far for me " (Perry, *op. cit.*, II, p. 430).

sense, as meaning also a certain *theory of truth*" (J.'s ital.).[1]
He was aware that in Peirce's original formulation pragmatism was a theory of meaning rather than a theory of
truth.   Yet the bulk of his two most important books on
pragmatism, *Pragmatism* and *The Meaning of Truth*, is concerned with the doctrine in the latter capacity.   James, like
Peirce, considered pragmatism implicit to a certain degree
in classical philosophy.   But in this matter he judged more
sanely than Peirce, holding that it was in the spirit of British
empiricism.   He regarded it as a temper underlying a kind
of philosophizing.   "Pragmatism represents a perfectly
familiar attitude in philosophy, the empiricist attitude. . . ." [2]
He identifies this with certain other points of view, prominent in but antedating British empiricism—nominalism,
positivism, utilitarianism.   Peirce, on the other hand, held
that "the most important consequence" of pragmatism is
that by its adoption "we must abandon nominalism",[3]
though this is obviously too strong a statement, even for
Peirce's own pragmatism.   While James found pragmatism
akin in spirit to the tendencies mentioned, he nevertheless
recognized that pragmatism "has no dogmas, and no doctrines save its method".[4]   In general, then, James regarded
pragmatism as a theory of meaning, a theory of truth, and
a general attitude of philosophizing.   As a theory of meaning
it was something he adopted almost exclusively from Peirce.
Some of his statements in connection with it are felicitous,
but on the whole it counted for little with him.   For Peirce,
on the other hand, pragmatism is a theory of meaning essentially, despite the fact that in later years he links it to
virtually everything else.   And while the meaning of 'truth'
depends upon pragmatism in the sense that the meaning of
any concept depends on the *theory* of meaning, it is hardly
the case, as with James, that the term 'pragmatism' is
primarily applied to a certain definition of the term 'truth'.

---

[1] *Pragmatism*, p. 55.   [2] *Ibid.*, p. 51.
[3] Letter to James, 1904 (in Perry, *op. cit.*, II, p. 430).
[4] *Pragmatism*, p. 54.

Peirce always retained a basic preference for his original statement of 1878, where pragmatism was a method of clarifying ideas, and he regarded his later developments of the doctrine as a drawing of implications from it.[1] "Pragmatism . . . as I understand it", he wrote to James, "is one of the propositions of logic."[2] We have seen enough to understand how steeped pragmatism was in the theory of signs, and how foreign such a procedure was to James. And while it cannot be doubted that pragmatism was for James a genuine and living conviction, one cannot help feeling that in his case it was not, as in Peirce's, a conviction born of considerable intellectual labour.

(2) Let us now confine ourselves to pragmatism as a theory of meaning, and compare the differences of formulation between Peirce and James. James's 'broader expression' of 'Peirce's principle' is that the "meaning of any philosophic proposition can always be brought down to some particular consequence, in our future practical experience, whether active or passive; the point lying rather in the fact that the experience must be particular, than in the fact that it must be active".[3] Now this statement, which at first sight seems clear, is in fact extremely vague; and although it is unfair to single out for analysis isolated statements, it happens to be the case that nowhere in James do we find a detailed statement of what he means by 'particular consequence' or 'future practical experience'. If we examine most of his statements of the maxim, we find not merely that important terms of this kind are unclear, but that his common language is also misleading, and that his metaphors are clever but overabundant for purposes of definition. What, in the present statement, is the import of the phrase that the meaning

---

[1] " Much as the writer has gained from the perusal of what other pragmatists have written, he still thinks there is a decisive advantage in his original conception of the doctrine. From this original form every truth that follows from any of the other forms can be deduced, while some errors can be avoided into which other pragmatists have fallen " (5.415).

[2] Letter, 1903 (Perry, II, p. 427).

[3] *Coll. Ess. and Rev.*, p. 412.

can be 'brought down' to some particular consequence? Consider also: "The pragmatic method . . . is . . . to interpret each notion by tracing its respective practical consequences";[1] and, A statement is "insignificant" if "no future detail of experience or conduct is to be deduced from" it.[2] In speaking of 'practical consequences' or 'conduct' James is indifferent to whether they mean (i) verifiable consequences from a statement, or (ii) personal reactions evoked by a statement. I believe it can be shown that on certain occasions James means something analogous to (i), and that on others he means (ii). In the following case there is a mixture of both.

He is discussing the metaphysical problem of 'theism versus materialism', and the applicability of pragmatism to this problem. Consider first, he says, the problem with respect to the world's past. According to the theist God made the world, according to the materialist it resulted from physical forces. Both theories (we suppose) explain the facts equally well. Both "have shown all their consequences and . . . these are identical. The pragmatist must consequently say that the two theories, in spite of their different-sounding names, mean exactly the same thing, and that the dispute is purely verbal".[3] Thus, all the sensible consequences of the two theories being the same, the theories themselves are identical, and there is no problem. But "theism and materialism, so indifferent when taken retrospectively, point, when we take them prospectively, to wholly different *outlooks* of experience" (my ital.).[4] In this case, even though the sensible consequences of the two theories should turn out to be the same, they would still be different theories, and a choice between them genuinely problematical; for they have different 'practical' consequences in *this* sense:

"A world with a God in it to say the last word, *may indeed burn up or freeze* [i.e. precisely as in the materialist world, so far as sensible effects are concerned], but we then

---

[1] *Pragmatism*, p. 45.   [2] *Coll. Ess. and Rev.*, p. 417.
[3] *Prag.*, p. 97.   [4] *Ibid.*, p. 103.

think of him as still mindful of the old ideals and sure to bring them elsewhere to fruition; so that, where he is, tragedy is only provisional and partial, and shipwreck and dissolution not the absolutely final things. This need of an eternal moral order is one of the deepest needs of our breast. . . . Here then, *in these different emotional and practical appeals, in these adjustments of our concrete attitudes of hope and expectation, and all the delicate consequences which their differences entail, lie the real meanings* of materialism and spiritualism. . . ." (my ital.).[1]

'Practical' consequences in the sense of personal reactions, whether in the form of feeling- or action-effects, are more precisely described by Peirce as 'emotional' and 'energetic' interpretants. But such effects Peirce explicitly excludes from the 'pragmatistic purport'.

But suppose that we eliminate from consideration, as constituting the 'meaning' of names and sentences, practical consequences of this kind. And let us also return to the 'broader' expression of pragmatism quoted on p. 169. We shall understand by it that, from any synthetic sentence some 'particular experiential consequence' (the terms 'practical experience' and 'particular consequence' combined) must be deducible if that statement is to be called meaningful; or in other words, that the meaning of a statement consists in its 'particular experiential consequences'. If, now, we can say what James understood by 'particular experiential consequence' we can state fundamentally wherein he differed from Peirce. I believe that the best suggestion for interpreting what he meant is to be found in the following passage:

". . . Metaphysical discussions are so much like fighting with the air; they have no practical issue of a *sensational*

---

[1] *Ibid.*, pp. 106-107 (also in *Coll. Ess. and Rev.*, p. 423). Likewise in discussing the problem of the ' One and the Many ' James says : " What exact thing do you *practically* mean by ' One ' when you call the universe One, is the first question you must ask. In what ways does the oneness come home to your own personal life ? By what difference does it express itself in your experience ? How can you act differently towards a universe which is one ? '' (*Coll. Ess. and Rev.*, p. 431 ; J.'s ital.).

kind. 'Scientific' theories, on the other hand, always
terminate in definite *percepts*. You can deduce a possible
sensation from your theory and, taking me into your
laboratory, prove that your theory is true of my world by
giving me the *sensation then and there*. Beautiful is the
flight of conceptual reason through the upper air of truth.
No wonder philosophers are dazzled by it still, and no
wonder they look with some disdain at the low earth of *feeling* from which the goddess launched herself aloft. But woe
to her if she return not home to its acquaintance. . . ."
(my ital.).[1]

The meaning of a proposition, for James, consists in a definite
set of feelings or percepts associated with that proposition.
When he insists that a proposition is meaningless because we
cannot deduce from it 'practical consequences', 'particular
experiential consequences', he means that we cannot deduce
other propositions with which percepts are directly associated. He appears to imply that from perceptual statements
we need not deduce practical consequences, for these *are*
directly associated with percepts, which is their meaning;
while from general statements perceptual statements must
be deducible, for their meaning consists in percepts indirectly
associated with them through the perceptual statements.
While I think that this is what James's view amounts to, I
do not mean to suggest that in his own terminology he did
make a sharp distinction between percepts and perceptual
statements. For he has no clear distinction between the
cognitive and the non-cognitive, between knowledge as
strictly judicative and feelings as emphatically non-cognitive,
between thought-signs and the material quality of thought-
signs. It is here that the misunderstanding of Peirce lies.
James did not see the necessity, when he read Peirce's 1878
paper, of interpreting the sensible translation of a name in
terms of a clearly defined formula; and the reason why he
did not see it was that he did not understand the papers of
1868. The theory of knowledge set forth in these papers is

[1] *Meaning of Truth*, pp. 40-41.

inseparable from Peirce's pragmatism and explains at once why the 'meaning' for him could not possibly be what it was for James.[1] He acutely and simply places his finger on the essential difference between James's pragmatic theory of meaning and his own when, in 1905, he says that James's definition "differs from mine only in that he does not restrict the 'meaning', that is, the ultimate logical interpretant, as I do, to a habit [interpretable as we have suggested], but allows percepts, that is, complex feelings endowed with compulsiveness, to be such" (5.494).

I want to call attention to a statement in Peirce by means of which we can express in another way James's relation to him. It is: "The Immediate Object of all knowledge and all thought is, in the last analysis, the Percept. This doctrine in no wise conflicts with Pragmaticism, which holds that the . . . Interpretant of all thought proper is Conduct. Nothing is more indispensable to a sound epistemology than a crystal clear discrimination between the Object and the Interpretant of knowledge" (4.539). It may be granted that Peirce's own distinction between object and interpretant is not always crystal clear, and that 'immediate object' sometimes means a sign and sometimes (as here) a 'percept'.[2] What I wish to point out, however, is that 'percept' may have two different meanings: (i) a quality regarded as the object of a perception, (ii) a quality regarded as a feeling associated with a perception. Strictly, perhaps, these are

[1] In harmony with the view underlying critical common-sensism, Peirce holds that pragmatism emphasizes especially "the point that there is no intellectual value in mere feeling *per se*, but that the whole function of thinking consists in the regulation of conduct" (Review of Engl. trans. of Wundt's *Prin. of Physiol. Psych.*, in *New York Post*, July 21, 1905, p. 4, and *Nation*, Vol. 81, 1905, p. 56). Compare this with the following by James: ". . . Whenever we intellectualize a relatively pure experience, we ought to do so for the sake of redescending to the purer or more concrete level again ; and . . . if an intellect stays aloft among its abstract terms and generalized relations, and does not reinsert itself with its conclusions into some particular point of the immediate stream of life, it fails to finish out its function and leaves its normal race unrun" (*Essays in Radical Empiricism*, p. 97).

[2] Cf. pp. 109-110 above.

not two different senses but rather two different points of
view from which a percept can be regarded; and although
in the above-quoted statement it has the first sense, it often
has for Peirce the second, as in the quoted statement at the
end of the last paragraph. Most often, however, it makes
little difference for Peirce which of the two senses it is used
in, since perception is a "two-sided consciousness" (5.607),
and the presence in it of the 'sense of duality' assures us that
in actual consciousness the two senses of 'percept' are
indissolubly connected. But we mention them only in order
to return to James. For we may now say that when 'percept', as the 'meaning' in James's pragmatism, is used by
him in the first sense, he confuses object and interpretant,
pragmatism properly being concerned with a certain kind
of *interpretant*; and when 'percept' as the meaning of a
statement is used by him in the second sense, he confuses
the *emotional* and the *logical* interpretant.

From the view that the 'experiential consequences' are
percepts, it is clear why James made the supplementary
emphasis that they must be 'particular'. For Peirce the
meaning of a proposition consists in a translation which is a
general formula, a formula for an *indefinite class* of confirmable consequences; for James the meaning of a proposition
consists in 'some' confirmable consequence—where by
'confirmable' he would mean 'associated with percepts'.
Whereas for Peirce the translating formula may be given for
any proposition, including a perceptual proposition, for
James the perceptual propositions would seem to be not
pragmatically translatable. And James is vague on the
question whether the 'meaning' consists in the *sum* of the
particular consequences, or in a *given* one, or in *any* one
so long as it is one.

43. **General Remarks on Parts I and II.** What Peirce
really thought of Jamesean pragmatism is not conveyed too
convincingly by his public statements, and the same holds
true for his opinion of other pragmatists, for instance,

Schiller and Papini. He professes enthusiasm for "the admirably clear and brilliant thinker", Schiller (5.414), and says that "in the main, I much admire Papini's presentation of the subject" (5.495). But one feels that when in 1905 he makes the announcement of "the birth of the word 'pragmaticism', which is ugly enough to be safe from kidnappers" (5.414), it is James, Papini and Schiller whom he has in mind no less than the amateurs of the literary journals. Despite his obvious attempts to show generosity to these philosophers, whether in public print or in papers designed for publication, he cannot conceal his distaste for their more or less emotional treatment of pragmatism. James, he says, "remodelled the matter" (6.482); Papini, surpassing in originality Schiller, who had offered seven different definitions of pragmatism (see 5.494-495), "discovered, to the delight of the Pragmatist school, that this doctrine was incapable of definition, which would certainly seem to distinguish it from every other doctrine in whatever branch of science" (6.482).[1]

Peirce's empiricism, as distinguished from that of his contemporary pragmatists and positivists, rests on a powerful analysis of knowledge, of meaning, and, in general, of signs. Unless it is examined with the roots of these doctrines borne in mind, it cannot be properly understood and the important characteristics differentiating it from other empiricisms will be obscured. Some years ago Messrs. A. E. Blumberg and H. Feigl wrote, in a well-known article summarizing the movement of 'logical positivism' (now better designated as 'logical empiricism'), that "by means of the theory of knowledge thus constructed, logical positivism goes beyond the Comtean and pragmatic rejection of metaphysics as useless or superfluous and shows that the propositions of metaphysics, in most senses of the term, are, strictly speaking, meaningless."[2] This is typical of the widespread ignorance (prevailing even to the present when

----

[1] It was when Papini made this 'discovery', Peirce reveals in 6.490, that he decided to change 'pragmatism' to 'pragmaticism'.

[2] "Logical Positivism", *Journal of Philosophy*, Vol. 28 (1931), p. 282.

the Collected Papers have been published) of Peirce's pragmatism and of his empiricism as a whole. Whatever the interpretation may be of the Comtean criterion of 'admissibility', we have seen that on the Peircean criterion the 'admissible' is the confirmable and the unconfirmable the meaningless, and that Peirce specifically applies the latter designation to much of traditional metaphysics. It is worth noting that the development of the principle of verifiability in the last few years has been in a Peircean direction. The most recent statements of the logical empiricist theory of meaning [1] sharply distinguish verifiability from conclusive verifiability; and in general it may be said that the relation between the logical positivism delineated in the Blumberg-Feigl article and that of the present day, is analogous to the relation between sensational positivism and Peircean pragmatism.

Another instance of how insufficient analysis of Peirce's theory of knowledge may permit a loose judgment is furnished by some remarks of Mr. R. B. Braithwaite in his otherwise discerning review of the Collected Papers. He says, "Peirce only differs from the orthodox account [of scientific procedure] in classifying the thinking of the hypothesis as itself a form of ampliative reasoning, and this difference is, I think, merely a verbal one, namely, that of whether 'an act of *insight* . . .' (5.181) is or is not called reasoning." [2] Now it may be that if what we are concerned with in scientific procedure is the hypothesis itself and not the way in which a mind arrived at it, Mr. Braithwaite is correct, although Peirce would doubtless hold that to better understand the process of abduction is both to better understand and to promote scientific method. We must point out, at any rate, that on our interpretation the concept of abduction, far from being a matter of small importance or of exclusively psychological bearing, is the very foundation of fallibilism. For on the Peircean analysis the bulk of thought,

[1] E.g. R. Carnap, " Testability and Meaning ", *Philosophy of Science*, 1936, 1937.   [2] *Mind*, N.S., Vol. 43 (1934), p. 510.

and all of thought in so far as it can be called 'new', is abductive in character; and every thought or positive judgment retains the status of a hypothesis capable of further confirmation. We have tried to show how large fallibilism looms in Peirce's empiricism. But it is of prime importance in its own right. Professor Dewey has suggested—and Peirce himself appears to have realized it—that fallibilism is of deeply revolutionary import; that the doctrine which calls for eternal scrutiny and correction is not destructive of a revolutionary ideology but wholly profitable to it, and has an immense moral significance.[1]

Peircean empiricism as revealed in these two Parts is a realistic and fallibilistic empiricism. It affirms the essential cognitive soundness of common sense and the artificial character of traditional scepticisms. By its analysis of knowledge in terms of the theory of signs it replaces naïve by critical common-sensism, the core of which is fallibilism. The more exact and more consciously methodological aspect of this empiricism is the doctrine of pragmatism,[2] which, by formulating a theory of meaning, concludes that all synthetic propositions are empirical propositions. By showing that translations must be general, not atomic or instantaneous, pragmatism introduces realism; and realism, in the form of prescriptive translations, further guarantees fallibilism. The view-point from which Peirce's empiricism may be approached is thus to a certain extent arbitrary; for from whichever angle we start we embrace the whole inevitably. This fundamental unity and cohesiveness is concealed by the fragmentary character of his remains. It is as the profoundest analyst in American philosophy that Peirce should continue to be known; but only by close attention to his writings can the significance of his analyses be appreciated and their results profitably employed.

[1] See his review of the Collected Papers, *New Republic*, Feb. 3, 1936.
[2] ". . . Pragmatism . . . is only an endeavour to give the philosophy of common sense a more exact development. . . ." (Review of Wundt, *loc. cit.*).

PART III

THE FORMAL AND THE EMPIRICAL

PRAGMATISM is the doctrine that all synthetic statements, all statements of fact, are empirical. Critical common-sensism is the doctrine that all empirical statements are at bottom statements of common sense in varying degrees of abstraction, and that no such statement is conclusively verifiable. Our account of Peirce's empiricism would be inadequate if we did not consider in detail what his opinions are on those realms of inquiry containing other than synthetic statements. In logic and mathematics there occur 'truths' commonly acknowledged to be necessary. It is incumbent upon an empiricist to explain this necessity, and in the present case, to exhibit its compatibility with pragmatism and fallibilism. If I speak to a great extent of Peirce's views with respect to *sentences* it is because (as it seems to me) only in this way can the character of his or any other empiricism be expressed with relative exactness.

As a connecting link between the previous Parts and this one, let us recall that Peirce called pragmatism 'the logic of abduction', or, what is the same thing, the logic of hypothesis. We interpreted this broadly to mean that, since on Peirce's view every synthetic statement is a hypothesis, pragmatism is the logic of synthetic statements. We quoted Peirce as having written to James that "pragmatism . . . is one of the propositions of logic". Clearly in order to understand this we need to know what Peirce's conception is of the nature of logic. There are a number of other remarks which go to show that he thought of pragmatism as a logical doctrine. "Pragmaticism", he says, "is a theory of logical analysis, or true definition" (6.490). Elsewhere he calls it a "maxim of logic" (5.18) [1] and a "logical rule" (5.465). In

---

[1] Cf. Letter to Ladd-Franklin (*J. of Phil.*, 1916, p. 720).

1908 he recalls that when he originally enunciated pragmatism in 1878, "the doctrine attracted no particular attention, for, as I had remarked in my opening sentence, very few
people care for logic" (6.482). He also claims (4.534, 534 n.)
that pragmatism is "closely connected" with his system of
graphs, a system of diagrammatization "by means of which
any course of thought can be represented with exactitude"
(4.530). The precise character of this connection is obscure,
but we may be able to see it in a general sense. Most significant is the statement, in a letter to Ladd-Franklin, that
"pragmatism is one of the results of my study of the formal
laws of signs. . . ."[1]

44. **The Nature of Logic.** 'Logic' is understood by Peirce
in a broad and a narrow sense, as he himself recognizes (1.444).
The latter, that of his earlier writings, is the traditional sense,
and treats "of the formal conditions of the truth of symbols"
(1.559), or in other words, of the conditions under which
conclusions may legitimately (in accordance with the pro-
fessed purpose of the argument) be derived from premisses.
Between logic in this sense and logic in the broader sense
there is no conflict, for the simple reason that the former
later becomes a branch of the latter. In this broader sense
logic is nothing else than the general theory of signs, which
Peirce calls, after Locke,[2] 'semiotic' (e.g. 1.191, 1.444, 2.227).
Semiotic, a field in which Peirce was a pioneer,[3] is the theory
of signs in all their aspects; it is the "philosophy of representation" (1.539). He also calls semiotic "the doctrine of
the essential nature and fundamental varieties of possible
semiosis" (5.488), and a considerable descriptive element
seems to be suggested. Peirce could profitably have distinguished between descriptive and analytical semiotic, the
former an empirical science concerned with the facts of the
sign-situation. Judging from its subdivisions, semiotic is

---

[1] *Ibid.*   [2] *Essay*, II, xxi, 4.
[3] ". . . Or rather a backwoodsman." ". . . I find the field too vast,
the labour too great, for a first-comer " (5.488).

essentially an inquiry of analysis, and Peirce says that it is the study of representation "so far as representation can be known without any gathering of special facts beyond our ordinary daily life" (1.539). Sometimes he conceives of it so broadly as to say that "logic . . . wholly consists, one might almost say, in exactitude of thought" (2.223). On the view of logic as semiotic, Peirce is untroubled by the question whether logic has as its subject-matter thoughts or words, since thoughts too are, as we have seen, conceived of as signs. He cannot admit "that logic is primarily conversant with unexpressed thought and only secondarily with language" (2.461 n.); for language, in the sense of signs, is "the woof and warp of all thought and all research" (2.220).

Semiotic or logic has three branches: 'speculative grammar' (which he sometimes also calls 'pure grammar', 'formal grammar', and 'stoicheiology' or 'stecheotic'), 'critical logic' (this alone constitutes 'logic' in the earlier and narrower sense, and is also called 'critic'), and 'speculative rhetoric' (also called 'formal rhetoric', 'pure rhetoric', and 'methodeutic'). Peirce is far from clear on details in the definition of these subdivisions, and consequently on their interrelationship. But in work the influence of which is being increasingly felt in contemporary investigation this is excusable, especially since the general distinctions are clear and details can be filled in. Roughly speaking, speculative grammar is concerned with the analysis and classification of *all* signs; critical logic, with the analysis and classification of a special category of signs, arguments; and speculative rhetoric, with "the methods that ought to be pursued in the investigation, in the exposition, and in the application of truth" (1.191). Critical logic assumes and depends upon speculative grammar, speculative rhetoric assumes and depends upon both of the others. According to Peirce, each of these three divisions lays down "formal conditions" for the attainment of its ends (1.559), and semiotic in general is the "quasi-necessary or formal" doctrine of signs (2.227). He is here using 'formal' in a sense somewhat different from that in which it is used when we contrast traditional 'formal' logic with 'scientific method', for the latter would be subsumed under speculative rhetoric. The interpretation of his usage is made more difficult by the fact that he also calls logic or semiotic the "science of the general *necessary* laws of Signs" (2.93, my ital.; cf. 4.9). I think that what he intends here by 'formal', 'quasi-necessary' and 'necessary' is 'standard': the formal conditions are standard conditions, in the sense that certain considerations determine them to be regulative or legislative. For he also speaks of the three departments as concerned with the 'general conditions' of significance, validity, and truth, respectively. Thus speculative grammar will be concerned with a set of regulative or standard conditions ('rules') under which signs are to be classified, and under which any semiotic relation is to be defined; critical logic will be concerned with the standard conditions, or rules, under which inferences are to be classified and weighed; speculative rhetoric will be concerned with the standard conditions, or methods, under which we can be led to determine the actual truth of propositions. We may add that the considerations determining a 'standard' set of conditions will differ in each of these divisions. In speculative grammar, for example, it is clear that an important consideration is traditional usage; and this branch of logic accordingly involves a greater conventional element than do the other two. I do not care to discuss this matter of what determines formal or standard conditions in speculative grammar and in speculative rhetoric, because Peirce is too fragmentary in proportion to the magnitude of the subject and the discussion would consist largely of conjecture. In critical logic, however, the question of regulative or standard conditions is traditionally known as the question of validity, and I do want to consider the view of Peirce. But first a few remarks on the divisions of semiotic in regard, not to what *determines* the rules they lay down, but to the *kind* of rules they lay down.

Speculative grammar "has for its task to ascertain what

must be true of the representamen [sign] used by every scientific intelligence in order that they may embody any *meaning*" (2.229); it is "the general theory of the nature and meanings of signs" (1.191). The contexts seem to indicate that 'meaning' is used in what we have called its general sense (cf. § 32), that is, as synonymous with the meaning- or sign-relation; so that speculative grammar would be concerned with the conditions under which the various signs function as signs. Speculative grammar is "the doctrine of the general conditions of symbols and other signs having the significant character" (2.93). Thus, for instance, the division of all signs into icons, indices and symbols (cf. § 47) belongs to speculative grammar. Critical logic is concerned with the types and degree of validity of inferences. Its classification of inferences is effected by laying down rules that define and govern them. For Peirce the analysis of both necessary and probable inference belongs to critical logic, though we shall see later that other semiotic issues are involved, chiefly belonging to speculative grammar. Speculative rhetoric, including what is ordinarily known as scientific method, and in particular the logic of discovery, is the study of methods for attaining 'truth'. But it is not confined to a study of methods for empirical science: Peirce regards the problem of discovering and perfecting techniques in mathematics as equally part of it. ". . . One of the main problems of logic" is "that of producing a method for the discovery of methods in mathematics" (3.364; cf. 3.454). In accordance with this broad conception of speculative rhetoric, it is in one place described as being concerned with "those general conditions under which a problem presents itself for solution" (3.430).

   In lieu of detailed examination of these divisions of logic we may make two or three general points. (1) What relation has the present classification to the conception of logic as 'syntax'? [1] General logical syntax abstains completely from any consideration of the conceptual content of signs and

[1] See R. Carnap, *The Logical Syntax of Language.*

confines itself to such matters as the classification of signs, the classification of types of systems (or 'languages', as Prof. Carnap prefers) in which signs occur, and in general the analysis of the properties of possible systems. On this conception we have not only general syntax but the syntax or logic of a given system, consisting in the formulation of its rules and in the set of all statements describing its properties. Peirce's semiotic is a much wider conception of logic than is syntax, which corresponds to no single division of it, except perhaps speculative grammar. But it is likely that speculative grammar would also consider questions that are today regarded as falling into 'semantics'. Semantics, unlike syntax, which confines itself to the analysis of sign-properties exclusively, analyzes the relations between signs and that which they designate; whence arises a special set of semantical concepts, such as 'definition', 'truth', 'satisfaction' (as when we say "the object a satisfies the description 'such-and-such'"), 'designation', and so on,—all of which concern some kind of relation between signs and what is signified by them.[1] Thus Peirce deals at length with the problem of 'the nature of propositions', which is largely semantical, as a problem of speculative grammar. It may be that he originally intended to limit speculative grammar to syntax. But it seems quite certain that he would regard semantical questions as within the domain of logic, and if they were excluded from speculative grammar they would appear to have no place in any of the three divisions. (2) Although the present-day view of semiotic might alter Peirce's classification in favour of a more sharply defined number of divisions, it would not very seriously modify his fundamental contributions to semiotic. He understood the primacy of speculative grammar, holding that the other departments of logic involved it. And while he never

---

[1] The inauguration of the field of formal semantics, as that word is understood in contemporary logical inquiry, is due primarily to A. Tarski. See, e.g., " Grundlegung der wissenschaftlichen Semantik ", in *Actes du Congrès International de Philosophie Scientifique,* fasc. III.

specifically analyzed the sense in which critical logic is grammatical or syntactical, the concept of the leading principle, which is the fundamental concept of critical logic, is today a most general fundamental concept of logical syntax. (3) Whatever the precise limits of semiotic, it is not difficult to see that in logic as thus conceived the doctrine of pragmatism bulks large. Pragmatism may be regarded as that branch of semiotic which studies the conditions governing the significance of synthetic propositions, and the question of which division of semiotic it actually falls into is relatively unimportant. A study of this kind in itself comprehends a vast field, and contemporary investigations are largely concerned with attacking the difficulties in formulation and expression that it involves. That Peirce should have been more detailed in his conception of pragmatism as essentially an inquiry of logic, is too much to ask. The very treatment of the doctrine as one falling in this domain, like the broad and fertile conception of logic itself, deserves much commendation.[1]

So much for Peirce's opinions on the general scope of logic. I want to turn, as I said, to the subject of what constitutes validity in inference. This problem will lead us continuously into the subjects of the succeeding sections. We shall see that while we appear at first to be in the realm of critical logic alone, grammatical or syntactical elements become increasingly prominent. Speculative rhetoric will enter in the section on induction, though in its broader sense it will already have been present during the discussion of 'ideal experimentation' in mathematics.

In the "Minute Logic" of 1902 Peirce makes a historical

---

[1] Prof. C. W. Morris, in his monograph "Foundations of the Theory of Signs" (in *International Encyclopedia of Unified Science*, Vol. I, no. 2, 1938), conceives of semiotic as divisible into the three branches of 'syntactics' (which is larger than syntax), 'semantics', and 'pragmatics'. Syntactics studies the relations of signs to one another ; semantics, the relations of signs to their objects ; pragmatics, the relations of signs to their interpreters (cf. *ibid.*, pp. 6-8, 16). Professor Morris builds on the fundamental semiotic conception of Peirce, and lays the foundations for a complex science of signs with the help of recent investigations (cf. *ibid.*, p. 59, for a selected bibliography).

review of various opinions on the question of validity. I shall summarize the essential points that he makes in this review, and then consider his own opinion. To the theories that sound reasoning depends upon divine inspiration, religious revelation or ecclesiastical authority (2.21, 2.72), or on the amount of influence which the reasoning contributes toward maintenance of the existing social order (2.71), Peirce gives comparatively little attention.[1] The basing of (critical) logic upon a system of metaphysics he holds to be a "vicious order of thought" (2.38). But the reason he gives for this is not quite the same as might be given today. For he believes that, contrariwise, metaphysics ought to be "founded on logic", as in Aristotle and Kant. I am unable to understand what it means for metaphysics to be founded on logic, unless it means that, owing to the difficulty of the subject, metaphysicians ought to be good reasoners. In one place Peirce seems to suggest that philosophical problems should be treated by the application of logical analysis (3.425). But as a rule he is remote from this opinion (e.g. 1.624-5, 2.168, 2.36-8). Much more important is his emphasis that the subject-matter and validity of logic are independent of psychology. The view, made popular by Mill, that logic's "theoretic grounds are wholly borrowed from psychology",[2] had to a certain extent been controverted, Peirce points out, by Kant and Herbart; and Venn, though a follower of Mill, did not assume it. Peirce himself, however, was among the first to dwell consciously and at length on its refutation.

"Logic is not the science of how we *do* think; but, in such sense as it can be said to deal with thinking at all, it only determines how we *ought* to think; nor how we ought to think in conformity with usage, but how we ought to think in order to think what is *true*. That a premiss should be pertinent to such a conclusion, it is requisite that it should relate, not to how we think, but to the necessary connections of different sorts of *fact*" (2.52).

[1] There are scattered references in the Papers to the form of this view held by Pearson. Cf. also *Pop. Sci. Mo.*, Vol. 58 (1900-1901).
[2] *Examination of Hamilton's Philosophy*, 5th ed., p. 461.

"How we think, therefore, is utterly irrelevant to logical inquiry" (2.55). (Cf. 5.157, 2.252, 2.210, 5.329.) [1]

A subtle intrusion of psychological considerations into logic lies in the view that the usages of speech determine the principles of logic (2.67). Though Peirce does not clearly distinguish two forms which this may take, he nevertheless implicitly refutes both. One—that which he is most conscious of—is that logical principles are based on ordinary grammatical principles; and against this he urges that those who hold it tacitly identify all language with the relatively small group of Indo-European languages. [2] The other recognizes the multiplicity of grammatical forms, and holds that there is no one logic but rather logics relative to these forms. This is a crude version of the argument for 'non-Aristotelian logic', and what Peirce has to say on this subject is best deferred to § 46 below. An argument by Peirce against the dependence of logic upon 'epistemology' amounts, I take it, to the declaration that epistemology, at least as traditionally conceived, is no autonomous discipline but consists either in general logic itself or in a branch of descriptive psychology. (Cf. 2.62-65.)

Peirce's own conception of logical validity is specifically directed against another, which assumes two forms, and

[1] In earlier writings Peirce is not so emphatic, and in 1883 he says: ". . . Formal logic must not be too purely formal; it must represent a fact of psychology, or else it is in danger of degenerating into a mathematical recreation" (2.710).

Peirce has a comment on Dewey: "[Professor Dewey] seems to regard what he calls ' logic ' as a natural history of thought. If such a natural history can be worked out, it will undoubtedly form valuable knowledge. . . . [But] if calling the new natural history by the name of ' logic ' (a suspicious beginning) is to be a way of prejudging the question of whether or not there be a logic which is more than a mere natural history, inasmuch as it would pronounce one proceeding of thought to be sound and valid and another to be otherwise, then we should regard this appropriation of that name to be itself fresh confirmation of our opinion of the urgent need of such a normative science at this day" (Review of *Studies in Logical Theory*, in *Nation*, 1904, Vol. 79, p. 220).

[2] In 2.358 he says: ". . . The entire purpose of deductive logic is to ascertain the necessary conditions of the truth of signs, without any regard to the accidents of Indo-European grammar. . . ."

which he is much concerned to refute. In one of these forms it is known since Aristotle as the criterion of 'self-evidence'. Peirce's distaste for it, which we have more than once described previously, is based chiefly on the ground that it fosters individualism in inquiry. Against the other form in which this criterion is stated, the same charge is not so easily brought. For it holds that the ultimate test of valid inference is an immediate, instinctive feeling of 'rationality'. This *Gefühl*-criterion Peirce associates most commonly with the name of Sigwart (5.85, 2.19-20, 2.209), and his respect for it is heightened by the fact that he finds it in Schröder. "Schröder", he says, "followed Sigwart in his most fundamental ideas of logic" (5.85), defining "logical consequentiality as *a compulsion of thought*" (3.432). The tradition that has arisen from the *Gefühl*-criterion, which is after all a species of psychologism, Peirce dubs the 'German' theory of logic, and the contrary theory, his own in the guise of another worthy tradition, is the "English, objective conception of logic" (2.185). The German doctrine supposes a non-cognitive faculty as final authority, and while this faculty appears to be social in that it is instinctively common in members of the human race, its claim to authority can be tested by nothing more than reiteration, by advice to exercise one's powers of rational insight,—that is, it cannot be tested at all. Peirce arrives at the expression of his own, the 'English' view, by making the criterion of logicality state the conditions of its own testing: Reasoning is valid when the facts are such as the conclusion represents them to be, whenever the facts are also such as the premisses represent them to be. The guarantee of validity is the *fact* that the conclusion is true when the premisses are true.

"Every reasoning holds out some expectation. Either, for example, it professes to be such that if the premisses are true, the conclusion will always be true, or to be such that the conclusion will usually be true if the premisses are true, or to be a method of procedure which must ultimately lead to the truth,[1] or makes some other such promise. If the facts bear out that promise, then, say the English, the reasoning is good. But if the facts violate the promise, the reasoning is bad, no matter how deliberately human reason may have approved of it. For the sole purpose of reasoning is, not to gratify a sense of rationality analogous to taste or conscience, but to ascertain the Truth. . . ." (2.153).

Thus in the case of necessary inference, which professes to be such that in any given class of such inferences the conclusions are always true when the premisses are true, and in the case of probable inference, which professes to be such that the conclusions are true a certain proportion of all the times the premisses are true, the criterion of validity is the actual fact that the conclusion *is* always, or *is* sometimes, true. ". . . The rationality of a reasoning, in the sense of that character of a reasoning at which the reasoner aims, does consist precisely in that necessary accord of the facts with the professions of the argument. . . ." (2.159).

But Peirce does not want to neglect the psychological aspect of reasoning, and in fact he bolsters his standard of validity by showing that this standard is the one tacitly assumed when men perform their multitudinous inferences. Instead of assuming an *instinct* of rationality by means of which reasonings are trusted, he holds that it is on *habits* of reasoning, tested by experience, that we rely. These habits are formed by our continually representing to ourselves what would ensue when we make certain suppositions, that is, what in fact would have to be the case, or probably be the case, if certain premisses were true. We form habits of reasoning by diagramming facts in the imagination. In so doing we need not exhaust all possible particular cases in order to perceive a necessary or probable relationship, but

---

[1] These three ' professions ', roughly described here, are those of necessary inference, probable deduction (probable inference proper) and induction, respectively (cf. § 50). In this section we mean by ' probable inference ' the second of these, but most often, up to § 49, we use it loosely, as covering induction too.

select cases that, by their generality, give us assurance of their representative character. This notion of imaginative experimentation by means of which we form the habits of, and check on the soundness of, our reasoning, is a pervasive and favourite theme of Peirce. When applying it to complex necessary reasoning such as mathematics—and we shall have more to say about it when we discuss this subject—he calls it "ideal experimentation" (3.528) or "abstractive observation" (2.227). The habits formed as a result of continually representing to ourselves experiential situations connected in certain ways are the factors that determine the validity of all reasoning. For there are (logically) good and bad habits, and the question of the logical goodness or badness of these habits is not itself a psychological matter (cf. 5.365). It is a question of whether they do in fact lead to true conclusions from true premisses. And the habits that we form are on the whole good habits, because we continue to improve them. In so far as they *are* habits of reasoning that *do* enable us to draw correct conclusions, they constitute our *logica utens*, the acriticial and implicit logic of the common man. It is when these habits become expressed linguistically as rules of inference, or conscious leading principles, that our logic ceases to be a *logica utens* and becomes a *logica docens*, or formulated, scientific and critical logic (cf. 2.186 ff.).

The presence of the foregoing empirical or pragmatic strain in Peirce's critical logic is perhaps wholesome as opposed to the subjectivist criterion of an infallible rationality-instinct. But it is open to serious difficulties, because it is not confined, as it should be, to a genetic account of what is involved in the reasoning process and how good reasoning comes to be distinguished from bad reasoning. Psychogenetically, the criterion of the validity of our arguments consists in the actual fact of whether or not the conclusions of these arguments are true when the premisses are true. Logically, however, the mere criterion of empirical success is not adequate to explain necessary reasoning. In the "Minute Logic" (and elsewhere) Peirce overlooks this distinction, and his confusion admits into empiricism a cancerous element. Necessary reasoning is there simply a limiting case of probable reasoning; since in the latter conclusions are in fact true a portion of the times that the premisses are true, indefinite increase in the magnitude of this portion is regarded as an approach to demonstration (cf. also 2.694). The application of a single standard to both necessary and probable inference, allowing for a difference in degree but not in kind, is a step in the direction of sensationalism. For it follows that the principles of logic are 'necessary' merely in the sense that they have never failed to be verified. And in admitting so unsatisfactory a consequence into a system of empiricism we open the door to a contrary contention, that in view of the indubitability of necessary inference, the principles of logic must be a priori laws of thought. We shall see that the application of the empirical standard of validity defines probable inference and constitutes a major contribution by Peirce to the subject. But its application to all inference misinterprets the character of necessary reasoning and identifies it with reasoning having the probability 1. That such reasoning should always lead to true conclusions from true premisses is not a sufficient condition for its definition. Peirce himself on occasion realized this (cf. 2.369, 5.24). An attractive explanation for his advocacy of the view in question would be that the distinction was not essential for the semi-pedagogical purposes of the "Minute Logic". But it is not characteristic of Peirce to modify for special purposes views that he would otherwise have considered important: even in his most popular writings he prefers to sacrifice interest to a high degree of accuracy. We shall see that apologies are not really necessary, and that a more fundamental conception of validity can be discovered in Peirce. By giving his treatment of inference in terms of leading principles linguistically expressed, the view we regard as objectionable can be better stated and at the same time the means of correcting it revealed. Unfortunately, we do not thereby rule this view out of existence: Peirce seems never to have been aware of the conflict.

45. **Leading Principles.** Let us speak, not of this or that inference, but of *classes* of inference; where by 'class' we shall understand "the *total* of whatever objects there may be . . . which are *of a certain description*" (1.204; my ital.). Then, in whatever way we differentiate necessary from probable inference, we shall at least say that an instance of necessary inference belongs to a different class of inferences from an instance of probable inference.

> " . . . In a logical mind an argument is always conceived as a member of a *genus* of arguments all constructed in the same way, and such that, when their premisses are real facts, their conclusions are so also. If the argument is demonstrative, then this is always so; if it is only probable, then it is for the most part so" (2.649).
> "To say that an argumentation is valid is to say that it is as truthful as it pretends to be. It is essential to reasoning . . . that it should be accompanied by the reflection that it belongs to a class of reasonings, few or none of which lead from truth to falsity. All reasoning, therefore, makes a pretension; and if that pretension is true, the reasoning is *valid*" (2.446).

In view of the above definition of 'class', where emphasis is laid not merely on a collection but on a collection of a definite description, the difference between the first of these quotations (649), in which Peirce speaks of a *genus* of arguments, and the second (446), in which he speaks of a *class* of arguments, is not important for our present purpose. We must bear in mind, however, that the latter, extensional emphasis, is much more important for probable than for necessary inference, and that the gist of Peirce's distinction will be found to consist in this point.

The defining principle of a class of inferences is called the leading principle of that class. A leading principle is a rule of inference, without which any inference is impossible, such principles usually being linguistic formulations of the habits employed in ordinary reasonings (3.164). An argument is valid if its leading principle is 'true' (2.463) (or in the words of the second quotation above, if its 'pretension' to lead to

true conclusions from true premisses is true). The leading
principle of an argument must be distinguished from the
premisses of that argument (2.465). Both premiss and
leading principle must be 'true' in order that an argument
should be valid (2.464). Let the premiss of an argument be
designated by 'P', the conclusion by 'C', the argument being
'P∴C'. Let the leading principle of this argument be
designated by 'P→C', which may be read 'P implies C',
abbreviated as 'M' (cf. 3.165; 2.466). Now when we assert
the argument 'P∴C', M is not expressed; but it is tacitly
assumed, else the argument cannot be valid. But we can
have the following argument: 'M and P∴C'. Thus a leading
principle may be added to the premisses of an argument;
and in the same way, a premiss may not be expressed as a
premiss but may be assumed as part of the leading principle.
In the argument 'Smith is a man, ∴ Smith is mortal', the
additional assumption usually made as premiss, 'All men
are mortal', is part of the leading principle. But we can
never entirely reduce the premisses to the leading principle,
or entirely reduce the leading principle to premisses. For
in the case of 'M and P∴C', this too has its leading principle
of inference, which may be designated by 'L' (cf. 3.168,
2.466). Here a fundamental distinction comes to be made
between two types of leading principles. 'Smith is a man
∴ Smith is mortal' is not a necessary argument; but if its
leading principle 'All men are mortal' is added to the
premisses and assumed as true, it becomes a necessary
argument. The principle of this (L) is: '(P→C, and P)→C'.
When this in turn is added to the premisses we get 'L and M
and P∴C'. But this does not differ from 'M and P∴C'.
The premisses of the latter argument are of themselves
sufficient to determine C necessarily, and therefore already
contain L. And the former argument, though it explicitly
contains L among the premisses, will nevertheless still have
L as its leading principle. A principle "which contains no
fact not implied or observable in the premisses" (3.166),
"which cannot be eliminated" from the leading principle

(2.466), Peirce calls a 'logical principle'. Thus in the fore-going L is a logical leading principle. At this point we may quote Peirce himself, from the article 'Leading Principle' in Baldwin's Dictionary.

> "Suppose that the leading principle involves two proposi-tions, L and L', and suppose that there are three premisses, P, P', P''; and let C signify the . . . conclusion. . . . Then, from the five premisses L, L', P, P', P'', the infer-ence to C would be necessary; but it would not be so from L, L', P', P'' alone, for, if it were, P would not really act as a premiss at all. From P' and P'' as the sole premisses, C would follow, if the leading principle consisted of L, L' and P. Or from the four premisses L', P, P', P'', the same conclusion would follow if L alone were the leading prin-ciple. What, then, could be the leading principle of the inference of C from all five propositions L, L', P, P', P'', taken as premisses? It would be something already implied in those premisses; and it might be almost any general proposition so implied. Leading principles are, therefore, of two classes; and any leading principle whose truth is implied in the premisses of every inference which it governs is called a 'logical' (or, less appropriately, a *formal*) leading principle; while a leading principle whose truth is not implied in the premisses is called a 'factual' (or *material*) leading principle" (2.589).

Thus the ordinary logical principles of inference are logical leading principles; while (to use the above example) 'All men are mortal' is a material leading principle. With greater economy we may now express (i) The criterion of validity: the validity of an argument is determined not by *Gefühl* but by the objective consideration of whether its lead-ing principle is 'true'; (ii) The distinction between necessary and probable arguments: a necessary argument is one governed by a logical leading principle, a probable argument is one governed by a material leading principle.

The details of probable inference will be dealt with later. One point must be noted here. Peirce speaks of the leading principle as a 'proposition' and as 'true'. This would imply that leading principles are sentences or assertions in the same sense as the sentences constituting the argument. If this were the case, there would be no point in using the concept of the leading principle at all. We should speak only of the sentences essential to an inference, and not go beyond classifying inferences as either complete or enthymematic. What follows will reveal that Peirce tacitly recognized this, and that his use of 'proposition' and 'true' to characterize leading principles is largely for the sake of convenience. The usage may seem to be justified to the extent that premisses may function as leading principles. But in so far as they do so function, they have a different status from that which they have as premisses. The expressions regarded as leading principles may from another viewpoint be regarded as assertions, true or false: they would then ipso facto belong to an inferential system with leading principles of its own. These considerations, which have been developed in detail only by comparatively recent logical theory, are not latent in the mind of Peirce. But let it be remembered that he looks most often on leading principles as habits that need not be expressed in order to be regulative of inference. Clearly a habit is not true or false: it can at most be called 'successful', 'useful' or 'desirable'. Those leading principles which he regards as purely conventional[1] have a fortiori no truth-value or assertiveness. With respect to the material leading principle, which governs probable arguments, it does not really act as a universal synthetic statement, the form in which Peirce most often states it. It acts as a propositional function the values of which must be statistically ascertained for that proportion which is true.[2] When we assumed in the preceding paragraph that its transfer to the premisses made the argument demonstrative, we assumed for simplicity's sake that it was in fact true for all values (and in any case it would have to have been statistically determined for some values in order to be a proposition and function as premiss).

---

[1] Cf. 4.361 and 4.361 n. For examples of such conventional principles, occurring in systems created by Peirce, cf. 4.485 ff., 4.359-363.
[2] Cf. p. 242, note 1.

Purely logical principles, Peirce holds, are "empty, or merely formal propositions" (3.168). And he also says, "We cannot recognize logical formulae as, properly speaking, assertions" (2.451). For if such a formula "be intended to state anything about real things, it is quite unintelligible" (2.315). Peirce suggests in one place that any such principle, in so far as it has any signification at all, "must be understood to mean something about symbols" (2.315). In the context what he seems to mean by this is that, for instance, the principle of identity 'A is A' (his example) defines the relation of reflexiveness; for he says, "the substantive verb 'is' expresses one of those relations that everything bears to itself". But elsewhere he is much more explicit in the conception of logical principles as linguistic. He says that "logical principles of inference are merely rules for the illative transformation of the symbols of the particular system employed. If the system is essentially changed, they will be quite different" (2.599; cf. 4.481, 2.467). In 1868 Peirce had in effect divided leading principles ('guiding principles' then) into material and logical by saying that such a principle might involve either "some matter of fact concerning the subject of argument, or merely a maxim relating to a system of signs" (5.280).

Now, it is in terms of this conception of logical leading principles as non-assertive rules for the translation of signs (sentences) that Peirce ought to have explained the validity of necessary as opposed to probable inference, rather than in terms of the view which the "Minute Logic" develops. It is not the degree of empirical success with which the two types of inference meet that will explain their difference. Necessary inference is not simply a limiting case of probable inference (as e.g. in 2.694), especially since on Peirce's own view an argument may have the probability 1 though it lead to false conclusions any finite number of times (cf. § 49). A given argument that purports to be necessary is guaranteed to be so by the form of its leading principle or rule. An argument that purports to be probable with a certain numerical value is determined to be so by empirically ascertaining whether its rule or leading principle, which refers to a whole class of similar arguments, holds for a percentage of those arguments equal to the numerical value. It is in this sense that the genus is what interests us in necessary arguments, and the class in probable arguments. Speaking of probable inference in the widest sense [1] (i.e. where 'probable' means simply 'not necessary'), it is essential, in weighing the conclusion of such an inference, to examine as many members as possible of a class of inferences to which it is considered as belonging. This examination will affect the 'strength', 'probability', or whatever the property may be, which is to be assigned the conclusion. In necessary argument, an inspection of the leading principle, to ascertain whether it is a logical principle or not, suffices to determine whether the conclusion does or does not follow necessarily. In a necessary argument alone does the defining principle also guarantee validity. "The only kind of reasoning which can render our conclusions certain . . . attains this certainty by limiting the conclusion . . . to facts already expressed and accepted in the premises" (2.664). The necessity of necessary reasoning consists not in the fact that it is always ratified empirically, but in the fact that it is analytic, the analyticity determined by a logical rule decreeing it. We shall find that on Peirce's view mathematical reasoning (which he regards as synonymous with necessary reasoning) actually derives its necessity from the fact that it is independent of all material interpretation. It is when this point of view concerning validity is uppermost in his mind that Peirce regards as a historical curiosity Mill's opinion that the principles of logic are inductive generalizations (5.167). Necessary reasoning is purely formal and independent of extra-systemical meaning: "What people call an 'interpretation' is a thing totally irrelevant, except that it may show by an example that no slip of logic has been committed" (4.130).

[1] See p. 189, note.

Peirce's concept of the leading principle, ill-expressed as it is in certain critical details, is a profound recognition of the distinction between a deductive system and the inferential rules governing it, and the dependence of the character of the system upon the character of the rules. Though the concept has been considerably refined since Peirce, it was in his day a notable advance over the concepts then analogous to it (employed chiefly by mathematicians), and its equivalent is the rule of transformation as understood to-day.[1] The extent to which Peirce sensed the importance of distinguishing between the sentences constituting a system and that system's rules is seen when, in constructing a Boolean calculus, he discriminates the "principles of logic themselves" (the rules regulative of the calculus) from the "maxims" of logic (which here, unlike a previous quotation, mean the logical propositions occurring within the calculus) (3.41). The need of the separation is expressed by Peirce when he says in medieval language that "reasoning moves in first intentions, while the forms of logic are constructions of second intentions" (2.599).[2] The view that logical principles are rules concerned with the systemic manipulation of signs is a consequence of the distinction between argument and leading principle. The defective element in Peirce's treatment of the leading principle is its lack of specificity. He fails to give enough examples of leading principles, and we are often uncertain how on his view they would be stated. This is especially the case in arguments that have material leading principles. It is uncertain, for instance, how the leading principle of an induction is to be stated. Although his accounts of the types of probable inference do enable us

[1] The distinction between logical and material leading principles corresponds to the present-day distinction between logical and physical transformation rules (' L-rules ' and ' P-rules '). See R. Carnap, *op. cit.*, § 51.

[2] These considerations correspond in a rudimentary way to the distinction between the ' object-language ' (e.g. the Boolean calculus) and the ' syntax-language ' (comprising sentences about the calculus). Cf. Carnap, *op. cit.*, p. 4.

to conjecture a statement of their rules, some instructive examples would render the accounts themselves the clearer.

In a manuscript of 1903 intended as an exposition of his system of 'existential graphs', Peirce makes a thorough-going attempt to construct a symbolic system by enunciating in detail the rules that are to govern it. Not only does he lay down rules of transformation but, surpassing ordinary mathematical practice, rules for the organization and construction of the system's elements.

"We frame a system of expressing propositions—a written language—having a syntax to which there are absolutely no exceptions. We then satisfy ourselves that whenever a proposition having a certain syntactical form is true, another proposition definitely related to it . . . will necessarily also be true. We draw up our code of basic rules of such illative transformations, none of these rules being a necessary consequence of others" (4.481).

The 'framing of the syntax' of the system, of its "grammar" (4.475), would today be called setting forth the 'rules of formation'. These analyze the type, number and inter-relation of the signs that constitute the system; they state "all the fundamental conventions of the system" and the conventions derived from these (4.423). Together with the "rules of transformation" (4.423, 4.475) they form the 'syntax' in the present-day sense. (Peirce says that his system is not intended as a 'calculus'. But what he under-stands by the word here is a mathematical instrument or mechanism for facilitating the drawing of conclusions. The system is, of course, a 'calculus' in the sense that its con-structions and inferential relations are determined by explicit rules or conventions. See § 46.) Peirce fails, however, in the system of rules that he lays down, to differentiate with any clarity at all just what is "eternal verity" from what "merely characterizes the special language of existential graphs" (4.477). We have already seen his statement that the so-called logical principles of inference become 'quite different' when the system is changed. Today it would be said that the system is by definition changed when its rules are changed rather than vice versa; but essentially the same point *seems* to be intended by Peirce here, where the 'logical principles of inference' become 'rules of illative transformation'. It is of interest and significance to note, in connection with Peirce's general purpose in the paper under consideration, what Benjamin Peirce, in his *Linear Associative Algebra* of 1870, edited by Charles in 1882, says, with similar purpose: "The symbols of an algebra, with the laws of combination, constitute its *language*. . . . The language of algebra has its alphabet, vocabulary, and grammar".[1] The alphabet and vocabulary are together equivalent to the rules of formation or construction, the grammar to the rules of transformation. "The *alphabet* of an algebra consists of its letters; the *vocabulary* defines its signs and the elementary combinations of its letters; and the *grammar* gives the rules of composition by which the letters and signs are united into a complete and consistent system".[2]

46. **On Fact and Formalism in Logic.** Another noteworthy insight of Peirce is his view that all logical propositions (as against rules) are "indistinguishable" (3.41). Between one analytic sentence and another there are no essential differences (cf. 3.148), so that the old view of three 'laws of thought' as being eminently the logical propositions is erroneous.

But in our general attempt to indicate Peirce's modernity we must guard against forcing the issue and reading into what are after all not fully elaborated writings too much of an anticipatory character. Although the conventional status of logical rules, both of formation and illation, is to some extent asserted by him, it is quite certain that he would not subscribe to so radical a conventionalism with respect to them as that of some contemporary logicians. In his conception of the possible types of such rules, and their relative importance, he is inadequate, holding for example (though in

[1] Pp. 2-3, ed. of 1882.   [2] P. 3.

1867) that substitution is not genuine "inference" (2.496); from which it would seem to follow that a rule of substitution is not a genuine transformation rule or is an unimportant one. But it is the nightmare of inconsistency that is Peirce's worst enemy and that threatens his conventionalism. Most significant is the fact that whereas for modern conventionalism the problem of 'non-Aristotelian logic' becomes a dead issue, Peirce does not seem to think so. In a letter to Francis C. Russell,[1] he says:

"Before I took up the general study of relatives, I made some investigation . . . supposing the laws of logic to be different from what they are. It was a sort of non-Aristotelian logic, in the sense in which we speak of non-Euclidean geometry. Some of the developments were somewhat interesting, but not sufficiently so to induce me to publish them. The general idea was, of course, obvious to anybody of sufficient grasp of logical analysis to see that *logic reposes upon certain positive facts, and is not mere formalism.* Another writer afterward suggested such a false logic, as if it were the wildest lunacy, instead of being a plain and natural hypothesis worth looking into (notwithstanding its falsity)" (my ital.).

This passage plunges us back at once into the view that the principles of inference depend upon fact. From speaking of transformation rules we return to 'laws of logic', by means of which we efficaciously draw true consequences from true assumptions. 'Non-Aristotelian logic' is neither equally admissible nor absurd; it is false; its laws are contrary to fact. This of course means that the drawing of true consequences from assumptions that are true is not due to a formal, syntactical guarantee but to a kind of faithfulness to reality on the part of the logical laws. This in turn means, contrary to a statement quoted above, that necessary inference must ultimately resort to interpretation to justify its necessity. The logical laws are "not absolutely certain" (4.77). Critical logic, unlike mathematics, "is categorical in its assertions"

---

[1] Quoted by P. Carus in the *Monist*, Vol. 20 (1910), p. 45.

(4.240). While it is a "normative science", it is also a "positive science" in that only "by asserting positive, categorical truth" can it show that good reasoning is really so (5.39). Elsewhere, "the logician does not assert anything . . . but there are certain assumed truths which he hopes for, relies upon, banks upon. . . ." (4.79).

To this vacillation between an unmistakably positive and an unmistakably conventionalistic conception of necessary inference, we must make an addition. This is the amazing circumstance that Peirce speaks of logic as 'reposing upon positive facts' in an altogether different sense from the one just stated. Consider the following: ". . . Logic does rest on certain facts of experience" (5.110); the "facts of which logic needs to take cognizance" are "the facts of doubt, truth, falsity, etc." (2.537; cf. 2.66). "That belief tends to fix itself under inquiry is . . . one of the facts with which logic sets out" (2.693). And, similarly, the 'facts' which logic must assume—and he calls them also 'logical principles'—comprise "all that is implied in the existence of doubt and of belief, and of the passage from one to the other, of truth and of falsehood, of reality, etc." [1] *This* conception of logic as reposing upon 'fact' occurs when Peirce has in mind the genesis of logic. It would be clear if we could quote the entire context of the following passage. Peirce is emphasizing that our beliefs, or belief-habits, are in large measure fixed or determined by 'peripheral excitations'.

> "Is there any law about the mode of the peripheral excitations? The logician maintains that there is, namely, that they are all adapted to an end, that of carrying belief, in the long run, toward certain predestinate conclusions which are the same for all men. This is the faith of the logician. *This is the matter of fact, upon which all maxims of reasoning repose* (my ital.). In virtue of this fact, what is to be believed at last is independent of what has been believed hitherto, and therefore has the character of *reality*. Hence, if a given habit, considered as determining an inference, is

[1] Review of C. Read, *The Theory of Logic*, in *Nation*, Vol. 28 (1879), p. 235.

of such a sort as to tend toward the final result, it is correct; otherwise not.   Thus inferences become divisible
into the valid and the invalid; and thus logic takes its
reason of existence" (3.161).

Here logic rests upon fact not in the sense that is validated
by fact but in the sense that the criteria of validity are
developed in experience. The 'maxims' of reasoning, which
are after all beliefs, come to be recognized as sound because
they inevitably compel universal agreement. The 'facts' of
belief, doubt and the like are thus essential to a genetic
account of logic.

Had Peirce come to realize that only in this second sense
does logic rest upon fact, he would have become conscious of
the positive and conventionalistic tendencies struggling side
by side in his writings. He might have called logical principles 'transformation rules' in any case, and then asked
himself whether these rules are legislative guarantees of
necessary inference, or somehow descriptive of experiential
testing of inference by interpretation. When we come to
discuss the analyticity of deduction in mathematics, we shall
have further corroboration of the former view. But peace
will not be for us, and we shall encounter a third, very
explicit, criterion of validity in necessary inference.

In the letter to F. C. Russell quoted above, Peirce states
that logic, by resting on facts, "is not mere formalism".
What this attack on formalism there amounted to was an
attack on conventionalism. There is an emphasis against
'formalism' in another sense, which is partly connected with
this one. The purpose of what is known as 'formal' or
'mathematical' or 'symbolic' logic, Peirce holds,

".   .   . is simply and solely the *investigation of the theory of
logic, and not at all the construction of a calculus to aid the
drawing of inferences.* These two purposes are incompatible, for the reason that the system devised for the
investigation of logic should be as analytical as possible,
breaking up inferences into the greatest possible number of

steps, and exhibiting them under the most general categories possible; while a calculus would aim, on the contrary, to reduce the number of processes as much as possible, and to specialize the symbols so as to adapt them to special kinds of inference" (4.373; my ital.).

The most important type of inference is mathematical inference, and the purpose of formal logic would seem to be largely the analysis of the structure of mathematics. Peirce declares this to have been the purpose of the logical algebras that he had constructed on previous occasions, and regards his system of graphs as a great improvement over them in this respect (4.429).[1] But what he means by 'analysis' and by 'breaking up inferences into the greatest possible number of steps and exhibiting them under the most general categories' is not clear. (*a*) In the above quotation and elsewhere it seems to be very much like a psychological analysis, aiming to discover every step that actually enters into the reasoning process, especially the complex instance of mathematics. That the analysis of the mathematical reasoning process interested Peirce greatly will be evident in § 48. (*b*) It may be that by denouncing 'mere formalism', which he characterizes as 'the mere construction of calculi', Peirce is warning against the duplication of mathematics by constructing systems and forgetting the rôle of semiotic analysis, the purpose of critical logic in its modern symbolic guise being the study of properties common to all systems. Thus he says that an interest in the essential elements of a mathematical hypothesis and of deductive processes "in their intellectal pedigrees and in their conceptual affiliations with ideas met with elsewhere . . . is the logical interest, *par excellence*" (4.370). And he says also that the logical analysis of an

---

[1] Thus also: " The principal desideratum in a calculus is that it should be able to pass with security at one bound over a series of difficult inferential steps. What these abbreviated inferences may best be, will depend upon the special nature of the subject under discussion. But in my algebras and graphs, far from anything of that sort being attempted, the whole effort has been to dissect the operations of inference into as many distinct steps as possible " (4.424).

algebra is "directed toward the essential elements of the algebra", while the mathematical interest is "toward the solution of problems" (3.322). In short, he finds speculative grammar too much neglected in critical logic (cf. 3.341).

I think that although both (*a*) and (*b*) represent Peirce's intent, the emphasis here is predominantly on the latter (cf. 3.451). But if so, why the attack on 'calculi', for would not the invention of new deductive [1] systems increase the understanding of the properties common to deductive systems in general? The answer is, of course, that Peirce uses 'calculus' in the mathematical rather than in the logical sense, and means by it 'calculus to aid the drawing of inferences'. ". . . The chief advantages of the new systems of formal logic" are the "broad and philosophical aperçus" that they make possible, "much more than any facilities they afford for drawing difficult conclusions".[2] The gist of Peirce's denunciation of formalism is really a plea for emphasis on the foundational as opposed to the purely technical aspect of symbolic logic.

"The employment of algebra in the investigation of logic is open to the danger of degenerating into idle trifling of too rudimentary a character to be of mathematical interest, and too superficial to be of logical interest. It is further open to the danger that *the rules of the symbols employed may be mistaken for first principles of logic*. An algebra which brings along with it hundreds of *purely formal theorems of no logical import whatever* must be admitted, even by the inventor of it, to be extremely defective in that respect, however convenient it may be for certain purposes" (3.619 ; my ital.).

The italicized portions of this passage show that Peirce's attack on formalism in the present sense is connected with that on linguistic and conventionalistic formalism. For

---

[1] 'Deduction', until otherwise specified, will continue to be understood in its traditional sense of necessary inference ("necessary deduction", 2.267).

[2] Review of Jevons, *Studies in Deductive Logic*, in *Nation*, Vol. 32 1881), p. 227.

clearly a conception of what constitutes the 'first principles of logic' affects the opinion of what is foundational and what purely technical. If Peirce had continued in the strain of his relativistic conception of transformation rules, the contrast between "the rules of the symbols employed" and "first principles of logic" would be nothing more than that between the rules of a given calculus and the concept of the transformation rule in general. But in this passage the contrast seems rather to be between the rules of a given calculus and the 'laws of logic'. When his inclination toward this emphasis is most prominent Peirce is certainly most vague, and just what he means by a theorem 'of no logical import' as opposed to a theorem 'of logical import' I am unable to say.

We must now go on to consider Peirce's philosophy of mathematics, including the question of the relation between mathematics and logic. For one who sharply distinguishes logic from psychology, Peirce is much concerned with the nature of mathematical *reasoning*, with the *process* of deduction. In fact, the bulk of his theoretical discussions on mathematics consists in an elucidation of this process. But he holds that the validity of mathematical inference is distinct from, and does not depend upon, the nature of its performance. This distinction is present in Kant, who recognized the analytical character of mathematical inference.[1] But in Kant (i) pure mathematics is conceived of as having a subject-matter, e.g. space in geometry, the properties of which it explains a priori; (ii) consequently, the individual axioms and theorems, as distinct from the inferential connection between them, are synthetic; (iii) and in any event, despite the application of the term 'analytic' to mathematical inference, this term is unsatisfactorily defined. On the question of subject-matter in mathematics, and on the analysis of mathematical propositions, Peirce disagrees radically with Kant; and he modifies considerably Kant's definition of 'analytic'. Before going into the subject of

[1] Cf. *Critique of Pure Reason*, B 14.

mathematics directly, I want to introduce a distinction needed for Peirce's account of the deductive reasoning-process.[1]

47. **Icon, Index and Symbol.** We said that, depending upon the point of view, Peirce makes different classifications of signs (there are in fact three basic classifications[2]). One of these is into term, proposition and argument. Another is into icon, index and symbol.

(1) An icon, generally speaking, is a sign that has a resemblance or similarity to its object. Thus any picture or diagram is an icon. "An Icon is a sign which refers to the Object that it denotes merely by virtue of characters of its own, and which it possesses, just the same, whether any such Object actually exists or not. It is true that unless there really is such an Object, the Icon does not act as a sign; but this has nothing to do with its character as a sign" (2.247).

(2) An index, as its name implies, is a sign that *indicates* its object in some manner or other. Various distinctions might be made of different kinds of index. For instance, a pointing finger, smoldering embers and a demonstrative adjective or pronoun are indices that can be distinguished as indicating in different senses. But these distinctions are beside our purpose. Suffice it that indices have no significant resemblance or similarity to their objects, as have icons; that they refer to individuals; and that they "direct the attention to their objects by blind compulsion" (2.306). It is the actual directing of the attention to its object that essentially distinguishes the index from the icon and the symbol. "An Index is a sign which refers to the Object that it denotes by virtue of being really affected by that Object" (2.248). As an icon retains the character making it significant even without the existence of its object, so an index retains its character even without the existence of an interpretant (cf. § 31 or 2.304).

---

[1] Kant's influence on Peirce's account of the mathematical reasoning-process is pointed out in § 51. [2] Cf. p. 20, note.

(3) A symbol is a conventional sign, which has no connection, whether of similarity or indication, with its object other
than its serving as that object's name. "A Symbol is a sign
which refers to the Object that it denotes by virtue of a law,
usually an association of general ideas, which operates to
cause the Symbol to be interpreted as referring to that
Object" (2.249). 'Cow', 'logic' and 'hit' are symbols
because they do not in themselves identify their objects (as
do the icon and index) but stand for their objects by conventional agreement. Thus the bulk of language, which in its
origin is essentially arbitrary, is symbolic. Any other sign
might just as well have been associated with a certain kind
of object as a given symbol. A symbol obviously loses the
character that renders it a sign if there is no interpretant.
For it acts as a sign simply and solely because it is understood
to do so; it acquires a meaning not by virtue of any qualitative
character but by social agreement. (Cf. 2.297-298, 304, 307.)

It is clear that in a mathematical system symbols occur,
and according to Peirce so do indices (e.g. 2.305), but it is in
the icon that we are mainly interested. When we say that
icons 'resemble' or are 'similar to' their objects, we must
not understand these words too narrowly. An icon may be
an icon of certain relations rather than of a particular thing.
Thus an ordinary geometrical diagram does not resemble its
'object' sensuously: there is "only an analogy between the
relations of the parts of each" (2.279; cf. 4.530). An algebraical *equation* is likewise an icon, because it exhibits relations between certain quantities, denoted by the algebraical
symbols that constitute it.[1] The equation does not photo-
graph, nor does it even diagram in the usual sense, but it
'exhibits' nevertheless (cf. 2.282).

"Particularly deserving of notice are icons in which the
likeness is aided by conventional rules. Thus, an algebraic formula is an icon, rendered such by the rules of

---

[1] The individual signs ' x ', ' y ', etc. usually employed as algebraical
variables are symbols: our convention might just as well be that ' α ',
' β ', etc. should serve as variables.

commutation, association and distribution of the symbols. It may seem at first glance that it is an arbitrary classification to call an algebraic expression an icon; that it might as well, or better, be regarded as a compound conventional sign. But it is not so. For a great distinguishing property of the icon is that *by the direct observation of it other truths concerning its object can be discovered than those which suffice to determine its construction.* Thus, by means of two photographs a map can be drawn, etc. Given a conventional or other general sign of an object, to deduce any other truth than that which it explicitly signifies, it is necessary, in all cases, to replace that sign by an icon. This capacity of revealing unexpected truth is precisely that wherein the utility of algebraical formulae consists, so that the iconic character is the prevailing one " (2.279; my ital.).

We shall shortly see, in expatiating the contents of this passage, that the diagrammatic or iconic character of mathematical reasoning is, according to Peirce, its most fundamental character.

48. **The Nature of Mathematics.** Peirce more than once calls attention to his father's definition of mathematics as "the science which draws necessary conclusions" (cf. 5.8, 4.229, 3.558), remarkable for the date (1870) at which it appeared. A glance at the context of this definition will indicate, I believe, that Benjamin Peirce's influence on his son was more than an inspirational one.

"Mathematics is the science which draws necessary conclusions.

"This definition of mathematics is wider than that which is ordinarily given, and by which its range is limited to quantitative research. The ordinary definition, like those of other sciences, is objective; whereas this is subjective. Recent investigations . . . make it manifest that the old definition is too restricted. The sphere of mathematics is here extended, in accordance with the derivation of its name, to all demonstrative research, so as to include all knowledge strictly capable of dogmatic teaching. Mathematics is not the discoverer of laws, for it is not induction;

neither is it the framer of theories, for it is not hypothesis; but it is the judge over both. . . .

"Mathematics, under this definition, belongs to every inquiry, moral as well as physical. Even the rules of logic, by which it is rigidly bound, could not be deduced without its aid.

". . . Symbols must be adopted which may serve for the embodiment of forms of argument, without being trammeled by the conditions of external representation or special interpretation." [1]

It will be convenient, in explaining Peirce's opinions, to outline five main points under which they fall. (1) With respect to its "method", mathematics is "the science which draws necessary conclusions"; with respect to its "aim and subject-matter", mathematics is "the study of hypothetical states of things" (cf. 4.238). (2) The way in which necessary conclusions are drawn is by means of experimentation upon diagrams or icons. (3) The relation between the axioms and theorems of a mathematical system is analytic. (4) Considered individually, the axioms and theorems of arithmetic, at least, are analytic; and in any case, no proposition of pure mathematics is synthetic. (5) Mathematics is independent of logic and, in a sense, prior to it.

(1) Pure mathematics Peirce holds to be a discipline void of any factual content whatsoever. We must constantly be on our guard to discriminate pure mathematics from inquiries with which it is likely to be confused. The definition by De Morgan and Rowan Hamilton, attempting to avoid the conception of mathematics as the science of quantity, and substituting an allegedly Kantian conception of mathematics as the science of pure time and pure space,[2] is guilty

---

[1] *Linear Associative Algebra*, pp. 1-2 in ed. of 1882.

[2] Peirce claims that the view which apparently influenced Hamilton and De Morgan is not the view of Kant, whoever else's it may be. A careful examination of the *Critique*, he says, especially the "Analytic of Principles", shows that space and time have no more to do with mathematics than with the subject-matter of other inquiries, and that Kant conceived of mathematics in terms of its method, which consists in the study of diagrams, rather than its subject-matter (cf. 3.557).

of this confusion. For there is a science of space and a science of time, but "these sciences are positive and experiential—branches of physics, and so not mathematical except . . . as calling in the aid of mathematics" (3.557). Mathematics is not a positive science; it "makes no external observations" (3.428); it makes no assertion about fact, and is consequently not concerned with the question of the existential truth of its statements (3.427, 1.245). We may go so far as to say that "a proposition is not a statement of perfectly pure mathematics until it is devoid of all definite meaning. . . ." (5.567). Pure mathematical propositions have meaning only in the sense that they have translations, i.e. other propositions deduced from them (cf. 4.132). "To say that algebra means anything else than just its own forms is to mistake an *application* of algebra for the *meaning* of it" (4.133). Mathematical statements are hypotheses, in the sense of mere assumptions, statements posited rather than asserted to be true; and the only purpose of employing these assumptions—any whatever—is to ascertain their necessary consequences. Mathematics "merely posits hypotheses, and traces out their consequences" (1.240); it "merely seeks to know what follows from certain hypotheses" (5.13 n.); it "deals exclusively with the consequences deducible from hypotheses arbitrarily posited" (6.182; cf. 4.132, 1.247).

The mathematician's hypotheses, Peirce says in very Lockean language, are "creatures of his own imagination" (5.567). And this fact, that mathematics assumes only what is "subject to the imagination", that it "deals exclusively with hypothetical states of things", explains the necessity of its inferences (4.232). The "objects which the mathematician observes and to which his conclusions relate are objects of his mind's own creation" (3.426; cf. 6.595). What does Peirce mean by these 'objects', and why is it that conclusions are drawn necessarily simply because they are 'of the mind's own creation'? In the first place, if a statement is regarded as belonging to mathematics, all material content is abstracted from, and an expression of formal character remains (cf. 4.234). Necessary conclusions can of course be drawn from statements with factual content, but this content is irrelevant so far as the inference is concerned (4.232). The hypothesis is a "pure" hypothesis, a "skeletonized" expression (3.559)—that is to say, a diagrammatized expression. Now the diagrammatic expressions called axioms are constructed arbitrarily: a certain order to the symbolic elements in the expression is assigned by the formation rules. And the necessary deduction consists in the picking out from this expression of properties not assigned to it by the rules but implicit in this assignment. The 'objects' of which Peirce speaks are the axiomatic expressions. They are 'creatures of the mathematician's imagination' in the sense that their diagrammatic structure is arbitrarily laid down by the formation rules. In Peirce's words, "a geometrical diagram or array of algebraical symbols is constructed according to an abstractly stated precept, and between the parts of such diagram or array certain relations are observed to obtain, other than those which were expressed in the precept" (2.216). The necessity with which a conclusion is drawn is due not to its stating a material property connected by some a priori intuition with a material property stated in the hypothesis but to its possessing *as an expression* (diagram) a configurative property hidden in the configurative properties assigned by the rules to the hypothesis-expression. The necessary character of mathematical reasoning "is due simply to the circumstance that . . . [its subject] . . . is a diagram of our own creation, the conditions of whose being we know all about"[1] (3.560). Without going further, we may note that if Peirce's opinion on this point were to be regarded as similar to a modern philosophy of mathematics, it would be to formalism and not to intuitionism. The axioms and definitions of pure mathematical systems should

---

[1] Peirce in fact says that "all diagrams, nay all pictures, depend upon conventions" (4.530).

not, he holds, be "contaminated with any substance" but should be "pure verbiage" (4.246). Thus, for instance, ". . . numbers are a mere series of vocables [elsewhere in the same paragraph, "meaningless vocables"] serving no other purpose than that of expressing . . . transitive relations. . . ." (4.154).

Thus mathematics is neither the science of quantity (3.554, 4.230) nor the science of pure time and space but the science that draws formal consequences. Peirce implies that although his father's definition did not take full cognizance of the other aspect of mathematics, as the 'study of hypothetical states of things', it entails the latter definition (4.232), and both "come to the same thing" (3.558). But he also feels inclined to think that despite this complementarity they are "two very different things" (3.559).

(2) Thus the necessity of mathematical reasoning is due to the fact that it deals with 'a diagram of our own creation' whose rules are set down in advance. ". . . The conclusion is compelled to be true by the conditions of the construction of the diagram" (2.778). But these 'conditions' strictly include the transformation rules as well as the formation rules. For the latter alone yield no inference, much less necessary inference. Accordingly we find Peirce to say that an algebra consists of "algebraical schemata" "with which are associated certain rules of permissible transformation" (4.246). We have already encountered Peirce's conviction of the strict analyticity of necessary reasoning (p. 197), and will presently have occasion to return to the subject. Here we want to say that diagrams are essential to validity in this sense only: that these diagrams are our hypothetical expressions arranged in definite orders by rules, and that necessary conclusions can be drawn only by applying rules of translation to these expressions. Very often, because of Peirce's psychological interest in mathematical processes, a different and erroneous impression is given of the relation between diagrams and validity. This impression is strengthened by the fact that Peirce declares himself to have

been much influenced by the views of F. A. Lange in the latter's *Logische Studien* (2.76). But Peirce as usual bestows credit where it is not due. Lange's view is that spatial intuition a priori is the source of necessity in mathematical inference, in which view he goes, as he says,[1] beyond Kant, for he thus holds logical as well as mathematical principles to be synthetic a priori. What Peirce thinks of such a view he reveals elsewhere. He finds fantastic the view, "not far from the opinion of Friedrich Albert Lange, a thinker of no ordinary force", that diagrams "prove the validity of the syllogistic formula" (4.354); and he explains, in almost so many words, that it is with Lange's account of the psychological process of reasoning that he is in agreement (cf. 4.355).

Not only mathematics but all reasoning that is necessary, according to Peirce, is carried on by means of diagrams, or more generally, icons. The popular conception is that icons are made use of only in geometry, doubtless because geometry is thus conceived of as the science of the properties of space. For Peirce pure mathematical geometry has nothing whatever to do with space, so that icons are not regarded by him as more important for this branch of mathematics than for any other. There are differences, but not fundamental differences, between a geometrical diagram and an array of algebraic equations.[2] Peirce likes to say that deduction is based on "observation and experiment" (e.g. 3.560), and that mathematics, while not a positive science, and while making no 'external observations', is yet an "observational science" (e.g. 2.65). Whereas the empirical sciences in so far as they are positive make use of probable reasoning, and of sensible experimentation as conducive to the success of such reasoning, mathematics, dealing only with necessary reasoning, employs "ideal experimentation" (3.527-528) or "abstractive observation" (2.227). Ideal experimentation

---

[1] *Logische Studien*, p. 9.

[2] ". . . Algebra is but a sort of diagram . . . language is but a kind of algebra" (3.419).

is that form of thought in which, for the purpose of determining the truth of a statement, we exhaust the possibilities, without recourse to experience. In sensible experimentation the attainment of our result always depends upon sampling which, though it continue to be improved indefinitely, will remain inconclusive. In ideal experiment we are (speaking in terms that will cover the simplest everyday, as well as the most abstract, inference) in the realm of possibility; we may freely choose samples that are absolutely representative of all cases, and we can safely draw conclusions "in advance of experience" (3.527). We know, with respect to material states of affairs, that certain combinations are possible and others are not, so that we can make decisions or draw conclusions not requiring to be empirically confirmed. Peirce himself gives an example of the distinction between ideal and sensible experimentation. ". . . The mathematician knows that a column of figures will add up the same, whether it be set down in black ink or in red; because he goes on the assumption that the sum of any two numbers of which one is M and the other one more than N will be one more than the sum of M and N; and this assumption says nothing about the colour of the ink" (5.8). But there is no such analytic guarantee in the case of a chemist expecting the appearance of a precipitate whether or not the Mayor of Hong Kong sneezes; for despite his experience that his results are not affected by such events, peculiar physical conditions may conceivably bring it about that they should be (cf. 5.8).

Mathematical inference, or deduction, is a process of ideal experimentation with hypotheses that happen to be devoid of material content. We draw conclusions by inspecting an icon and noticing properties implicit in it. We discover "hidden relations among the parts" (3.363). The diagram, being constructed according to a rule, is so selected that it is representative of all other diagrams to which the rule would apply; that is, it is general. The reasoning, while based on an individual schema, is necessary in that it applies to all possible cases (4.233). Thus we reason on individual figures and individual formulae, but in geometrical reasoning the figure is constructed according to the most general directions of the rule, and the formula in algebraical reasoning avails itself of variables (cf. 3.92). The figures of traditional syllogism are icons, exhibiting the relations of M, S and P, in particular the occurrence of M in both the premisses. We must repeat that the notion of iconization is broad: icons which are expressions of pure mathematics exhibit their 'object' fully as much as other icons. They exhibit relations —relations of quantities, or, in non-quantitative mathematics, relations of order.

What Peirce means when he says that the conclusion is drawn by noticing relations among the parts of the diagram is that we notice the applicability of one of our transformation rules. The intuitive or observational element in deduction, the ideal experimentation, consists largely in noticing this applicability. This is especially seen if we consider mathematical reasoning from the point of view of proving a given theorem. The insight which we credit to the mathematician who accomplishes the proof is that of ideal experimentation, 'proof' being another way of saying that the theorem is deduced from the axioms in accordance with the transformation rules. Even in ordinary reasoning concerning commonplace matters, when, as I said, we 'exhaust the possibilities', we tacitly apply a transformation rule, for instance, the principle of the transitivity of the class-inclusion relation; and it is in the insight that this applies that our ideal experimentation consists. According to Peirce, the process of inference can be analyzed into three basic steps: the first is colligation (Whewell's term), the conjunction of the premisses into a compound proposition or composite icon; the second is the contemplation of this icon in order to detect new relations of its parts; the third is the thought, when the inference is drawn, that it is one of a class of inferences, in other words, "the judgment that what we observe in the colligated data follows a rule" (2.444; cf. 2.442-444). It seems clear that Peirce does not regard these three steps as temporally successive; and certainly the rule of an inference in mathematics, if not elsewhere, is not something that we wake up to when the conclusion has been drawn.

The notion of experimentation presupposes the notion of experience, and Peirce accordingly speaks, in what he regards as a perfectly legitimate usage, of "inner experience" (4.91), where ideal experimentation takes place. ". . . All knowledge comes to us by observation. A part is forced upon us from without and seems to result from Nature's mind; a part comes from the depths of the mind as seen from within. . . ." (2.444). We draw necessary conclusions "not by a simple mental stare, or strain of mental vision" but by "manipulating on paper, or in the fancy, formulae or other diagrams—experimenting on them, *experiencing* the thing" (4.86). From sensible experience we derive the "Outward truth", from inner experience, the "Inward truth" (4.87). This usage of the word 'experience' we have covered under the fourth sense in § 26. While it is, of course, not inadmissible, the combination of the concepts of necessary inference and experience is awkward. We hasten to point out, therefore, that in Peirce's usage it is subordinate to his ordinary sense of 'experience', which is not linked but opposed to mathematical inference. Mathematics, he says, "is not obliged to resort to experience for the support of the laws it discovers and enunciates. . . ." (2.65). And further, "in any world in which there is such a thing as the course of experience—an element which is absent from the world of pure mathematics—in such world a certain kind of reasoning must be valid which is not valid in the world of pure mathematics" (2.193). Experience remains for Peirce primarily compulsion from without, something imposed upon us by the external world and clothed with abstraction. In a passage dealing expressly with the advisability of broadening the meaning of the word, Peirce declares himself opposed to the idea. The basis of its meaning was given, he says, by Locke. Rather than stretch it to embrace new considerations, invent a new word (cf. 5.611-613).

(3) The validity of mathematical reasoning depends upon diagrams, then, only in the sense that it depends upon expressions being manipulated according to rules. Peirce holds that the so-called truths of mathematics follow "syllogistically" from certain propositions which may be regarded as definitions (3.20, 3.252), and that these propositions involve no assumption "in reference to experience or intuition". The question whether there "actually are such objects in experience or pure intuition is not in itself a part of pure mathematics" (3.20). Now although Kant expressed the doctrine of the explicative or analytic character of necessary reasoning, his view suffers from an unsatisfactory conception of analyticity. He regards those assertions as analytic where the predicate (consequent, conclusion) is thought in the subject (antecedent, premiss), albeit thought unclearly or confusedly.[1] Peirce regards this conception as unduly psychological, and moreover, as psychologically absurd when we consider the complexities of certain mathematical inferences (cf. 4.51-52, 4.86). Whether a theorem is consistent with a hypothesis is the question "of whether they are logically compossible or not" (4.86), not whether the theorem is thought in the hypothesis. In general, all the truths of a mathematical system may be said to be "involved" in the axioms, but not thought in them (*ib.*). Accordingly Peirce is forced to conclude that "deductive reasoning is really quite different from what it was supposed by Kant to be" (6.595), although in saying this he is also thinking of the fact that the individual propositions of mathematics are by no means synthetic. On his view, "an analytical proposition is a definition or a proposition *deducible* from definitions; a synthetical proposition is a proposition not analytical" (*ib.*). Analytical propositions thus reduce to "mere affairs of arrangement" (2.690). The assertion that the premisses of a deduction imply the

---

[1] Cf. *Critique of Pure Reason*, B 11.

theorems is for Peirce an analytical proposition in this sense. We are thus led back to what we have already concluded, namely, that the analyticity of a necessary inference consists in this inference being governed by a logical leading principle, a rule certifying that nothing is asserted in a theorem which has not already been asserted in axioms and definitions. In mathematics, then, none but logical leading principles occur. To such an account we arrive both by express statement and internal evidence. In (5) we shall encounter the view which jars with this account and is not easily reconcilable with it.

According to Peirce deductive reasoning enlarges our knowledge, though it does not increase our information. By virtue of the view that such reasoning is iconic, he has no difficulty in explaining how it can both enlarge our knowledge and be analytic. We must not confuse the extension of our knowledge which the proof of a difficult theorem accomplishes with the relation in which this theorem actually stands to the assumptions from which it is deduced. While Peirce believes that discovery and novelty are truly characteristic of mathematical inquiry, he neither feels nor has any need of, for instance, ascribing to the principle of mathematical induction a synthetic a priori character, as does Poincaré. The possibilities of deduction are rich, and there is an indefinite number of interesting theorems derivable from a suitable set of axioms.[1] The art of the mathematician is the art of ideal experimentation.

(4) What kind of statements are the so-called truths of pure mathematics? Peirce holds that they are not what Kant thought they are, that is, both a priori and synthetic, nor what Mill thought they are, that is, inductively well-established empirical propositions; nor that they are analytic in Kant's sense of the word (cf. 4.91, 4.232). He

---

[1] Peirce regards logical machines as not wholly faithful replicas of the cognitive process of inference. They cannot duplicate the diversity and indefinite choice of conclusions that characterize the latter. (Cf. 6.595 and " Logical Machines ", *Am. Jour. Psych.*, Vol. 1, 1888.)

shows how the relations of arithmetic can be defined in terms of 'logical' relations, and that the propositions of arithmetic can be derived from logical propositions (3.20 ff.), and regards the fact of such a derivation as sufficient proof of the view that arithmetical propositions are not synthetic (cf. 4.88-91). These propositions, he declares explicitly, are "analytical", they are "corollaries from definitions" (6.595). Against the argument of Mill that arithmetical propositions are experiential because we can conceive of a world in which a fifth thing should arise when two things are added to two other things, he answers that this actually does happen in the existing world, "and the fact that nobody dreams of its constituting any infringement of the truths of arithmetic shows that arithmetical propositions are not understood in any experiential sense" (4.91). In other words, Peirce is saying that the proposition '2 things plus 2 things equal 4 things' is by no means the same as '2 plus 2 equal 4'. The former is indeed a synthetic proposition, but the latter is a proposition of pure arithmetic. The former may or may not be true; the latter is analytic, or as Peirce says here, 'logically necessary'.

With respect to the axioms and theorems of geometry, distressingly little can be found in Peirce. It appears that he would not understand the axioms in such a way that they amount to definitions and are accordingly analytic (cf. 3.632-633). On the other hand, he seems to class geometrical with arithmetical propositions in the place where he calls the latter 'logically necessary'; but this is far from certain, because only the arithmetical propositions are considered explicitly (cf. 4.88). Two other possibilities remain. One is that they are synthetic sentences; but in this case the distinction between pure and physical geometry becomes muddled, and this distinction is undoubtedly primary in Peirce's opinions on mathematics. The other is that they are not propositions at all but 'rhemes' or propositional functions; and of this there is no discussion. Peirce says that "the postulates of geometry must go into the number of things approximately true" (1.131; cf. 1.401 and Century Dict. art. "Axiom"), but he doubtless has physical geometry in mind. The question, then, remains in the air, and I do not believe that the choice of any of the alternatives has satisfactory evidence in its favour.

(5) On the provocative subject of the relation between mathematics and logic, Peirce has very definite convictions, all the more surprising because they are incompatible with the theory of logic that we have examined and with the foregoing opinions on the essential character of mathematical inference.

Peirce was acquainted with the thesis that mathematics is a branch of logic through Dedekind's *Was sind und was sollen die Zahlen*. He believes that this thesis is erroneous, for he makes the distinction—which he says was intended by his father—between the science that *draws* necessary conclusions and the science of *drawing* necessary conclusions (4.239). The former is mathematics, not the latter, which is critical logic. An algebra interests the mathematician for its power as a 'calculus'; the logician, on the other hand, is interested in the structure of the algebra and analyzes the inferences which it performs. The mathematician draws consequences, the logician studies and classifies the conditions under which these consequences are drawn.[1] Far from mathematics being a branch of logic, it "is almost . . . the only science which stands in need of no aid from a science of logic" (2.81). Logic is a "science of reasoning", mathematics a "science that reasons" (4.242). Mathematics is

---

[1] Peirce sometimes makes much of the point that mathematics is hypothetical and deductive whereas logic is ' positive ', ' categorical ', ' a science of fact ', etc. (e.g. 1.247, 4.240, 5.126, 3.428). We do not here concern ourselves with this, because we are comparing mathematics and logic as *subject-matters*. It does not really matter to the present discussion whether we regard Peirce's view as being that critical logic is positive or that it is conventionalistic. The question is, what functions belong to the domain of logic and what functions to the domain of mathematics ? (We should also call attention to the following discrepancy. 4.240 says : " Logic . . . is categorical in its assertions " ; 2.65 says that " the laws it discovers and enunciates . . . are merely conditional, not categorical ".)

interested only in reaching a conclusion, and seeks the speediest and most convenient method of doing so; logic is interested only in analyzing diagrams in as great detail as possible (4.533). The function of logic is the "analysis and theory of reasoning", the function of mathematics is "the practice of it" (4.134). Thus for Peirce mathematics becomes a kind of art, and he says as much. "Mathematics may itself be regarded as an art of reasoning. Perhaps this is not the highest conception of it. But at any rate, mathematics has no occasion to inquire into the theory of the validity of its own argumentations; for *these are more evident than any such theory could be*" (2.120; my ital.). ". . . Logic does not go into the business of doing people's reasoning for them . . . mathematics undertakes that business" (2.532). We ought not to call a system of mathematics 'logical' but rather a calculus of logic 'mathematical'. Thus Peirce speaks of "the employment of algebra in the investigation of logic" (3.619) and says that "formal logic is nothing but mathematics applied to logic" (4.263). Logic, "like every other science", has its mathematical aspect, so that we have "a mathematical logic just as there is a mathematical physics and a mathematical economics" (1.247; cf. 4.240). ". . . True mathematical reasoning is *so much more evident* than it is possible to render any doctrine of logic proper—without just such reasoning—that an appeal in mathematics to logic could only embroil a situation" (4.243; my ital.). There are and have been disputes over whether a conclusion follows logically from certain premises, but there have been none over whether a conclusion follows "mathematically" (*ib.*). If a supposed inferential blunder occurs in mathematics, it is subsequently determined to be either correct or fallacious "without appeal to logic, but merely by the careful review of *the mathematics as such*" (1.248; my ital.) Mathematics is thus a self-sufficient discipline. "Mathematics is not subject to logic. Logic depends on mathematics" (2.191). ". . . Mathematics performs its reasonings by a *logica utens* which it develops for itself, and has no need of any appeal to a *logica docens*" (1.417). "We simply recognize a mathematical necessity. . . . The recognition of mathematical necessity is performed in a perfectly satisfactory manner antecedent to any study of logic. Mathematical reasoning derives no warrant from logic. It needs no warrant. *It is evident in itself*" (2.191; my ital.).

Summarizing this in a word, (i) logic is the theory of deduction; mathematics is the practice of deduction; (ii) mathematics has its own criteria of validity; it is independent of logic, which, on the contrary, makes use of it; it is 'self-evident'. To prepare the ground at this point for an argument in favour of Peirce's consistency by saying that mathematics is here contrasted with logic in the narrower sense, critical logic, rather than semiotic, has little force. For critical logic on Peirce's view involves speculative grammar; and in any case, its principal concept, that of the leading principle, is as general a semiotical concept as any could be. Benjamin Peirce, by whom Charles Peirce must certainly have been influenced on the relation between mathematics and logic, had said, in addition to what we have quoted above, "The symbols of an algebra, with the laws of combination, constitute its *language*; the methods of using the symbols in the drawing of inferences is its *art*".[1] That is to say, the logic of an algebra is its language or speculative grammar; the mathematics of the algebra is its art. We may also note that if logic is the theory of deduction while mathematics nevertheless has its own criteria of validity, then logic can be a theory only in a descriptive sense: it presumably observes the modes of mathematical inference, generalizes from a great many species of mathematics, and then simply categorizes valid forms of argument to which it also applies semiotic analysis. Logic, from this point of view, does not construct mathematical systems by means of rules but simply dissects systems properly mathematical. We may ask, as a final preliminary point, whether the present conception of the relation between mathematics

---

[1] *Op. cit.*, p. 2, ed. of 1882.

and logic is contradicted by Peirce's attempts to derive arithmetic from 'logic'. I do not think it is by *this* that it is contradicted at all. For in this case (cf. e.g. 3.20 ff., 3.372) the term 'logic' is used to denote not a theory of rules but a calculus, such as that of Boole, in which the constituent sentences are analytic. Were it not for the fact that the variables *a*, *b*, etc. had been construed as classes, 'class' being a 'logical' concept, Peirce would doubtless have called the calculus a 'mathematical' or a 'logical' calculus indifferently. Thus he says, "quantitative algebra is only a special development of logical algebra. On the other hand, it is equally true that the Boolean algebra is nothing but the mathematics of numerical congruences having 2 for their modulus" (4.136). And in more general fashion, "If there is any part of logic of which mathematics stands in need . . . it can only be that very part of logic which consists merely in an application of mathematics, so that the appeal will be, not of mathematics to a prior science of logic, but of mathematics to mathematics" (1.247). Peirce's studies toward defining traditional mathematical relations in terms of 'logical', and deriving mathematical propositions from a small set of analytic propositions, is an important contribution, foreshadowing modern logistic and culminating in the work of the Whitehead-Russell *Principia Mathematica*.[1] But it is not incompatible with the view under consideration. For although mathematical propositions may be derived from logical propositions, the process of derivation is on this view itself a 'mathematical' process, with a mathematical criterion of validity independent of logical analysis.

The concept of a self-sufficient criterion of 'evidence' to sustain the validity of mathematics is contrary to the Peircean conception of semiotic as well as to the general Peircean theory of inquiry. Semiotic analyzes every deductive system as something which ceases to be a system when the rules responsible for its construction and operation

---

[1] See C. I. Lewis, *A Survey of Symbolic Logic*, pp. 100 ff., for an account of Peirce's work in this direction.

are neglected. The legislation of the rules is logic, and the rules of a given system constitute the 'logic' of that system. The rules by which a deductive system functions are its leading principles, and are, moreover, formal or logical leading principles. On this view the validity of mathematics is determined by the fact that it has logical leading principles. How often Peirce emphasizes that the validity of an inference depends on the character of its leading principle, need not be repeated. A consequence of this is that we cannot speak of an inference as being 'mathematically' valid except colloquially. Peirce says that mathematics reasons by means of a *logica utens*; but a *logica utens* remains an uncriticized and pre-scientific logic even though it be dignified with the title of the instrument of mathematics. Dr. W. V. Quine has said that Peirce's criterion of validity in necessary reasoning [1] is nothing else than the *Rechtsgefühl* which he criticizes in the German logicians.[2] While we cannot agree with this so far as to ignore the other side of the story, which we have gone to some length to set forth, it is certainly supported by the views under present consideration. If the reasoning of the mathematician is 'evident' and requires no standards set up by logic, then his sole guarantee that his reasoning is valid is a feeling that it is so. Since mathematics is regarded by Peirce as the science of deduction *par excellence*, we have here a third criterion of validity in necessary reasoning. The first was (i) that the validity of deduction consists in the empirical fact that its premisses, when true, always lead to true conclusions; the second (which we would like to think is Peirce's view in the last analysis) was (ii) that the validity of deduction consists in its analyticity, or conformity to 'empty' logical principles; the present one is (iii) that the validity of deduction consists in the standards of the mathematician's practice.

The view that logic preaches what mathematics practises has a somewhat childish sound. It may be objected that

[1] ". . . All necessary reasoning . . . is mathematical reasoning " (5.148).
[2] Review of Vol. II of Collected Papers, *Isis*, Vol. 19 (1933), pp. 221-2.

what Peirce intends is that the standards of mathematical procedure are determined not simply by intuitive practice but by the rules which the mathematician (not the logician) lays down for his purpose. Let us see what this implies. Mathematics presumably operates by a *logica utens* or indigenous logic rather than by a *logica docens* or theory of logic. To say that reasoning operates by a *logica utens* is ambiguous: it may mean that the reasoning is carried on by a kind of trial and error process, profiting from the previous methods under which empirical success, or the attainment of true conclusions, has been obtained; or it may mean that the reasoning is carried on intuitively by a feeling that the possibilities have been exhausted.[1] That the *logica utens* of mathematics cannot be one in the former sense is settled by Peirce's view of pure mathematics as empty of content and as actually attaining the necessity of its conclusions in virtue of this. What are the leading principles of this *logica utens*? They cannot be explicit principles, for then we have by definition not a *logica utens* at all; and moreover, if they are really logical leading principles, then to say that they are 'mathematical' is a play upon words. The only alternative is that they are habits in the proper sense of the word, which when formulated are merely descriptive of mathematical practice. But how deductions can be made from meaningless signs without explicit and quasi-mechanical rules is quite mysterious. Peirce seems to be unaware, in his comparison of mathematics with logic, that ideal experimentation is the discernment of the applicability of transformation rules, and seems to regard it as itself guaranteeing validity by intuitively discerning what necessarily follows from a diagram given by formation rules.

The view of the autonomous character of mathematics is the more unsatisfactory the further its implications are car-

---

[1] The *logica utens* of the common man is a combination of both these senses. He intuitively represents the facts in a given inference to turn out as they have in previous inferences that seem to be of the same kind (cf. § 44).

ried. Although, as I said, I would like to think of Peirce as perhaps finally holding to the second view (ii), it is not easy to dismiss what is repeated so often and so plainly. What we are entitled to say is that the general character of Peirce's philosophy militates against criteria of 'evidence' in the present objectionable sense. That this does not wholly damn the objectionable view or render its presence less conspicuous, goes without saying. One thing should have been revealed by the foregoing sections, namely, that Peirce's speculations on the foundations of mathematics and logic do not form a systematic body of opinion. The many valuable and anticipatory insights that punctuate them represent gropings in a domain which Peirce apparently never had the leisure to contemplate as a whole.

I want to say a word on a matter which I have consciously deferred lest it breed confusion. This is what seems to be an extension by Peirce of the principle of fallibilism to mathematics. For example, he says: "It is often said that the truths of mathematics are infallible. So they are, if you mean practical infallibility. . . ." (1.248). But since mathematicians may err, we can never be sure of the certainty either of mathematical propositions or mathematical inferences. Thus "Twice two may perhaps not be four" (2.192) and "Mathematical certainty is not absolute certainty. For the greatest mathematicians sometimes blunder, and therefore it is *possible*—barely possible—that all have blundered every time they added two and two" (4.478). And again he says that mathematics is only "susceptible of attaining a practical certainty" (6.595). But in amazing reversal— which introduces some intelligibility into the situation—he says: "*Theoretically*, I grant you, there is no possibility of error in necessary reasoning"; there is error only in practice and in fact (5.577). On this last admission, deduction is analytic, and 'fallibility' in mathematics refers only to the fact, quite obvious, that the mathematician is capable of calculation errors. For Peirce well knows that the proof of a theorem is something different from the confirmation of a material statement, which is an implicit prediction or reference to the future and must always lack complete evidence. A trace of plausibility can be manufactured for this 'fallibilism' as a serious view if we adopt the position considered just now, that mathematical reasoning is autonomous, and that ideal experimentation by itself suffices to determine validity. Thus when Peirce says "Deduction is really a matter of perception and of experimentation. . . . The operations of perception and of experimentation are subject to error, and therefore it is only in a Pickwickian sense that mathematical reasoning can be said to be perfectly certain" (6.595)—we may offer something like this: Mathematics by virtue of its ideal experimentation is "more evident" than "any doctrine of logic" (4.243). Yet nothing experimental is infallible, so that mathematics is not *perfectly* evident. The lie to this interpretation is given when the quotation from 6.595 is placed in its context. For that paragraph, above all others in Peirce, stresses the analytic character of deduction and most clearly defines analyticity (cf. p. 218 above). The passage refers to 'deducing', not to 'deduction', and if it meant anything but that mathematicians, like all other men, are fallible, it would be absurd.

In both logic and mathematics we have found disturbing inconsistencies in Peirce. Logical principles of inference sometimes appear to be validated by empirical testing, at other times to be formal rules with a linguistic character. Mathematical inference by the internal evidence is valid in virtue of its analyticity, or government by logical principles in the latter sense; at other times it is a discipline with self-imposed norms. Yet if we survey as a whole Peirce's work on logic and mathematics, we have an unmistakable impression of their formal character. The simple question, What is the relation of these domains to experience? is answered by pointing to two cardinal distinctions: the distinction between logical and material leading principles, and the distinction between pure mathematics and natural science.

Although general logic or semiotic may contain synthetic sentences, it is, as an inquiry, concerned solely with analysis, and will not of itself increase our information on matters of fact. On the other side, Peirce rigidly excludes from positive inquiry all a priorism and necessity. Questions of logic are non-empirical and are decided by analysis and convention; questions of positive science are empirical and the answers to them have always some residue of fallibility. In applying the term 'formal' to logic as semiotic, we are guilty of using the term loosely—but not more guilty than Peirce himself (cf. pp. 181-182 above). There is, after all, no good reason why the term may not be opposed simply to 'positive', as the term 'analytical' often is; and in this broad sense the pragmatic theory of meaning and the inquiries of semantics, employing semiotic concepts, are formal.[1] Speculative rhetoric, in evaluating methods of obtaining evidence, will not itself be positive, and will likewise in this sense be formal (cf. 1.559).[2]

One of the best illustrations of a concept into the analysis of which all the branches of semiotic enter, is the concept of probability. In this analysis the concept 'experience' is employed, but it is not itself an experiential inquiry except in so far as it accepts empirical data concerning the actual usages of the term 'probability'. Peirce's theory, which we now want to discuss, will reveal the basic difference between probable and necessary inference. In the drawing of neces-

[1] See Wittgenstein, *Tractatus Logico-Philosophicus*, and Carnap, *op. cit.*, pp. 280-2.

[2] Among Peirce's technical contributions to symbolic logic (a discussion of which has necessarily been omitted by us) are his conception of the rheme (propositional function) and the free variable, his introduction of the class-inclusion relation into a Boolean algebra, his generalization of such an algebra to apply to propositions, his clear distinction between what is now called material implication and implication in the ordinary sense, his important elaboration of the logic of relatives or calculus of relative rhemes (i.e. propositional functions of more than one variable), his contributions to the calculus of probabilities, and his contributions (already mentioned) to the logistic thesis. For an account of this and other work by Peirce, see C. I. Lewis, *A Survey of Symbolic Logic*, pp. 79-106. In Peirce, see Volumes III and IV of the Collected Papers.

sary conclusions by means of a logical leading principle no resort to experience is required. The case is altogether different in probable inference, where, in order to speak of degrees of probability, we must resort to statistical investigation.

49. **The Empirical Interpretation of Probability.** The aim of this and the following section is a modest one, and necessarily so. The subjects dealt with are so large, and a detailed treatment of Peirce's views alone involves so many comparisons, that we cannot avoid being both brief and arbitrary in the selection of points for discussion. Fortunately, the details omitted are not essential to our general purpose, which is to delineate the structure of Peirce's empiricism. For this it is sufficient to indicate the empirical import of his theory of probability, and I propose to do just that.

That Peirce was influenced, in his 'frequency' theory, by Venn, there is no doubt. In the 1878 paper on "The Doctrine of Chances" he says: "The conception of probability here set forth is substantially that first developed by Mr. Venn, in his *Logic of Chance*. Of course, a vague apprehension of the idea had always existed, but the problem was to make it perfectly clear, and to him belongs the credit of first doing this" (2.651 n.). This is not incompatible with another statement, that his opinion concerning the nature of probability "was fully made up before I saw the book. I do not think I learned anything from that except a classification of the philosophies of probability" (6.590). Peirce's claim of independently arriving at the theory is not difficult to believe, especially since it is true that, as he says, the central idea "had always existed." In his review of *The Logic of Chance* in 1867,[1] shortly after its appearance, he is fully prepared to restate Venn's thesis in his own terms. His views on induction do not coincide with Venn's in early writings (long papers of 1867 and 1868), and can be discerned to develop gradually. In general, we may say that if

_____
[1] *North American Review*, Vol. 105, pp. 317-21.

Peirce's work on probability lacks the coherence and illustrative material of Venn's book, it extends the frequency analysis in significant respects.

Venn calls his interpretation of probability the 'materialistic' one; Peirce calls his the 'objective' interpretation, "the conception of probability as a matter of *fact*" (2.673). Venn commonly speaks of probability as a property of events, the central conception being that of a series of events; Peirce speaks of it as a property of propositions, his central conception being that of a class of inferences. While this difference is not a profound one, since the theories of Venn and Peirce are mutually translatable, the difference in possibility of refinement is great; so that although Peirce himself speaks often of events as probable, he does so for the purpose of simplicity and realizes that he is speaking in elliptical terms.[1] As a result of the more accurate terminology, he is able to make certain useful classifications of inference, and in effect to facilitate the discussion of the relation between probability and induction.

Peirce does not distinguish between the calculus of probabilities, a branch of pure mathematics in which from the assumption of certain probability-values certain other probability-values are demonstratively inferred, and probable arguments. What he does clearly comprehend is that the term 'probability' need not be interpreted within the calculus, and that an analysis of the meaning of this term must be based on its usage in the fields of physical science and common sense. These two types of distinction are closely related but are not the same. For Peirce most often thinks of the calculus *as* interpreted, and when he comes to define a probable argument in the Johns Hopkins paper of 1883 he confuses such an argument with an argument within the interpreted calculus. (Cf. Appendix I.)

[1] ". . . When an ordinary man says that it is highly probable that it will rain, he has reference to certain indications that it will rain—that is, to a certain kind of argument that it will rain—and means to say that there is an argument that it will rain, which is of a kind of which but a small proportion fail " (3.19).

In the review of Venn, Peirce says that although the analysis of probability is not simply one of words, what we must do in order to give a correct analysis is to inquire "into the manner in which the *terms* probable, likely, and so forth, have been *used*" (my ital.).[1] He thus implies that the interpretation of 'probability' depends upon an analysis of the contexts in which it acquires meaning. When these are examined, we find that 'probability' refers to a 'genus of argument'. Peirce points to Locke as having given the most suggestive hint in this direction. Locke says that something is called 'probable' when supported by a "proof . . . such as for the most part carries truth with it".[2] Peirce's view is that a proposition is probable if it is the conclusion of an inference which is one of a class of inferences-with-true-premisses leading to true conclusions in a certain proportion of cases. This is the same as saying that probability is a property of a class of arguments, or better, of a leading principle, which governs a class of arguments. It might be imagined that this drives us into infinite regress, for if 'probability of a proposition' is an elliptical expression, referring to a leading principle, must not the leading principle itself be the conclusion of an argument, and so on? This, however, is not the case; for when we speak of probability as a property of leading principles, we do not mean that it is the leading principle itself which is probable. The given proposition is probable, and the leading principle, as we shall see more clearly below, is an expression having a numerical value, so that the probability of each inference which it governs (and one of these concludes the given proposition) has the same value. Now the probability determined by a leading principle is the number of times in which the premiss and conclusion are both true, divided by the number of times in which the premisses are true (2.669). Thus in analyzing probability we analyze the nature of probable inference; for the probability of a proposition depends upon "the strength of the argument in its favour"

---

[1] P. 317, *loc. cit.*   [2] *Essay*, IV, xv, 1 ; cf. 2.649, 2.696.

(3.19). The classification of inference into necessary and probable is a well-established distinction in the history of logic, especially since the medieval period, but on that distinction a probable inference is simply one whose conclusion does not follow apodictically (cf. 4.45). To imagine that a given inference by itself renders a conclusion probable is superficial. An inference is probable only in so far as it is a member of a class of inferences. Its probability is the relative frequency with which this class of inferences is found to yield true conclusions; and since this frequency will be expressed by a ratio which can vary, the inference can not only be called probable but probable in a certain degree. But how do we determine the ratio of true conclusions to true premisses? There is only one way, namely, empirically or statistically. Probability "essentially refers to a course of experience" (5.169). A probability, Peirce says in his review of Venn, is a "statistical fact".[1] Thus the probability that a given man with poor posture will live to the age of seventy is ascertained by empirically investigating as many cases as we can of men with poor posture living to be seventy, and making this number the numerator of a fraction in which the denominator will be the number of all the cases we have examined of men with poor posture regardless of their age at death. Or in other words, the probability will be the ratio of the frequency with which propositions asserting that given men have poor posture and live to be seventy are true, when propositions asserting that the same men have poor posture are true. Probability is "that character of an argument . . . which consists in the frequency with which like . . . arguments are found true in the course of experience".[2] It is thus a ratio of the frequency with which a leading principle is successful. To take still another statement, in which the use of 'event' for expedience is shown, "probability depends solely upon the relative frequency of a specific event (namely, that a certain kind of argument yields a true conclusion from true

---

[1] *Loc. cit.*, p. 319.
[2] Article " Probability " in Century Dictionary.

premisses) to a generic event (namely, that that kind of argument occurs with true premisses)" (3.19). Before defining probability more precisely, a few words on the empirical character of Peirce's conception.

The term 'probability', like any other term not purely logical, is subject to the scrutiny of the pragmatic criterion. If it can be defined in such a way that what is called a 'probability' is publicly ascertainable, and differences in degree of probability are discriminable to general satisfaction, then and under no other conditions is it an admissible sign. Probability, if the term is to mean anything, "must be of the nature of a *real fact* and not a mere *state of mind*" (5.21). Consequently, "that real and *sensible* difference between one degree of probability and another, in which the *meaning* of the distinction lies, is that in the frequent employment of two different modes of inference, one will carry truth with it oftener than the other. It is evident that this is the only difference there is in the existing fact" (2.650, my ital.; cf. 2.649). Opposed to this pragmatic or empirical interpretation of probability is that which Peirce calls, after Venn, the 'conceptualistic'. The basis of the frequency theory had been laid when, for the purposes of mathematics, probability was defined as a fraction. But the fraction had been described as one in which the numerator was the number of cases favourable to the event and the denominator the total number of cases both favourable and unfavourable, all the cases being 'equally possible'. The Laplacian theory had assumed that when, of a given number of alternatives with respect to an event, we know nothing of any, then since all are 'equally possible', the probability of any one is the same as that of any other, that is, $1/n$. Thus under conditions of complete ignorance, we assume, a priori, equal probabilities for each of the alternatives. Peirce considers the conceptualistic theory best expounded by De Morgan, who explicitly rejects the notion of objective probability and holds the word 'probability' to mean "the state of the mind with respect to an assertion, a coming event, or any other matter on which absolute knowledge does not exist".[1] On this view, "by degree of probability we really mean, or ought to mean, degree of belief",[2] and, in development of the classical conception, the probability of each of a pair of exhaustive alternatives about which we know nothing at all is 1/2, this value representing "perfect indecision, belief inclining neither way, an even chance".[3] When we speak of propositions rather than events, we find that "every proposition . . . puts the hearer into some degree of belief . . . including, of course, the intermediate state, which is as clearly marked upon our scale as any other".[4] We regard the conclusion of an inference in similar subjective manner, according as we believe that "like [arguments] will prove their conclusions to be true in the particular modes asserted" in a certain proportion of instances.[5] I make the last quotation in order to point out that it is not simply a notion of 'genus of argument' that is Peirce's distinctive emphasis, but rather the notion of such a genus determined empirically and expressed in a ratio of arguments to one another. De Morgan too, and no doubt others before him, weigh an argument by referring it to some group of arguments, but there is all the difference in the world between weighing probability a priori and determining it statistically.

Like Boole and Venn, Peirce effectively criticizes the conceptualist view, and shows in an original manner that the feeling of belief is not always in fact proportional to the values of chances, that the assumption of probability 1/2 in cases of complete ignorance leads to absurd results, and that in general the conceptualistic definition has difficulty in interpreting the calculus of probabilities (cf. 2.674-679).[6] He

---

[1] *Formal Logic*, p. 173.   [2] *Ibid.*, p. 172.
[3] *Ibid.*, p. 182.   [4] *Ibid.*, p. 193.   [5] *Ibid.*, p. 193.
[6] Peirce says, in objecting to the conceptualist view : " Credence and expectation cannot be represented by single numbers. Probability is not always known ; and then the probability of each degree of probability must enter into the credence. Perhaps this again is not known ; then there will be a probability of each degree of probability of each degree of probability ; and so on " (Review of Venn, *loc. cit.*, p. 320). (Cf. Keynes, *A Treatise on Probability*, p. 373.)

points to the evil effects of the Laplacian tradition (2.101, 2.764, 2.785), is keenly aware of the fact that Boole himself, in defining independent events, illustrates the influence of this tradition, and criticizes Venn for having "fallen into some conceptualistic errors of his own".[1] But he overlooks, in all this criticism, the most potent and general argument that he could have used, especially against De Morgan, namely, that from the pragmatic criterion. For all the features of De Morgan's view follow from the assumption that probability is a "state of the mind",[2] whereas it is essential for pragmatism that probability is "a *real fact* and not a mere *state of mind*" (cf. above). The conceptualistic notion "is strictly not probability, but a sense of probability".[3] Peirce's theory of probability is a genuinely empirical theory because it is formulated by the founder of pragmatism. Not that the formulation of pragmatism preceded that of the definition of probability. They originate simultaneously. But the development of the one keeps pace with that of the other, and the theory of probability, since it deals with a complex concept, is pragmatism's best exemplification.

Peirce and Venn, retaining the conception of probability as a ratio, substitute for the notion of 'equally possible' cases the notion of 'equally frequent' cases (cf. 2.673). Probability is a statistical ratio, "the statistical ratio of the number of experiential occurrences of a specific kind to the number of experiential occurrences of a generic kind, in the long run" (5.21). ". . . To say . . . that a proposition has the probability ρ means that to infer it to be true would be to follow an argument such as would carry truth with it in the ratio of frequency ρ" (2.697). To repeat what we have already said, the numerator of this ratio consists in the number of times both premiss and conclusion are true, the denominator, in the number of times the premiss is true. Now in speaking of a ratio we might be thought to speak of something that remains fixed and presents itself to us, upon

---

[1] *Loc. cit.*, p. 319 ; cf. 319-321.
[2] *Op. cit.*, p. 173.   [3] Century Dictionary.

statistical inquiry, as the empirical probability-value. But obviously as our examination of inferences increases there may be considerable fluctuation of the ratio in the series of ratios that results; and it is in order to indefinitely decrease the fluctuations, and center them about a stable value, that Peirce refers to instances of arguments (as Venn did of events in a series) examined 'in the long run'. If we continue the examination long enough, he holds, the ratio "will approximate toward a fixed limit" (2.650). Almost thirty years later, he is somewhat more precise. The value which a ratio will have 'in the long run' he calls the 'probability-limit', which is the limit of an endless succession of values. He defines this as "the only possible value from o to ∞, inclusive, about which the values of the endless succession will never cease to oscillate" (2.758). Whatever place in the succession is chosen, values both above and below the probability-limit will follow; and if V represent any possible value from o to ∞ other than these values, and other than the probability-limit, "there will be some place in the succession beyond which all the values of the succession will agree, either in all being greater than V, or else in all being less" (*ib.*). I do not want to enter here into the objections which have been raised since Peirce's time to this conception of probability as a limit. The general objection which relates most to our purpose is that since the succession of values constitutes, in the first place, an empirical series, and in the second place, an infinite series, we can never know what the limit is which is alleged to be the 'probability'; for we cannot examine all the values in the series, and we cannot say what the empirical results of future examinations will turn out to be. In Peirce's last manuscript on the subject of probability (1910, 2.661-668), he raises a somewhat similar objection. Reviewing his procedure in 1878, he says:

" . . . When I . . . define probability [in that paper], I repeatedly say that it is the quotient of the *number* of occurrences of the event divided by the *number* of occurrences of the occasion. Now this is manifestly wrong, for

probability relates to the future; and how can I say how
many times a given die will be thrown in the future? . . .
If probability be the ratio of the occurrences of the specific
event to the occurrences of the generic occasion, it is
the ratio that there *would be* in the long run. . . . This
long run can be nothing but an endlessly long run; and
even if it be correct to speak of an infinite 'number', yet
$\frac{\infty}{\infty}$ (infinity divided by infinity) has certainly, *in itself*, no
definite value" (2.661).

By stating the difficulty in this way Peirce is unjust to himself. Although the 'occurrences of the generic occasion' that
are examined continue to be examined endlessly, it does not
follow that the *ratio* must have ∞ as its denominator.
Peirce seems, in spite of himself (cf. 5.169), to be confusing a
ratio of the specific occurrences to all *possible* occurrences
with a ratio of the specific occurrences to the generic occurrences *examined*. The examination will, to be sure, continue
without end (or more accurately, indefinitely), but an infinite
number of cases cannot have been empirically examined.
Thus Peirce says, in 1901, "An objective probability is the
ratio of frequency of a specific to a generic event *in the
ordinary course of experience*" (2.777).

But the effect of the 1910 objection is to ask what is asked
by the objection stated above, not, Can we assign numerical
probabilities? but, Which, among the numerical ratios that
we can and do discover, is the limiting-value that we wish to
call the probability? The 1910 note goes on to answer the
objection. It could, however, be answered on the basis of
Peirce's empiricism in general. The substance of the note,
supplemented by considerations from the latter source, is, I
think, somewhat as follows: We can never determine an
absolute value for the probability, because the concept of
probability refers to an endless succession or 'long run' of
ratios. But what we can determine, and what serves our
purpose fully as well, is a *habit* in the subject-matter about
which we make a probability-statement. This habit will be
expressed by the statistical ratio. Now a habit will not

necessarily continue to prevail in an indefinite examination. But then we have already seen that *no* assertion that refers to the future (and all synthetic statements do) is true necessarily. Thus let the habit of a coin be its falling head in approximately one-half of all examined instances of tossing. It will not continue to fall head necessarily: it may in fact fall tails in every instance henceforth examined. But we are justified nevertheless in ascribing to the coin, on the basis of its homogeneous composition and its behaviour in a very large number of observations, the habit of falling head one-half the time. The probability-statement 'The probability that this coin will fall head is 1/2' expresses the fact that the coin falls head in one-half of all examined instances, that is, it expresses the habit. This probability-statement is a *hypothesis*, a statement never completely confirmable. The essential unfinality of the value which it states, far from being a vicious state of affairs, is a consequence of the principle of fallibilism. Any tentative statistical ratio expressing the truth-frequency of a class of inferences is derived from an empirical examination of these inferences. This ratio will be modified by subsequent examination of new instances of similar inferences, in the same way that any hypothesis is modified by empirical observation.[1] The probability-statement will not, however, be undermined by the mere fact that, in the course of a large portion of new cases examined, exceptions to the stated value turn up. Since the probability-statement refers to an endless series, the value which it states will be modified only after a very large number of cases to the contrary (i.e. after an unusually extended fluctuation in the ratio), an ever larger number with the increase of the total number of instances examined.[2] Even the assignment of the value 1 to a probability will not necessarily be affected by any finite number of exceptions, so long as in the endless

[1] See E. Nagel, " The Meaning of Probability ", *Jour. Amer. Statist. Assoc.*, 1936, p. 21.

[2] The amount of deviation requisite for alteration of the probability-value must be partially determined by conventional considerations. (Cf. Nagel, *loc. cit.*)

succession this number remains finite and does not increase indefinitely (cf. 2.357). Peirce's empiricism, then, finds worthy exemplification in his general theory of probability. That probability is a statistical ratio objectively and publicly ascertainable follows from the doctrine of pragmatism. That this ratio can never be finally and conclusively ascertained follows from the complementary doctrine of fallibilism.[1]

Peirce's analysis well illustrates how any significant theory of probability springs from a general methodological viewpoint. If we glance at a theory quite different from his, this becomes clear. On the view of Keynes,[2] probability is likewise a property of arguments rather than individual propositions, and he perhaps brings home more emphatically than Peirce the fact that the same proposition acquires different degrees of probability relative to different premises serving as evidence. But according to him 'probability' is a logical relation between propositions (premiss and conclusion), which, though of equal status with a relation like implication, is not capable of analysis or definition; it is an ultimate simple and must be intuited, 'perceived directly'. We determine a given probability not by statistically examining cases where we have similar conclusions from similar evidence, but by directly apprehending the evidential weight of the given argument. Consequently the probability of one argument is determined to be greater than that of a second by intuitive realization of its greater evidential force rather than by com-

---

[1] In the second edition of the *Logic of Chance* (1876), although it is implicit also in the first, Venn says : " The conception of an ultimate limit in the ratio between the numbers of the two classes in the series necessarily involves an absolute fixity of the type. When therefore nature does not present us with this absolute fixity, as she seldom or never does except in games of chance (and not demonstrably there), our only resource is to introduce such a series, in other words, as has so often been said, to substitute a series of the right kind " (§ 36, ch. 5 ; ch. 6 in 3rd ed.). " The substitution . . . is really equivalent to saying, Let us assume that the regularity is fixed and permanent. It is making a hypothesis which may not be altogether consistent with fact, but which is forced upon us for the purpose of securing precision of statement and definition " (§ 13, ch. 1, 2nd and 3rd ed.).

[2] J. M. Keynes, *A Treatise on Probability*. (Cf. pp. 3-22, 34, 86.)

paring two probability-ratios; for on this view probabilities cannot be numerically ordered. Keynes's conception of probability employs the much wider assumption that we do have intuitive knowledge. He believes that certain propositions are "self-evident",[1] and speaks of that which we "really know"[2] as against mere belief. Denying that the concept of intuited probability generates individualistic confusion, he defends the probability-relation as objective on the ground that a proposition is more or less probable according as the evidence is augmented or is lacking. But granted this objectivity, the *determination* of it cannot well be defended as public, and Keynes's defence is in fact lame and no more than a kind of faith.[3] We need go no further into this view to see how far removed are its presuppositions from those of Peirce. For Peirce all relations are analyzable and theoretically definable, and feeling alone is immediate. Probability is public; it is measurable, though often only theoretically and always only approximately. And it is in virtue of its factual character, empirically determinable, that it can be called objective at all.

50. **Probability and Induction.** The following discussion rests on the assumption that Peirce uses the word 'deduction' in two senses, to cover both necessary inference and probable inference proper, and that the latter is called 'probable deduction'. The justification of this assumption is given elsewhere.[4] All that I would say here is that if it is not what Peirce means, then I do not know what he means, and I can make no sense of the comparisons he makes between probable deduction and induction. Our discussion will at first center around some points of the 1883 paper "A Theory of Probable Inference", noteworthy among Peirce's papers for its suggestiveness, but in my opinion one of the least satisfactory in point of execution and clarity.

Suppose that from the proposition 'This man has been

---

[1] *Ibid.*, p. 17. [2] *Ibid.*, p. 18.
[3] Cf. *ibid.*, p. 18. [4] Cf. Appendix I.

wounded in the liver' we conclude 'This man will recover'. Since this does not follow necessarily, the inference must be made in virtue of some material leading principle, and we may state this principle, roughly, as 'x is wounded in the liver and x recovers'.[1] 'x' is a free variable: when certain arguments are substituted for it, we get a true sentence; when others are substituted, we get a false sentence. This leading principle acquires a numerical value if we regard it as stating the percentage of true sentences resulting from the substitution, e.g. 'Half the men wounded in the liver recover'. The probability of the inference is the ratio of the number of times the leading principle is true to the number of times the premiss is true; in other words, it is a fraction with 'x is wounded in the liver and x recovers' as numerator and 'x is wounded in the liver' as denominator. Most simply expressed, probability is the ratio of the number of true values of the leading principle to the total number of values. Consider now the following inference, which occurs in Peirce (2.694):

> About two per cent of persons wounded in the liver recover;
> This man has been wounded in the liver;
> Therefore, [there are two chances out of a hundred that] he will recover.

Now in this argument, which Peirce calls a 'simple probable deduction', something like what we have just said is presupposed. (a) The first sentence is the leading principle, transferred to the premisses after having been given a numerical value by statistical investigation; (b) Since the investigation of similar inferences continues indefinitely, the sentence is not asserted as being *fully* determined numerically, and this is the reason for Peirce's 'about'; (c) I have inserted brackets around part of the conclusion as stated by

[1] In § 45 we gave as example of a material leading principle ' All men are mortal ', which means ' If x is a man, x is mortal '. In strictness, we should have used the present formulation, ' x is a man *and* x is mortal ' ; it enables us to express the frequency with which both premiss and conclusion are true. Peirce himself, however, uses the universal sentence when he gives examples of material leading principles.

Peirce, for if the bracketed words are regarded as belonging to the conclusion, then by the definition of probability it is a necessary inference and not probable[1] (cf. 2.720 n.); (*d*) The bracketed words, when fully expressed, constitute a probability-statement, in this case, 'The probability that a man wounded in the liver will recover is 1/50'. The leading principle of the argument above remains 'x is wounded in the liver and x recovers'. The probability-statement is a hypothesis; it states that one-fiftieth of the leading principle's values are true (i.e. that 'This person will recover' results from 'This person has been wounded in the liver' once in every fifty cases empirically examined[2]). The proportion of true values for the leading principle may subsequently be found to change, and the probability-statement would then have to be modified.

The 'simple probable deduction' is called by Peirce deductive because, like a necessary syllogism, it applies a rule to a particular case. Thus 'Every man dies; Enoch was a man; hence, Enoch died' applies a universal rule to a particular case; the probable deduction above applies to a particular case "a rule not absolutely universal but subject to a known proportion of exceptions. Both may alike be termed deductions, because they bring information about the uniform or usual course of things to bear upon the solution of special questions; and the probable argument may approximate indefinitely to demonstration as the ratio named in the first premiss approaches to unity or to zero" (2.694).[3]

[1] An argument is defined as ' probable with probability q ' if the leading principle's truth-frequency has the numerical value q. (See above in this paragraph.) Thus the conclusion without the brackets (the specification of the argument's probability-value) follows by definition from the major premiss (the specification of the leading principle's truth-frequency).

[2] Or, put somewhat differently, ' This person will recover ' is found to be true once in every fifty times that ' This person has been wounded in the liver ' is true.

[3] The fact that an argument may have the probability 1 and yet lead to false conclusions a large number of times renders the last part of this statement false, even though emphasis be laid on ' indefinitely '. For once there are exceptions, we cannot be said to approach demonstration.

Besides simple probable deductions, Peirce discusses (as other species of probable deduction) 'complex probable deductions' and 'statistical deductions', and intensive as well as extensive forms of these. We are not interested in all of these forms. We state the following as they are stated in Peirce, except for the brackets and other slight modifications:

The simple probable deduction:

The proportion q of the M's are P's;
S is an M chosen at random;
It follows, [with probability q that] S is a P.

The statistical deduction (in breadth):

The proportion q of the M's are P's;
The S's constitute a numerous random sample of the M's;
Hence, [probably about] the proportion q of the S's are P's.

An induction is an inverse form of the statistical deduction:

The proportion q of the S's are P's;
The S's constitute a numerous random sample of the M's;
Hence, [probably about] the proportion q of the M's are P's.

An example of the statistical deduction is:

A little over half of all human births are males;
The births in New York constitute a numerous random sample of all human births;
Hence, [probably] a little over half the births in New York during any one year are males.

If the first and third sentences are interchanged this becomes an induction.[1]

---

[1] According to Peirce in 1883 an induction is the apagogical inversion of some statistical deduction. The premiss and conclusion are interchanged and negated, so that if ' The proportion q of the S's are P's ' is the conclusion of the statistical deduction, it occurs in the premiss of the induction as ' The proportion r of the S's are P's ', where q and r are logical negatives (cf. 2.720, 722).

Now one of the main points of the 1883 paper is that
although both probable deduction and induction are instances
of probable reasoning, they are probable in different senses.
In order to make this intelligible, we must restate the
statistical deduction. For as it stands it has no specified
probability, and there seems to be no way of determining for
it a numerical probability. I believe that not only ought the
'probably about' to be bracketed, but also 'the proportion
q'. If this is done in the statistical deduction, then what it
states is that

> If the proportion q of a class M has the property P, [it
> follows with probability q that] a member of a sub-class
> S chosen at random from M will have the property P.[1]

This is not the same as the simple probable deduction, which
states that

> If the proportion q of a class M has the property P, [it
> follows with probability q that] a member of M chosen at
> random from M will have the property P.

But I do not think that any change ought to be made in
the induction, which states that

> If the proportion q of a sub-class S chosen at random
> from a class M has the property P, [then probably] the
> proportion q of the class M has the property P.

It will be found that, the probable deduction and the induction stated in this way, Peirce's opinions on the relation
between them are satisfied. Before considering these
opinions, two other points should be mentioned.

(i) Peirce gives two rules for the validity of probable
deduction and ampliative inference (the latter comprising
abduction and induction). First, the sampling must be
'fair', that is, the samples must be independent and drawn
at random. To attain the requirement of randomness, "the

---

[1] q may, consistently with the frequency theory, be indeterminate.
Instead of being exactly specified, it may for instance mean ' not very
large ' or ' well over one-half '.

sample must be taken according to a precept or method which, being applied over and over again indefinitely, would in the long run result in the drawing of any one set of instances as often as any other set of the same number" (2.726). Beyond saying that randomness is achieved by minimizing all acts of volition and choice, and employing game-of-chance mechanisms whenever possible, Peirce lays down no precise specifications. The second rule, interesting especially as applied to induction, is that of predesignation: we must designate, before sampling a class, what the property is for which we propose to sample. Thus, it is specifically for the property P that we sample the M's. If this rule is not observed, it will always be possible to find some character, however obscure, in which the instances sampled agree, and whether the same proportion of the entire class M has the property will be simply a matter of accident. Peirce's development of this rule and the implications of its abuse is acute and worthy of attention, but a discussion of it would take us afield. (Cf. 2.735-740, 6.408-409, 2.790.) (ii) One of the traditional foundations of induction, Laplace's rule of succession, is rejected by Peirce on grounds already familiar to us. The rule asserts that if an event has been observed to occur in a certain way m times, the probability that it will occur in this way the next time is $(m+1)/(m+2)$. This assumes the conceptualist principle of a priori probabilities. For when m=0, the probability of the event becomes 1/2, thereby implying that alternatives of which we know nothing are equally probable. In view of the fact that the conceptualist principle is regarded by Peirce as absurd, the rule has for him no basis in experience and its application to induction mistakes the character of that type of inference. (Cf. 2.681 ff., 2.744-745, 2.764, 5.346.)[1]

We restated the statistical deduction in such a way that all probable deduction is seen to be capable of assigning a numerical probability to its inference, and induction, though

[1] It would seem that on Peirce's view the prediction of the character of a single instance ought not to be an induction at all (but see 2.680).

'probable' in some sense, incapable of so doing. If we now turn to Peirce's views on the relation between probability and induction, starting with the 1883 paper, we find that induction has no 'probability' if this word is retained in its frequency interpretation. The conclusion of probable deduction follows with probability q because the leading principle (major premiss) is true in q proportion of cases. Suppose that in a given leading principle the proportion of M's that are P's has been found to remain stable at q, and suppose that we want to test q as being the probability-value correctly assigned; that is (taking the statistical deduction as typical), suppose we want to find out whether, if among the M's the proportion that is P is q, the probability that a member of a random sub-class will be P is q.[1] Then, on continuing to sample other sub-classes we find that in each the number of members turning out to be P tends to be q. In a given sub-class sampled, individual members may turn out not to be P, but on the whole about q will be found to be P, and the exceptions will be increasingly minimized as the number of sub-classes sampled increases. In probable deduction, then, "on continuing the drawing sufficiently, our prediction of the ratio will be vindicated at last" (2.703). What about induction? If induction were probable in the same sense we should be able, at least theoretically, to substantiate the ratio asserted by its generalization. But this is not the case. Induction does not confirm or vindicate a conclusion when the sampling is continued; it *modifies* the conclusion "so as to become true" (2.703). In probable deduction, "though the predicted ratio may be wrong in a limited number of drawings, yet it will be approximately *verified* in a larger number"; in induction, "the ratio may be wrong, because the inference is based on but a limited number of instances; but on enlarging the sample, the ratio will be *changed* till it becomes approximately correct" (2.709; my ital.). In

---

[1] It is in virtue of the fact described in the next three sentences that we *define* the probability as being q when the number of M's that are P's is q. (Cf. p. 243, note 1.)

induction, on increasing the number of sub-classes from which we take samples, we approximate always closer to the entirety of the class M, and consequently we approximate to the correct proportion of the class having property P. Thus it appears that the frequency interpretation holds for probable deduction but not for induction (or ampliative inference in general).

> "The theory here proposed does not assign any probability to the inductive or hypothetic conclusion, in the sense of undertaking to say how frequently *that conclusion* would be found true. It does not propose to look through all the possible universes, and say in what proportion of them a certain uniformity occurs; such a proceeding, were it possible, would be quite idle. The theory here presented only says how frequently, in this universe, the special form of induction or hypothesis would lead us right" (2.748).

The leading principle of an induction, unlike that of a probable deduction, does not produce a conclusion on the basis of statistical information which it brings to bear. In induction we *conclude* a generalization. And since it concludes something about an entire class, to make it one of a group of inferences with similar conclusions would require, as Peirce says, an investigation of possible universes. According to Peirce the justification of induction is that it is a self-corrective process: "This is of its essence" (2.729). But notice the last sentence in the above quotation, which seems to say that an induction is probable in some way analogous to probable deduction, namely, that we can give the 'frequency' with which it will 'lead us right'. This is different from the view that induction is probable only in the sense that it approximates to the truth by correcting its own errors, the view Peirce was to develop from this time (1883). The meaning of the other view and its presence here are explained if we glance at what Peirce's view was before this time.

In 1867 and 1868 we find no distinction between probable deduction and ampliative inference. The latter alone is

synonymous with 'probable inference'. Peirce's concept of
a probable argument as referring to a class of arguments true
with a relative frequency is, as we have noted, already
explicit at this early date. But he does not specify precisely
enough what *kind* of similarity the arguments constituting
the class must have. Accordingly the class to which an
induction belongs is the class of *all inductions*, that is, the
class of inferences whose leading principle is the inductive
method. And an induction is probable in the sense that the
majority of inductions are successful. It is this view that is
vestigial in 1883.[1] (Cf. 2.508 ff., 5.346 ff.) In the 1878
paper on "The Probability of Induction" the view of induction as concluding a ratio of frequency persists,[2] the reason
being Peirce's opposition to conceptualist interpretations
of the probability of induction. Peirce, however, confesses
a certain puzzlement. He gives two examples of arguments,
one an induction, the other what he was later to call a
probable deduction (2.689). In the latter, "I know that
reasoning similar to that would carry truth 99 times in 100
[the ratio specified had been 99%]"; but in the induction,
"I do not in the least know how often such reasoning would
carry me right". What we do know is that the concluded
proportion "can be probably approximated to" (2.689). In
a deductive inference "we infer with certainty or with the
appropriate degree of probability", but not so in induction
(2.692). We do not know "the probability of our conclusion", "we only know the degree of trustworthiness of
our proceeding" (2.693).

The reinforcement, after 1883, of the view that induction
is not probable on a frequency interpretation, is influenced
by the development of the positive doctrine, that induction
is a successful approximative process. As far back as 1868
Peirce emphatically declares that induction does not depend

[1] But the roots of the view that induction is a progressive approximative
process are also to be found in 1868 (e.g. 5.275).
[2] In fact it always persists (cf. 2.369, 5.194), in no flattering tribute to
Peirce's consistency.

for its validity on any assumption about the uniformity of nature, or in general, on any assumption of "a particular constitution of the universe" (5.345). To add, for instance, such an assumption to the premises of an induction, is to produce a demonstration and hence beg the question (cf. 2.770). If, moreover, induction depended on the uniformity of nature, we should be able to conceive of a world in which it could not be practised. But the notion of an absolutely chance universe is absurd (2.750, 5.345). *Whatever* the constitution of the universe, some kind of regularity must always be discriminable in it (*ib.* and 6.403). There is no such thing as greater or lesser uniformity of nature. All that we can mean by this is that we are to a greater or lesser degree *adapted to our surroundings* (2.750). ". . . There is no possibility of a series of experiences so wanting in uniformity as to be beyond the reach of induction, provided there be sufficiently numerous instances of them, and provided the march of scientific intelligence be unchecked" (2.769). The fact that we are adapted to our surroundings is important, because it is in virtue of this that we hit 'instinctively' upon fruitful hypotheses that induction is to test (cf. 2.753-754). In Peirce's discussion of Mill he distinguishes several senses of 'uniformity' (6.98-100, 2.761-769, 1.92). One of these is the 'special uniformity' which consists in the common character that defines the members of a species. That there should be such special uniformities undoubtedly contributes, Peirce admits, to the strength of our inductions; but even this "is not essential to induction" (1.92). He goes so far as to say that induction does not depend for its validity "upon any material assumption whatever" (2.784). He does, however, admit elsewhere that "even upon my theory some fact has to be supposed" to make induction a valid process (2.749). This supposition is not one about the constitution of things but rather that in the process of sampling no abnormal conditions should suddenly arise; that is, the factual conditions prevailing during the sampling must remain as stable as at the outset of the sampling. This condition met, together with the rules of randomness and predesignation, induction is its own guarantee. The character of its sampling is such that errors are inevitably discovered (5.576, 2.269). An induction does belong to a class of inferences, for it must have a leading principle; and this leading principle may, moreover, be regarded as the inductive method. The class of inferences to which it belongs is not, however, the class of all inductions, but the class of inferences describing the sampling of a given subject-matter. The conclusions of these inferences are not similar and different but the same conclusion correctively modified. In this way the inductive method approximates to the truth. ". . . All that induction infers is what would be found true in the usual course of experience, if it were indefinitely prolonged" (6.100).

After 1883 Peirce does not even regard induction as 'probable' in this specially qualified sense, but rather as not probable at all (since he usually refrains from employing 'probability' in more than one sense). It simply conforms "to the formula of induction" (2.780). ". . . It may be conceived, and often is conceived, that induction lends a probability to its conclusion. Now that is not the way in which induction leads to the truth. It lends no definite probability to its conclusion. It is nonsense to talk of the probability of a law, as if we could pick universes out of a grab-bag and find in what proportion of them the law held good" (*ib.* cf. 1.92). Elsewhere, likewise, Peirce regards the view "that the affirmative experiments impart a definite probability to the theory" as not just false but meaningless, that is, contrary to the proper employment of the term 'probability' (5.169). "You can ask what the probability is that the next chemical element to be discovered will have an atomic weight exceeding a hundred. But you cannot ask what the probability is that the law of universal attraction should be that of the inverse square until you can attach some meaning to statistics of the characters of possible universes" (*ib.*). Probability "essentially refers to a course of experience, or at least of real events; because mere possibilities are not capable of being counted" (*ib.*). Although an inductive conclusion cannot be said to have degrees of probability, it can be said to have degrees of 'strength', a concept from which Peirce confesses that he cannot remove the vagueness. "But we may say that an induction from more instances is, other things being equal, stronger than an induction from fewer instances. Of probable deductions the more probable conclusion is the stronger" (2.780). We may sum up the relation between probable deduction and induction by the following quotation, which defines the different types of validity involved in them, and in necessary deduction to boot:

[a] ". . . An argument professing to be necessary is valid in case the premises could not under any hypothesis, not involving contradiction, be true, without the conclusion being also true. . . .

[b] "A probable deductive argument is valid, if the conclusions of precisely such arguments (from true premises) would be true, in the long run, in a proportion of times equal to the probability which this argument assigns to its conclusion; for that is all that is pretended. . . .

[c] "The validity of induction is entirely different; for it is by no means certain that the conclusion actually drawn in any given case would turn out true in the majority of cases where precisely such a method was followed; but what is certain is that, in the majority of cases, the method would lead to *some* conclusion that was true, and that in the individual case in hand, if there is any error in the conclusion, that error will get corrected by simply persisting in the employment of the same method." (2.781).

In 1910 Peirce attempts to distinguish "three ways of falling short of certainty" (2.662), namely, 'probability', 'likelihood' (or 'verisimilitude') and 'plausibility'. These three properties appear to belong to probable deduction, induction, and abduction, respectively. The property of being plausible applies to hypotheses; it is in virtue of their plausibility alone that we entertain them problematically as possible scientific truths. "By Plausible, I mean that a theory that has not yet been subjected to any test, although more or less surprising phenomena have occurred which it would explain if it were true, is in itself of such a character as to recommend it for further examination. . . ." (2.662; cf. 6.469). Likelihood is the property of a hypothesis which already has inductive evidence in its favour. "I call that theory *likely* which is not yet proved but is supported by such evidence that if the rest of the conceivably possible evidence should turn out upon examination to be of a *similar* character, the theory would be conclusively proved" (2.663).[1] Peirce does not regard the three properties as three stages of certainty. It happens to be true that a probability is more stable than a likelihood, and a likelihood more stable than a plausibility, but a probability is not equal to some high likelihood. If it were, then some degrees of likelihood would be capable of assuming numerical values. But Peirce says that "any numerical determination of likelihood is more than I can expect" (2.663); and moreover, we may have low degrees of probability and high degrees of likelihood, so that likelihood and probability are not continuous but generically different. According to Peirce, the history of science shows "only too grievously how great a boon would be any way of determining and expressing by numbers the degree of likelihood that a theory had attained" (*ib.*). Some years earlier he had distinguished an aspect of induction which he called 'qualitative induction'. Qualitative induction, after testing a theory, "goes on to judge of the combined value of the evidence, and to decide whether the hypothesis should be regarded as proved, or as well on the way toward being proved, or as unworthy of further attention, [etc.]" (2.759). In qualitative induction, "relative evidential values . . . have to be estimated according to our sense of the impressions they make upon us" (*ib.*

---

[1] Peirce admits his loose employment of the last two words.

cf. 2.772). Lacking the resource of assigning to induction a probability, it is this preoccupation with some other kind of scale for inductive evidence that leads Peirce in 1910 to introduce the notion of 'likelihood'. That he does so signifies a permanent recognition of the mistake of characterizing induction as probable.

51. **Peirce and Kant.** No philosopher, with the possible exception of Aristotle, is so often mentioned by Peirce as Kant. This is hardly an accident, because Kant's influence upon him is greater than that of any other individual. Among the classics of the past, none was so thoroughly studied by him as the first *Critique*; he "almost knew the whole book by heart" (1.4), and for a period of years he analyzed it with his father (1.560, 3.405) and Chauncey Wright (1.4). In his youth he was a "passionate devotee of Kant" (4.2), who was his "revered master" (1.563). From Kant he first learned to grapple with philosophical problems (5.12). There grew up in him a deep respect which he never relaxed, believing, in spite of criticisms which he made, that "Kant possessed in a high degree all seven of the mental qualifications of a philosopher" (1.522).[1] It is as easy to overestimate this influence as to underestimate it. But having completed our account of Peirce's empiricism, we have some perspective by which to judge it.

[1] " 1. The ability to discern what is before one's consciousness ; 2. Inventive originality ; 3. Generalizing power ; 4. Subtlety ; 5. Critical severity and sense of fact ; 6. Systematic procedure ; 7. Energy, diligence, persistency, and exclusive devotion to philosophy." Mr. Braithwaite (*Mind*, 1934, p. 511) believes that Peirce's own deficiencies were in 1 and 5. I am not certain that I should agree, even if they be considered as deficiencies relative to the other five. It is in clarity and consistency, which do not appear on his list, that Peirce is deficient. Consistency he must have thought too obvious a qualification to list. But there is an interesting remark by him on clarity : " Crystal clearness, such as we justly require in mathematics, in law, in economics, is in philosophy the characteristic of the second-rates. The reason is that the strongest men are able to seize an all-important conception long before the progress of analysis has rendered it possible to free it from obscurities and difficulties " (*Nation*, Vol. 59, 1894, p. 344).

We have seen that Peirce differs completely from Kant on the nature of mathematical sentences, holding that they are not synthetic. This means that they have no subject-matter, and there arises the distinction between purely formal and applied mathematics—a distinction foreign to Kant. But apart from this, Peirce was strongly influenced by Kant's theory of mathematical reasoning, much more than by F. A. Lange's. "What really distinguishes mathematics, according to [Kant], is not the subject of which it treats, but its method, which consists in studying constructions, or diagrams" (3.556; cf. 3.560). I should like to quote a good deal from chapter 1, section 1 of the Transcendental Doctrine of Method, but the following may suffice to show what Peirce and others among present-day thinkers have learned from it.

". . . Mathematical knowledge is the knowledge gained by reason from the *construction* of concepts. To *construct* a concept means to exhibit a priori the intuition which corresponds to the concept. For the construction of a concept we therefore need a *non-empirical* intuition. The latter must, as intuition, be a *single* object, and yet none the less, as the construction of a concept (a universal representation), it must in its representation express universal validity for all possible intuitions which fall under the same concept. Thus I construct a triangle by representing the object which corresponds to this concept . . . completely a priori, without having borrowed the pattern from any experience. The single figure which we draw is empirical, and yet it serves to express the concept, without impairing its universality. For in this empirical intuition we consider only the act whereby we construct the concept, and abstract from the many determinations (for instance, the magnitude of the sides and of the angles), which are quite indifferent, as not altering the concept 'triangle'." [1]

". . . Whatever follows from the universal conditions of the construction must be universally valid of the object of the concept thus constructed." [2]

---

[1] *Critique of Pure Reason*, A 714, B 742 (trans. Kemp Smith).
[2] *Ibid.*, A 716, B 744.

". . . Mathematics does not only construct magnitudes (*quanta*) as in geometry; it also constructs magnitude as such (*quantitas*), as in algebra. In this it abstracts completely from the properties of the object that is to be thought in terms of such a concept of magnitude. It then chooses a certain notation for all constructions of magnitude as such (numbers), that is, for addition, subtraction, extraction of roots, etc. Once it has distinguished in the universal concept of magnitudes the different relations in which the magnitudes may stand, it exhibits in intuition, in accordance with certain universal rules, all the various operations through which the quantities are produced and modified. When, for instance, one quantity is to be divided by another, their symbols are placed together, in accordance with the sign for division, and similarly in the other processes; and thus in algebra by means of a symbolic construction, just as in geometry by means of an ostensive construction (the geometrical construction of the objects themselves), we succeed in arriving at results which discursive knowledge could never have reached by means of mere concepts." [1]

What applies to mathematics does not, on Kant's view, apply to all necessary reasoning. Peirce's extension of this view consists essentially, as he says (3.560), in holding that all necessary reasoning is iconic.

Turning to another phase of Kant's influence, we find that while critical common-sensism is "a variety of the [Scottish] Philosophy of Common Sense" (5.439),

". . . it has besides some claim to be called Critical from the fact that it is but a modification of Kantism. The present writer was a pure Kantist until he was forced by successive steps into Pragmaticism. The Kantist has only to abjure from the bottom of his heart the proposition that a thing-in-itself can, however indirectly, be conceived; and then correct the details of Kant's doctrine accordingly, and he will find himself to have become a Critical Common-sensist" (5.452).

[1] *Ibid.*, A 717, B 745.

Elsewhere Peirce says:

"Kant (whom I *more* than admire) is nothing but a somewhat confused pragmatist. . . . The *Ding an sich*, however, can neither be indicated nor found. Consequently,
no proposition can refer to it, and nothing true or false can
be predicated of it. Therefore, all references to it must be
thrown out as meaningless surplusage. But when that is
done, we see that Kant regards Space, Time and his Categories just as everybody else does, and never doubts or has
doubted their objectivity. His limitation of them to possible experience is pragmatism in the general sense; and
the pragmaticist, as fully as Kant, recognizes the mental
ingredient in these concepts. Only (trained by Kant to
define), he defines more definitely, and somewhat otherwise,
than Kant did, just how much of this ingredient comes
from the mind of the individual in whose experience the
cognition occurs. The kind of Common-sensism which
thus criticizes the Critical Philosophy and recognizes its
own affiliation to Kant has surely a certain claim to call
itself Critical Common-sensism" (5.525).

That Kant's limitation of the proper exercise of 'speculative reason' to objects of 'possible experience' had a considerable influence on positivism and on Peirce cannot be
denied.[1] It is "pragmatism in the general sense"—but in
a very general sense. ". . . To experience alone do all a
priori synthetic propositions relate", says Kant;[2] but we
ought not to be misled by the mere presence of the word
'experience'; the a priori synthetic proposition cannot be
so easily dismissed by Peirce as the *Ding an sich*, because
it is the most fundamental concept of Kant's philosophy.
Looked at from this point of view, Kantism is actually
contrary to pragmatism, which, if it condemns anything,
condemns the view that there are a priori synthetic propositions. The a priori synthetic proposition rests on the
notions of the forms of intuition and the categories of
thought. A remark from his article "Kantianism" for the

[1] See p. 156, note 1, where the first quotation amounts to an implied
criticism of the way in which Kant formulated the limitation.

[2] *Critique*, B 294.

Century Dictionary shows Peirce's appreciation of the difficulties which a pragmatist must find in Kant: "In attributing an unchangeable character to these conceptions [categories], Kant is profoundly hostile to the spirit of empiricism; but in limiting human knowledge strictly to objects of possible experience, he seemed to strike a severe blow to metaphysics." When in 1877 Peirce distinguishes the four methods of attaining belief, he ascribes in general terms the use of the 'a priori method' to traditional metaphysicians. But in a note of 1893 he shows specifically how some of them, notably Kant, have followed this method.

> "Many critics have told me that I misrepresent the a priori philosophers, when I represent them as adopting whatever opinion there seems to be a natural inclination to adopt. . . . Perhaps I shall be told . . . that since Kant, that vice has been cured. . . . Kant proceeds to reason as follows: Geometrical propositions are held to be universally true. Hence, they are not given by experience. Consequently, it must be owing to an inward necessity of man's nature that he sees everything in space. Ergo, the sum of the angles of a triangle will be equal to two right angles for all the objects of our vision. Just that, and nothing more, is Kant's line of thought. But the dry-rot of reason in the seminaries [1] has gone to the point where such stuff is held to be admirable argumentation. I might go through the *Critic of the Pure Reason*, section by section, and show that the thought throughout is precisely of this character" (5.382 n.; cf. 2.31).

He finds that distortions of pragmatism are due to "many writers, especially of the starry host of Kant's progeny" (5.464).

Peirce exercises complete independence in his criticism of Kant and is equally ready to give praise and blame. For instance, he often finds unsatisfactory nominalism in Kant (1.19, 4.50, 6.506); but on the other hand, he finds suggestions for a proper statement of the principle of induction

---

[1] Peirce distinguished 'laboratory-philosophy' from 'seminary-philosophy' (e.g. 1.129).

(2.691, 4.92, 5.223 n.). The really strong point of influence upon him is Kant's distinction between passive sensation and cognition. In 1868, when, as we saw, this takes the form of a distinction between the material quality of a thought-sign and the thought-sign itself, he is most under Kant's influence. In 1885 he speaks of Kant's

> "sharp discrimination of the intuitive and the discursive processes of the mind. The distinction itself is not only familiar to everybody but it had long played a part in philosophy. Nevertheless, it is on such obvious distinctions that the greater systems have been founded, and [Kant] saw far more clearly than any predecessor had done the whole philosophical import of this distinction" (1.35).

These words are equally applicable to Peirce himself, whose restatement of the distinction is couched in original and useful terms.

But we must give proper recognition to the rôle of Kant in the genesis of Peirce's pragmatism. The anti-Kantian criticisms cited above are those of one who has reflected on the problems of pragmatism, who has become aware of the deficiencies which a pragmatist must point out in Kant, and who is familiar with the conflicting strains that are to be found in that philosopher. But that there *is* an experimental emphasis in Kant is an inescapable fact; it impressed Peirce prior to his enunciation of pragmatism, and it caused him later to say that he "was led to the maxim by reflection upon Kant's *Critic of the Pure Reason*" (5.3). Recalling the naming of his doctrine, he says that "the writer, along with nineteen out of every twenty experimentalists who have turned to philosophy", thought most readily in Kantian terms (5.412). The name 'pragmatism' he derived from Kant's word '*pragmatisch*': he rejected the suggestion that the name 'practicism' or 'practicalism' be adopted, because the terms '*praktisch*' and '*pragmatisch*' in Kant are "as far apart as the poles" (5.412). This assertion is of course borne out by a glance at the *Critique* (A 800, B 828): 'pragmatic' is synonymous with 'empirical' or 'experimental', 'pragmatic laws' being opposed to "pure practical laws, whose end is given through reason completely a priori". The actual word 'pragmatic' is fairly old in the English language, but it is Kant's sense alone that Peirce follows.

From Kant's famous parallel between a philosophical doctrine and a piece of architecture Peirce draws pragmatic implications. This parallel, he says, recognizes "the cosmic character of philosophy", and he uses 'cosmic' because '*cosmicus*' is Kant's own word; "but I must say I think *secular* or *public* would have approached nearer to the expression of his meaning" (1.176). The terms 'secular' and 'public' Peirce opposes to "individualistic" (1.177). Philosophy, like a building, though ultimately produced by individuals, "is meant for the whole people, and is erected by the exertions of an army representative of the whole people" (1.176). True and significant thought does not consist simply in a collection of individual *tours de force*. It is a fabric, built by that form of co-operative inquiry which is called scientific. No teaching more characteristic and fundamental than this can be found in Peirce.

52. Conclusion. In Part I we showed, with as much detail as possible, that there is no segment of knowledge which can be called incorrigible, self-evident, or absolutely primary. What does serve as a substructure for our positive knowledge is a set of beliefs, formed by the activities of the individual and society, which may be called the beliefs of common sense. When the former emphasis, fallibilism, is merged with the latter, the theory of common sense, we obtain our critical common-sensism, which distinguishes sharply the indubitable knowledge that we possess from the incorrigible knowledge that philosophers of the most diverse schools have thought us to possess or have felt it necessary to assume. In Part II we showed that if, on the basis of the way in which men actually communicate with one another, we formulate a theory of meaning, the conclusions of Part I

are ratified.   For in the first place, all synthetic statements must be capable of experimental investigation, and it is on the bedrock of common sense that such investigation rests; and in the second place, these verifiable statements all implicitly refer to the future, so that they cannot be conclusively verifiable.   Thus all synthetic statements possess some degree of generality, and this is a form of realism.   In Part III we showed that our conclusions with respect to synthetic sentences have no bearing when we enter the realms of mathematics and logic, which, though they may make use of synthetic sentences, cannot be said to increase our knowledge of fact.   A sound empiricism demands that this separation be made, for we cannot otherwise reconcile the element of 'necessity' in mathematics and logic with the principle of fallibilism.

If the empiricism of Peirce were to be characterized by a designation just to all the doctrines that constitute it and sharp enough to distinguish it from other historical conceptions that are to some extent similar, 'public empiricism' would be reasonably accurate.   This empiricism proclaims, as its most fundamental principle, the public character of knowledge, truth, and meaning.   Common-sensism, fallibilism, and pragmatism in *Peirce's* sense reflect his theory of common or co-operative inquiry.   The scientific method, on his view, is more than a set of stilted precepts.   It is an attitude, applicable to inquiry in any sphere whatever.   It embraces analytical as well as positive investigation, so that we can speak of scientific logic, meaning logic conceived in a way that favours its development by the method of co-operative solution of problems.   Since individualism retards inquiry, whereas the public attitude promotes it, the distinction between them is clearly of moral as well as of methodological importance.

Public empiricism is, I think, a point of view essentially sound.   It is a considerable advance over nineteenth-century positivism and the great tradition of British empiricism, and it is an original product at the same time that it synthesizes the best in three—Locke, Reid and Kant—whom Peirce admired most among modern philosophers. Like the work of all first-class minds, it suffers from obscurities and inconsistencies, defects which ought never to be condoned. But its cardinal merit is the manner in which it lends itself to inevitable translation and modification—a merit which belongs, after all, only in lesser degree to its predecessors in the empirical tradition. There are indications that contemporary studies directed toward the formulation and precision of an empirical viewpoint have awakened to the importance of Peirce. From his empiricism, certainly, there is much to learn.

APPENDIX I

I WANT to justify here the assumption I have made that Peirce uses 'deduction' equivocally. Sometimes he distinguishes between 'necessary deduction' and 'probable deduction', and sometimes he employs 'deduction' as synonymous with 'necessary inference'. Neither of these facts is by itself conclusive. First I want to state the evidence for the univocality of 'deduction', and then to state the evidence for its equivocality.

I. If 'probable deduction' is identical with logistic deduction, then what Peirce must mean by it is an inference the constituent propositions of which happen to be about probability-statements. It would then belong to the mathematical theory of probability, even though the term 'probability' be regarded as interpreted in a definite way. In a probable deduction we would thus simply lay down one assertion of a probability-value and conclude necessarily another from it. Now in 2.783-787 Peirce says just this. He distinguishes three kinds of 'probable inference', the first induction, the third abduction. "The second kind of probable inference is, by the definition of it, necessary inference. But necessary inference may be applied to probability as its subject-matter; and it then becomes, under another aspect, probable inference. . . . This is probable deduction. It covers all the ordinary and legitimate applications of the mathematical doctrine of probability" (2.785). (Cf. 2.564.) A second consideration is the fact that in a great many places Peirce divides all inference into deduction, induction and abduction, where 'deduction' clearly means necessary inference (e.g. 5.145, 6.474). A third consideration is that if 'deductive' is to be equivocal, then so must 'analytic' and 'explicative', which are synonymous with it (e.g. 2.680).

These points seem quite conclusive—until we turn to the other side of the picture.

II. We may note first a passage at least partially contradicting the one quoted above. In 2.268 Peirce divides probable deduction into 'statistical deduction' and 'probable deduction proper'. "A Statistical Deduction is a Deduction whose Interpretant represents it to reason concerning ratios of frequency, but to reason concerning them with absolute certainty. A Probable Deduction Proper is a Deduction whose Interpretant does not represent that its conclusion is certain, but that precisely analogous reasonings would from true premises produce true conclusions in the majority of cases, in the long run of experience". I suggest that these kinds of deduction cannot both belong to the calculus of probabilities. Most important is the fact that whereas in the passage just quoted, from an unpublished ms., 'statistical deduction' is necessary, in the Johns Hopkins paper of 1883 Peirce does not thus distinguish it from 'probable deduction proper', and says, in the plainest terms,

> "The conclusion of the statistical deduction is here regarded as being 'the proportion r of the S's are P's', and the words 'probably about' as indicating the modality with which this conclusion is drawn and held for true. It would be equally true to consider the 'probably about' as forming part of the contents of the conclusion; only from that point of view the inference ceases to be probable, and becomes rigidly necessary, and its apagogical inversion [the induction] is also a necessary inference presenting no particular interest (2.720 n.).[1]

Even in 2.269 induction is compared, not with a necessary inference (i.e. 'statistical deduction' as *there* defined) but with 'probable deduction proper'. The interpretant of the induction "does not represent that from true premises it will yield approximately true results in the majority of

[1] Peirce says also in this paper that the " validity " of the statistical deduction and the induction " is the same ". It is " the *nature of the probability* in the two cases " that " is very different " (2.703 ; my ital.).

instances in the long run of experience [this is the probable deduction], but does represent that if this method be persisted in, it will in the long run yield the truth, or an indefinite approximation to the truth, in regard to every question". We may also call attention to the quotation of p. 252 above, where the validity of probable and necessary deduction are different things. Using 'probable inference' in the broad sense of inference which is not necessary, Peirce says in 6.147: "The inductive and hypothetic forms of inference are essentially probable inferences, not necessary; while deduction may be either necessary or probable". Furthermore, "Necessary Deductions are those which have nothing to do with any ratio of frequency, but profess . . . that from true premisses they must invariably produce true conclusions" (2.267). How deductions which do *not* invariably produce true conclusions from true premisses can belong to the calculus of probabilities I do not know. Further, "A Necessary Deduction is a method of producing Dicent Symbols [propositions] by the study of a diagram" (2.267)— thus clearly implying that in probable deduction the study of a diagram is not sufficient.

Perhaps the plainest evidence that Peirce uses 'deduction' in two senses, and consciously, is to be found in definitions for the Century Dictionary. His article on "Inference" shows clearly that 'explicative inference' and 'necessary inference' are quite different, the former being wider than the latter. Necessary inference is defined as "an explicative inference in which it is logically impossible for the premisses to be true without the truth of the conclusion". On the other hand, probable inference (i.e. inference not necessary) is defined as "a kind of inference embracing all ampliative and some explicative inference, in which the premisses are recognized as possibly true without the truth of the conclusion, but in which it is felt that the reasoner is following a rule which may be trusted to lead him to the truth in the main and in the long run". In the article "Deductive", Peirce says: "Deductive reasoning is commonly opposed to inductive, and is meant to include all necessary reasoning (even mathematical induction), together with those probable reasonings which predict results as true in the long run [i.e. probable deductions], but excluding those inferences which are regarded as being open to correction in the long run [i.e. inductions]". In the article "Induction", he says: ". . . Every kind of reasoning which is neither necessary nor a probable deduction, and which, though it may fail in a given case, is sure to correct itself in the long run, is called an induction." It seems to me that a great deal of explaining must be done to erase these clearly intended distinctions between necessary reasoning, probable deduction (both of these 'deductive') and induction.

On p. 231 above I have suggested the confusion in Peirce's mind which I believe accounts for the passage in 2.785 that goes counter to our assumption. I do not pretend to glibly explain every other such passage. All that may be added is that if probable deduction is not the probable argument in the sense demanded by the frequency interpretation, it is not clear just what is, since ampliative inference is excluded by the account in § 50. But once the fact of Peirce's equivocal use of 'deduction' is admitted, the undesirability of this use may be granted.[1]

---

[1] Many inconsistencies in cognate matters could be described. For example, consider the definition of a 'complete' argument. 2.466 says: ". . . Every argument has, as portion of its leading principle, a certain principle which cannot be eliminated from its leading principle. Such a principle may be termed a *logical principle*. An argument whose leading principle contains nothing which can be eliminated is termed a *complete*, in opposition to an *incomplete*, *rhetorical*, or *enthymematic* argument." And 2.471 says: "A valid, complete, simple argument will be designated as a syllogistic argument."

Compare these with 5.270: "A complete, simple, and valid argument, or syllogism, is either *apodictic* or *probable*."

Thus, on the one hand, a complete argument is a necessary one, governed by a logical principle; on the other hand, a probable argument (one not necessary) may also be complete.

APPENDIX II

A. The following table, giving the year of publication (or of composition, in the case of mss.) of all writings in the Collected Papers, will supply those who are interested with the date of any paragraph cited above.

Volume I

Paragraphs	Year	Paragraphs	Year
		313	c. 1905
		314-316	1903
1-2	c. 1898	317-321	c. 1910
3-14	c. 1897	322-323	c. 1903
15-26	1903	324	1903
27	1909	325	?
28-34	1869	326-329	c. 1894
35	1885	330-331	?
36-39	c. 1890	332-336	c. 1905
40-42	c. 1892	337	1875
43-125	c. 1896	338-339	?
126-129	c. 1905	340-342	c. 1895
130-132	c. 1893	343-349	1903
133-134	c. 1894	350-352	?
135-140	c. 1899	353	c. 1880
141-175	c. 1897	354-416	c. 1890
176-179	c. 1896	417-520	c. 1896
180-202	1903	521-544	1903
203-283	1902	545-559	1867
284	1905	560-562	c. 1905
285-287	1904	563	c. 1898
288-292	1908	564-567	c. 1899
293	c. 1894	568-572	1910
294-299	c. 1905	573-574	1906
300-303	c. 1894	575-584	1902-3
304	c. 1904	585-590	c. 1903
305-311	1907	591-615	1903
312	1910	616-677	1898

Volume II

Paragraphs	Year
1-218	1902
219-226	1903
227-229	c. 1897
230-232	1910
233-272	c. 1903
273	1902
274-277	c. 1902
278-281	c. 1895
282	c. 1893
283-284	c. 1902
285	c. 1895
286-291	c. 1893
292-294	c. 1902
295-296	c. 1893
297-302	c. 1895
303-304	1902
305-306	1901
307-308	1902
309-331	c. 1902
332-356	c. 1895
357-390	1902
391-426	1867
427-430	1893
431-434	1902
435-444	c. 1893
445-460	1893
461-516	1867
517-531	1883, 1893
532-535	1893
536-549	1902
550	1876
551-592	1902
593-600	1901
601-602	1902
603-604	1901
605-608	1902
609-611	1901
612-617	1902

Paragraphs	Year
618	1901
619-660	1878
661-668	1910
669-693	1878
694-754	1883
755-772	c. 1905
773-791	1902
792-807	1866

Volume III

Paragraphs	Year
1-44	1867
45-149	1870
150-151	1875
152-153	1877
154-251	1880
252-305	1881
306-327	1882
328-358	1883
359-403 M	1885
404-424	1892
425-455	1896
456-552	1897
553-562 I	1898
563-570	1900
571-608	c. 1903
609-615	1901
616-645	1902
646-648	1883

Volume IV

Paragraphs	Year
1-5	1898
6-10	1906
11	?
12-20	c. 1880
21-152	1893
153-169	c. 1897
170-226	1897

Paragraphs	Year
227-323	1902
324-330	c. 1904
331-340	c. 1905
341-346	1905
347-349	1901
350-371	c. 1903
372-393	1902
394-417	1903
418-509	c. 1903
510-529	1903
530-584	1906
585-642	1908
643-646	1909
647-681	c. 1909

Volume V

Paragraphs	Year
1-4	1902
5-10	c. 1905
11-13	c. 1906
14-212	1903
213-357	1868
358-387	1877, 1893
388-410	1878, 1893
411-463	1905
464-496	c. 1906
497-537	c. 1905
538-545	c. 1902
546-548	c. 1908
549-564	1906
565-573	1902
574-589	1898
590-604	1903
605-606	1901
607-609	1902
610-614	1906

Volume VI

Paragraphs	Year
1-5	1898
6	c. 1903
7-34	1891
35-65	1892
66-87	1898
88-97	1903
98-101	1902
102-163	1892
164	1889
165-167	1903
168	?
169-173	1902
174-176	1906
177-184	1911
185-237	1898
238-271	1892
272-286	c. 1893
287-317	1893
318-348	c. 1909
349-352	1902-3
353-383	1902
384	1901
385-394	1902
395-427	1878
428-448	1893
449-451	c. 1895
452-485	1908
486-491	c. 1910
492-493	c. 1896
494-521	c. 1906
522-547	c. 1901
548-556	1887
557-587	c. 1905
588-618	1893
619-630	1868

B. A biographical sketch of Peirce (by Paul Weiss) is to be found in the *Dictionary of American Biography*. An excellent bird's-eye view of Peirce's general philosophy can be obtained from two reviews: one by Ernest Nagel (*Journal of Philosophy*, 1933), the other by John Dewey, (*New Republic*, Feb. 3, 1937). The most complete bibliography of Peirce's published writings (mentioning papers not printed in the six volumes of the Collected Papers) is that of M. R. Cohen, in his 1923 edition of Peirce, *Chance, Love and Logic*. This bibliography appeared also in the *Journal of Philosophy*, partly in 1916 and partly in 1918. The published writings not mentioned by it include the following:

1. Extracts from correspondence with Lady Welby, in Ogden and Richards, *The Meaning of Meaning*, Appendix D, sec. 6. London and New York, 1923. (4th ed. rev., 1936.)

2. Correspondence with Christine Ladd-Franklin, in *Journal of Philosophy*, 1916, pp. 717-722.

3. "Guessing", in *The Hound and Horn*, 1929 (Vol. II), pp. 267-282.

4. "Training in Reasoning", *ibid.* 1929 (Vol. II), pp. 398-416.

5. Letters to William James, in Perry, *The Thought and Character of William James* (see Index in Vol. II, p. 783). Boston, 1935.

6. "Questions on William James's *Principles of Psychology*", *ibid.* II, pp. 105-108.

INDEX

Abbot, F. E., 94, 124-5
Abduction, 36-44, 64, 128, 131-6, 139, 176, 179, 245, 252, 263. See also Hypothesis
Achilles paradox, 17, 43
Acritical inference, 7, 42
American philosophy, 177
Ampliative inference, 36 f., 37 n., 136 n., 176, 245, 248. See also Abduction, Induction
Analytic statements, 90, 200, 218 ff., 224
Analyticity, 197, 203, 206, 213, 218 ff., 225, 227 f.
A priori method, 67 f., 69 n., 258
Aristotle, 186, 188, 254
Arithmetic, 210, 220, 224
Associational suggestion, 7, 10, 41 f.
Atomism, sensationalistic, 122 f., 125 f., 161
Attention, 15, 44
Authority, method of, 66 ff., 75
Axioms, 210, 212, 218 ff.

Bain, A., 96
Baldwin's Dictionary of Philosophy and Psychology, 24, 94 f., 167, 194
Belief, nature of, 54-6, 62, 65, 69-70
Bentham, J., 149 n.
Berkeley, G., 12, 28, 95 n., 96, 121 n.
Blumberg, A. E., 175 f.
Boole, G., 224, 236
Bowditch, H., 3 n.
Braithwaite, R. B., 176, 254 n.
Breadth, 24 ff., 100
British empiricism, 168, 261

Carnap, R., 87 ff., 176 n., 183 n., 184, 198 n., 229 n.
Cartesianism, 2, 45, 56, 78-9
Carus, P., 201
Categories, 49, 50 n.

Century Dictionary, 24, 94, 133, 258, 265
Class, 192, 224
Clifford, W. K., 76
Cognition, 2 n., 3-18, 20 ff., 31-6, 43, 50, 52, 82 f., 101, 105, 110
Cohen, M. R., 270
Common sense, 2, 33 n., 47 f., 57, 60 f., 79-80, 84, 93, 177, 260 f.
Communication, 155-6, 163 ff.
Comte, A., 75, 121 f., 128 ff., 175 f.
Conventionalism, 89, 91, 139-49, 196, 198 f., 200-3, 205 f.
Corrigibility, 33, 35, 59, 65, 74, 79, 86, 119. See also Fallibilism
Critical common-sensism, Part I, 93, 173 n., 177, 256 f., 260 f.
Critical logic, 181 ff., 201, 205, 223
Critique of Pure Reason, 95, 210 n., 254, 258 f.

Dedekind, R., 221
Deduction, 36, 135, 136 n., 205 n., 214 f., 225, 241, 243, 249, 263-266. See also Necessary inference, Probable deduction
Deductive systems, 30, 198-200, 203-6, 224 f.
Definition, 108 f., 111, 114, 184
De Morgan, A., 210, 234 ff.
Depth, 24 ff., 100
Descartes, R., 45, 56, 65 n., 78 f., 96 f.
Descriptive signs, 98, 107
Determinateness and Indeterminateness, 23 ff., 27 f.
'Determination', 4, 6-8, 10, 21 n.
Dewey, J., 177, 187 n., 270
Diagram. See Icon
Dogmatism, 75-6
Doubt, nature of, 54-6, 59
Duns Scotus, 123
Dynamic object. See Object (of a sign)

271